Adapting to Teaching and Learning in Open-Plan Schools

Adapting to Teaching and Learning in Open-Plan Schools

Edited by

Vaughan Prain, Peter Cox, Craig Deed, Debra Edwards, Cathleen Farrelly, Mary Keeffe, Valerie Lovejoy, Lucy Mow
La Trobe University, Australia

Peter Sellings
Federation University, Australia

Bruce Waldrip
University of Tasmania, Australia

and

Zali Yager
Victoria University, Australia

SENSE PUBLISHERS
ROTTERDAM/BOSTON/TAIPEI

A C.I.P. record for this book is available from the Library of Congress.

ISBN: 978-94-6209-822-0 (paperback)
ISBN: 978-94-6209-823-7 (hardback)
ISBN: 978-94-6209-824-4 (e-book)

Published by: Sense Publishers,
P.O. Box 21858,
3001 AW Rotterdam,
The Netherlands
https://www.sensepublishers.com/

Printed on acid-free paper

All Rights Reserved © 2014 Sense Publishers

No part of this work may be reproduced, stored in a retrieval system, or transmitted in any form or by any means, electronic, mechanical, photocopying, microfilming, recording or otherwise, without written permission from the Publisher, with the exception of any material supplied specifically for the purpose of being entered and executed on a computer system, for exclusive use by the purchaser of the work.

TABLE OF CONTENTS

Acknowledgments		vii
Acronyms		ix

Section One: Overview of Research

1. Researching the Outcomes of the Bendigo Education Plan — 3
   Vaughan Prain, Peter Cox, Craig Deed, Debra Edwards, Cathleen Farrelly, Mary Keeffe, Valerie Lovejoy, Lucy Mow, Peter Sellings, Bruce Waldrip & Zali Yager

2. Quantitative Research on Personalising Learning and Wellbeing in Open-Plan Up-Scaled Learning Communities — 19
   Bruce Waldrip, Peter Cox & Jeong Jin Yu

3. Personalising Learning: Theory and Enactment — 43
   Vaughan Prain, Peter Cox, Craig Deed, Debra Edwards, Cathleen Farrelly, Mary Keeffe, Valerie Lovejoy, Lucy Mow, Peter Sellings, Bruce Waldrip & Zali Yager

Section Two: School Leaders and Teachers: Challenges in Adaptation and Reasoning

4. Restructuring Teaching and Learning in Open-Plan Schools — 61
   Peter Cox & Debra Edwards

5. Learning in Technologically-Mediated Spaces in Open-Plan Settings — 79
   Debra Edwards, Craig Deed & Anthony Edwards

6. Distributing Leadership in Open-Plan Schools — 95
   Mary Keeffe

7. Adapting to Teaching in Open-Plan Up-Scaled Learning Communities — 107
   Valerie Lovejoy, Lucy Mow, Debra Edwards, Bruce Waldrip & Vaughan Prain

8. Preparing Pre-Service Teachers for Open-Plan Learning Environments — 125
   Craig Deed, Peter Cox & Debra Edwards

TABLE OF CONTENTS

Section Three: Learner Effects and Implications

9. Student Views of Personalising Learning in Open-Plan Up-Scaled Learning Communities   141
Valerie Lovejoy

10. Building relationships: Teacher Advisor Programs in BEP Schools   159
Mary Keeffe

11. Student Wellbeing in Open-Plan Up-Scaled Learning Communities Including Gendered Effects   173
Cathleen Farrelly

Section Four: Conclusion and Implications for Teaching and Learning in Like Settings

12. New Practices, New Knowledge and Future Implications for Learning in Open-Plan Settings for Low Socio-Economic Background Students   195
Vaughan Prain, Peter Cox, Craig Deed, Debra Edwards, Cathleen Farrelly, Mary Keeffe, Valerie Lovejoy, Lucy Mow, Peter Sellings, Bruce Waldrip & Zali Yager

13. Epilogue: The End of the Beginning   205
Anne Edwards

References   211

Index   227

ACKNOWLEDGMENTS

This research was supported under the Australian Research Council's Linkage Projects funding scheme (Grant LP100200179). We would also like to thank participant schools, staff and students.

ACRONYMS

ACARA	Australian Curriculum Assessment and Reporting Authority
BEP	Bendigo Education Plan
BLPCP	Bendigo Loddon Primary Care Partnership
DEECD	Department of Education and Early Childhood Development (Victoria)
ICSEA	Index of Community Socio-Educational Advantage
NAPLAN	National Assessment Program-Literacy and Numeracy
PLEQ	Personalised Learning Experience Questionnaire
SAR	Students as Researchers
SES	Socio-economic Status
SRC	Students' Representative Council
SSC	Student Support Centre
TA	Teacher Advisor

SECTION ONE
OVERVIEW OF RESEARCH

VAUGHAN PRAIN, PETER COX, CRAIG DEED, DEBRA EDWARDS, CATHLEEN FARRELLY, MARY KEEFFE, VALERIE LOVEJOY, LUCY MOW, PETER SELLINGS, BRUCE WALDRIP & ZALI YAGER

1. RESEARCHING THE OUTCOMES OF THE BENDIGO EDUCATION PLAN

CHANGING SCHOOL SETTINGS

For many reasons educators in this century are increasingly concerned about how to imagine and enact successful secondary education (Fullen, 2007; Good & Brophy, 2008). This is partly due to broad recognition that education systems play a key role in enabling or constraining individual, subgroup, and national capabilities (Hallinger, 2011; OECD, 2010, 2014). Another contributor to this concern is the rise of comparative accounts of educational success within and between nations in high stakes subjects, such as science and mathematics, leading to calls for new approaches for under-performing cohorts (PISA, 2012; Tienken, 2013). At the same time, multiple uncertainties and contested views about what knowledge, skills, and values might count as evidence of success now, and in the future, influence curricular prescriptions. This is evident in debates about appropriate topics and sequences in national curriculum documents on compulsory subjects, such as mathematics and literacy (Green & Beavis, 2013; Oates, 2011).

Research over the last thirty years has also amplified our sense of how much individual learners differ within and between ethnic and other subgroups, posing increasingly complex demands on curricular design for all students. Within the challenge of achieving equitable educational outcomes, improving regional students' academic performance and wellbeing remains a concern for many education systems worldwide, including in Australia. As often noted, the health and career prospects of these students tend to remain inferior to their metropolitan counterparts, especially in the case of students of low socio-economic status (SES) (Bradley, Noonan, Nugent & Scales, 2008; Lyons, Cooksey, Panizzon, Parnell, & Pegg, 2006; Thomson & De Bortoli, 2008).

Education researchers also claim that systems and methods developed for a different century's conditions and agendas now seem inadequate to address the new and complex needs of all students, as well as national and global aspirations. This inadequacy results in a widespread rhetoric regarding the need for education systems to be adaptable in producing life-long learners who can team, communicate,

V. Prain et al. (Eds.), Adapting to Teaching and Learning in Open-Plan Schools, 3–17.
© *2014 Sense Publishers. All rights reserved.*

be creative and critical problem-solvers, and have a sense of global responsibility. However, translating this rhetoric into workable curricular practices remains an ongoing matter. In a world of increased unpredictability, techno hyper-connectivity, accelerating social and economic change, highly stratified life chances, and profound concerns about sustainable futures, educators agree on the pressing need to rethink what and how students learn. These new ways include fresh curricular content in some subjects, altered teaching and learning methods, and changes to the physical/ virtual settings for secondary education, including up-scaling learning communities into open-plan layouts. All these changes interact in some school contexts to produce predictable and unexpected challenges, opportunities, and necessity for adaptation, and new knowledge about teaching and learning in these settings.

THE BENDIGO EDUCATION PLAN

It is one such context and this new knowledge that we focus on in this book. We report on a three-year Australian Research Council study (2011-2013), *Improving Regional Secondary Students' Learning and Wellbeing* (IRL), where we aimed to identify and analyse the outcomes of an ambitious, large-scale approach to address these curricular demands and challenges. The context is a cohort of over 3000 predominantly low SES secondary students in regional Australia. This approach, the Bendigo Education Plan (BEP), was devised by a group of local educators to provide a more effective, innovative, future-oriented secondary education in this city for these students (Bendigo Education Plan Steering Committee, 2005). The Plan entailed many strategies, including designing and building four new open-plan schools, extensive work on curriculum reform to enable differentiation and personalised learning, systematic teacher professional learning, and attempts to link the schools more closely to their communities. Our research also included a comparative study of two like regional schools in Australia with similar socio-economic profiles to the schools in Bendigo, but where students learnt predominantly in traditional classroom settings.

Given the well-known difficulties of improving the life chances of low SES students in many western countries (see Domina & Saldana, 2011), our research is timely in providing new knowledge about enablers and constraints to achieve effective student learning and wellbeing in these settings. Inasmuch as there is an agreed orthodoxy about teaching disadvantaged students, many educators prescribe a singular approach of explicit teacher-directed instruction with minimal student choice on learning methods and topic focus (Halliday & Martin, 1994). These students, these educators assert, are not ready for, or capable of gaining from, any alternatives. However, evidence of success for this singular approach is at best patchy (see Domina & Saldana, 2011). Thus, our study is a complex story of considerable teacher and student experimentation over time with new blended approaches under various constraints and opportunities. We track attempts in these schools to develop effective, diverse practices in open-plan settings where students were expected to engage meaningfully in large groups, smaller subgroups and as individuals.

This question of the ways in which effective collective and individualised learning and wellbeing for both teachers and students can be organised and achieved in these new settings is fundamental to this story, and to education systems more broadly. It is the question of the extent to which institutionalised learning can be tailored to individual, group and community needs, thus meeting multiple expectations in ways that engage and prove workable for participants. In this case, it is a story of varying degrees of effective adaptation and successful learning in an initial transition phase in these new settings. So often in the last ten years, schools have been exhorted to become adaptive, dynamic learning networks (Akinsanmi, 2011; Ledward & Hirata, 2011), and our study highlights one creative, extensive, collaborative, community-building approach to try to achieve this outcome.

In this book we focus particularly on teacher and student adaptation to the idea/ practice of an up-scaled learning community in a setting that includes an open-plan layout. While all the curricular initiatives of the BEP posed challenges and demands for teachers and students, and influenced outcomes, the new settings were a significant catalyst to prompt and support teacher change in beliefs and practices. Teachers were compelled to consider how to optimise their potential to enhance student learning, while at the same time minimising potential obstacles or difficulties created by these new spaces. These included teacher/student resistance to change, increased noise levels, student distraction, and lack of a history of proven practices. Our book is a record of what was tried, why, and what participants learnt from these attempts.

In tracking and explaining these changes, our research expands on the limited research literature around the effects of open-plan settings on teachers' practical reasoning, student learning gains, and wellbeing. While there is an extensive research literature on factors promoting successful teacher and whole-school change in traditional settings (Fullan, 2007), our study is novel in looking at how these factors play out in these new settings. Past researchers have claimed only modest gains in such settings, mainly in terms of improved student wellbeing (see Hattie, 2009). However, we develop a case for explaining what, and how, the new settings, combined with the practical reasoning of teachers, contributed to changes to student learning processes, outcomes, and wellbeing, as teachers and students transitioned to productive new practices.

INTERPRETING CHANGES IN THE OPEN-PLAN SETTINGS

Our research team consisted of nine teacher educators with expertise in inclusive education, literacy education, mathematics and science education, curriculum development, and qualitative and quantitative research methods. A research officer and two doctoral students also contributed to our research design, enactment, and analyses. None of us had participated in the design of the BEP, but we were broadly sympathetic to the need for significant curricular change to alter learning outcomes for this student cohort. In characterising and explaining changes to teachers' and students' beliefs and practices, we saw the necessity to draw on complementary socio-cultural, ecological, pedagogical, psychological, and philosophical theoretical perspectives. We elaborate on each of these frameworks in subsequent chapters, but the following points provide an introduction to our thinking on key aspects of each lens.

Socio-cultural Perspectives

We were interested in the effects of a community focus in these schools, where each school was organised into four learning communities of 150-300 students in separate buildings. From an activity system perspective, participants needed to act out new roles, rules, goals, outcomes, and new divisions of labour, drawing on new and old material, and symbolic tools to shape the scope and nature of activities (see Engeström, 1999). In traditional schools, labour is divided in the activity system into hierarchies of control and responsibility in school administration, where the curriculum is 'managed' through tight organisation of time, space, and student movement during the school day. Responsibility for learning normally devolves to teachers who enable and monitor learning and wellbeing in 'private' classes of up to 30 students.

The new up-scaled communities necessitate review and possible take-up of fresh practices, altering both teachers' and students' spheres of influence. In the past, a sphere of influence has been loosely defined in terms of school/community links around influences on practices (see Epstein, 1996). For the purposes of our study, we define spheres of influence as teacher and student perceptions, and exercise of their individual and collective agency. This can be defined both in terms of the degree (amount of influence on, and responsibility for, others in maintaining or changing individual/collective practices/learning over time), and areas of focus (influence on pedagogical decisions around what, when, where, how, why, with whom, and at what pace, students learn). We recognise that both teachers' and students' spheres of influence can also include broader cultural matters such as contributions to the ethos and values that shape (and form the bases for judging) participant behaviour.

In a traditional school setting, a teacher's sphere of influence is usually clearly prescribed, predictable, and often entails reproducing a school's history of practice and ethos around curricular processes, whether these are traditional or innovative. Teachers and students have unfolding individual and collective understandings of what practices are thinkable and doable in the context of their school's culture and history, often embedded in narratives of accepting or resisting externally-imposed or locally-initiated changes. Spheres of influence in the new settings, we argue, are more malleable, especially in the early years of transition. Roles of leader, staff member, student advocate, subject coordinator, student, and school council member are more emergent, improvised, and pragmatically rationalised. The new settings unsettle past expressions of school culture and agency, and stimulate or necessitate new possibilities. This implies that a sphere of influence is multi-dimensional in terms of areas of application, but also in terms of scale, duration, and stability, or susceptibility, to alteration (both perceived and actual). For example, in an open-plan setting, teachers may exercise a new or enhanced sphere of influence when they (a) team to negotiate levels of noise in adjacent learning activities in an open space during a class, (b) advocate with colleagues for an individual student around a personal or academic problem, (c) design, enact and evaluate a team-generated cross-curricular or co-curricular learning experience, (d) seek, receive and act upon explicit student feedback on the effectiveness of their teaching, and (e) propose changes to the structuring of time and space in their open-plan setting. Students also exercise spheres of influence in many ways, individually and collectively, including when they (a) contribute to effective group learning sequences and (b) make suggestions about changes to, or provide feedback on, teaching/learning and communication practices. The new settings provide scope for community leaders and other teachers to attempt to adapt old curriculum practices and resources to new contexts, or envisage and enact fresh ones.

In theorising teamwork in these settings, we were interested to see the extent to which Edwards' (2011, p. 34) account of "relational agency", understood as negotiated mutual responsibility between expert participants, could explain the character of (and the means to develop) new expressions of agency in these new settings (see especially chapter 3 for elaboration of this case). This raises sharply the question of the degree to which students' 'expertise', including their rights and experiential knowledge of their own learning, should influence school practices and the development of teacher expertise (see chapters 3, 6, 9, and 10 for further discussion). For Edwards (2011), relational agency is about effective co-ordination/ integration of diverse professional expertise for the benefit of the student/child, and clearly this applies to teacher teamwork; however, in the school setting students can also support peer and teacher learning.

We were also interested in how these new expressions of agency relate more broadly to change processes. We agree with Engeström (2001, p. 137) that major changes to activity systems can arise from attempts by agents to address perceived internal contradictions and conflicts (see chapters 6, 9 and 10). However, our three-year research identified multiple catalysts leading to both large and incremental changes. These included: individual or group dissatisfaction with the practicability of an approach or organisational feature (see chapters 5 and 10); experiential prompts from working in these new open-plan settings leading to collaborative experimentation (see chapters 5 and 7); extensions of prior teacher teamwork (see chapter 7); external pressures on performance in high stakes subjects (see chapters 7 and 10); staff employment changes leading to advocacy by new staff of imported 'proven' new methods (see chapter 11, and Prain et al., in press); and student inputs to curricular matters (see chapter 10).

Ecological Perspectives

We were interested to explain how interactions between participants and physical/cultural resources and tools influenced adaptive and interactive practices in these settings. In explaining these reciprocities, we drew on affordance theory (see Gibson, 1986; Greeno, 1994) (see chapters 7, 8 and 10), and on Dunbar's (1993) account of optimal scales for community building (see chapters 3 and 5). Drawing on Gibson (1986), Greeno (1994) Norman (1999) and others, we define affordances as features in the environment that prompt and sustain an agent's or team's goals, where primary affordances such as increased visibility and larger space enable secondary affordances such as reconfigured group sizes. By 'features', we mean both physical properties, (such as a large open-plan space as an affordance for curricular differentiation, by enabling complex, temporary, flexible groupings of students working with a team of teachers), and also properties of culturally-designed objects (such as a computer program feature that affords teachers opportunities to customise/constrain/expand circulation of feedback by controlling recipient access of online messages to particular students, their parents and relevant teaching staff). We well know that the concept of 'affordance' has been stripped of explanatory power in recent times by being applied to anything that can be understood as an enabling effect or object (eg. my foot is an affordance for walking). Thus we use this concept in our study to interpret precise influences of features, as discussed above, on adaptive changes to curricular enactment.

Pedagogical Perspectives

The settings prompted many new insights for us and the participant teachers into curriculum development in these new settings, but in this study we were particularly interested in how differentiation and attempts to personalise learning were understood and enacted (see Prain et al., 2013). In seeking to conceptualise effective learning in this context, and account for teacher development of a curriculum with depth, and provision of differentiated learning tasks and experiences, we develop our case for how personalising learning can be understood and experienced. We claim that personalising learning should be understood multi-dimensionally, and include academic, social, and cultural dimensions (see Prain et al., in press).

Philosophical Pragmatism

As individual researchers, we use different but related frameworks to guide our insights into curricular design and effects. These include feminist critical discourse analysis (Farrelly, O'Brien, & Prain, 2007), phenomenological studies of participant meaning-making (Keeffe & Andrews, 2011), and socio-cultural and socio-semiotic theories about learning and meaning-making (Alterator & Deed, 2013; Tytler, Prain, Hubber, & Waldrip, 2013).

However, in interpreting teacher and student adaptive processes and experimentation to address problem-solving around curricular design and enactment, we draw broadly on pragmatist theories of meaning in this study. By 'pragmatist' perspectives we do not mean common-usage understandings of actions based on expediency or compromise. Rather, we view a pragmatist theory of meaning as understandings produced by and for participants through their engagement in cultural/ material practices and their analyses of these practices' effects in a particular historical context (see Dewey, 1996; Wittgenstein, 1972; Peirce, 1931–58; Engeström, 1999; Edwards, 2005; Billett, 2006; Vygotsky, 1986). From this broad umbrella of cultural/ historical perspectives, new knowledge is understood as justified beliefs derived from analyses of past accounts of knowledge/values/practices, and their application to attempted new practices and subsequent outcomes. Following Dewey (1996), we conceptualise teacher adaptive processes in this context as a pragmatist sequence of problem/value recognition, analysis of key elements, creative development of possible solutions, trialling, and review.

Our own form of inquiry paralleled these teacher processes as we aimed to understand and explain changes to participant practices, beliefs and outcomes in these learning communities. We adopted this approach because it provides both fine-grain and larger perspectives and methodologies for interpreting teachers' and students' practical reasoning around new roles, altered activities and interactions, and their effects. The approach is also inherently flexible for interpreting fresh practices in the context of mainstream schooling, and the rationales for changes to, or maintenance of, practices over time. In focusing on adaptation, we do not presume that these new activity systems are moving teleologically to an ideal version of schooling practice, or that past approaches/structures are always inferior approximations. The idea of an optimal learning community as the basis for conducting effective schooling has a very long history in educational theory/practice (Lee & Smith, 1997; Battisch, Solomon, Watson, & Schaps, 1997). In the BEP, up-scaling the human and physical resources is the way in which an optimal learning community has been conceptualised. In this book we track the practices, participant reasoning, and learning and wellbeing outcomes arising from these new conditions for schooling for this student cohort.

Sociocultural Theories about Distributed Leadership

We draw on Gronn's (2002) notion of hybridised, distributed leadership, and on Andrews et al.'s (2011) account of the principles of parallel leadership to examine the way that leadership in these schools is enacted and links with a sense of belonging, trust, and school-wide capacity to enable learning (see chapter 6). Our study explores the way that traditional boundaries of leadership between teachers and students become blurred by pedagogical principles determined by the co-construction of knowledge, the differentiated curriculum, and student autonomy. As teacher and student agency develops in each learning community, the momentum turns towards leadership as a form of personal and professional autonomy. A hybrid form of distributed leadership is required that gives constructive support to teachers, colleagues, and students as they practise and share decision-making in complex educational contexts. The influences of pedagogical change and the affordances of the open-plan settings inform the transition from top-down, hierarchical leadership to more democratic and distributed leadership. Gronn (2009) describes the co-existence of a centralised authority and collegial, democratised, shared interests in leadership activities and responsibilities as a form of hybridised leadership that develops over time. The schools in this study, experience this form of leadership as an emergent process that fluctuates from traditional and reactive to flexible and responsive leadership in various phases and contexts. Student voice, for example is an emergent feature of changing patterns of leadership that challenge school structures for an authentic place and purpose. Keeffe and Andrews (2011) emphasise the importance of a school-wide pedagogy that is core to all leadership actions and decisions, particularly as it relates to a shared vision of learning. It is in this space that the link between school leadership and learning is made explicit and explored.

THE EDUCATIONAL CONTEXT OF THE BEP

The BEP was devised in 2005 to address concerns typically associated with a predominantly low SES regional secondary student cohort. These included low rates of school attendance, modest student academic performance when compared with metropolitan counterparts, and persistent signs of poor student wellbeing (BEP, 2005). These are evident in high rates of teenage pregnancy, bullying, high levels of psychological distress, and disengagement (see Bendigo Loddon Primary Care Partnership Population Health Profile, 2013). The real retention rate in 2005 from Year 7 to Year 12 was estimated to be approximately 75% (BEP 2005). (In 2011, when we began this study, the student retention rate from Year 7 to Year 12 had fallen further to approximately 72.6%, below the state average of 82.6%). Average study scores for the Year 12 Victorian Certificate of Education at the Senior College (Years 11-12) over the period 2002-4 had been static in the modest range 29.5 to 29.7 out of 50, and below a like school average of 31. The Plan also entailed the demolition of five Years 7-10 schools, and rebuilding four Years 7-10 schools, with each school structured into four open-plan communities. The four Years 7-10 schools have a significant number of students in the lowest SES group, as judged by youth allowance payments (ranging from 32 to 52% per school). These payments are part of an Australian government scheme to provide financial support to low income families to meet student education costs. Very few students from the Years 7-10 schools enrol in higher-level mathematics and physical science subjects at the Senior College. In the Attitudes to School Survey 2004-2005, reported in the BEP (2005), students rated highly the quality of teacher instruction and feedback, while teacher effectiveness, fairness, firmness, energy, and willingness to help with personal problems were consistently rated less positively. Students rated their connectedness to peers, motivation to learn, and self-esteem highly, but rated connectedness to school and teachers lowest. The BEP was formulated to address these conditions, and was developed over two years with input from various steering committees for each school, and from the Regional Office of Education, with input from local university educators, principals, teachers, community leaders, and health service providers.

Aims of the BEP

The BEP aimed to improve educational outcomes by ensuring:

- substantial improvement in student retention from Years 7–12;
- significant increase in the range of subjects available to students in Years 9–10;
- significant improvement in student attendance in Years 7–10;
- greater challenge for all students, particularly high-achieving students;
- improved student engagement and interest in subjects, particularly for average-achieving and low-achieving students, and those from lower socio-economic backgrounds;
- improved teaching methods, classroom management, discipline and wellbeing of students.

Given the educational context, we consider this set of aims appropriate for this education system, and a reasonable starting point for characterising success, even if precise accounts of how gains were to be measured were not specified in the Plan.

BEP Strategies

To achieve these goals, the BEP writers proposed major strategies as well as a range of curricular innovations. The major strategies focused on (1) rebuilding four schools using contemporary design principles, (2) curricular reform leading to a more explicit, differentiated curriculum that replaced a traditional age-based curriculum with a stage-based one, based on the state-mandated curriculum; and (3) the development of teacher professional knowledge to enable effective teaching, learning and student wellbeing in these new settings. The budget for implementing these strategies included capital investment in building the new schools on existing school sites ($94 million 2005-2012), and recurrent additional staffing and teacher professional learning investment in curricular change ($600000 annually in 2007, 2008, 2009). While each strategy is complementary in principle, they represent collectively a significant change to schooling practices in this context, and posed major challenges to teachers' professional knowledge and adaptive skills.

Drawing on Nair (2006), the design principles for the new schools entailed building large flexible spaces to allow teams of teachers to work with up to 125 students at a time, where each school consisted of four self-contained learning communities, each with two learning neighbourhoods per community. The idea of up-scaling the traditional classroom community of 30 students (by five- to ten-fold) was based on several considerations. These included a belief that the larger community-based organisation of schooling was justified, based on Dunbar's (1993) anthropological claim that there was an optimal community size of 250 people for building personal relationships and achieving bonding. This design was intended to maximise student access to a rich communal learning environment, where every student would know, to a greater or lesser extent, the members of their learning community, as well as learn how to be an active, integrated member of that community. The students would have more freedom of contact with a larger group of teachers and students, facilitating more informal learning. Spaces were designed to accommodate multiple users and multiple purposes concurrently and consecutively, with use of formal and informal furniture pointing to possible usage. In these neighbourhoods, ICT access was intended to be ubiquitous, where movable furniture would further enhance usage and support flexibility. The buildings were to be designed to integrate previously discrete functions, so that eating areas and formal/informal areas could support sharing and learning throughout the school day. Design features and functions were intended to enable optimal teacher-student relationships, with open staff rooms, visual links between all areas, and minimal exclusion zones.

In 2013 the four schools vary in size from 553 to 1223 students, but the following diagram (Figure 1.1) represents an initial blueprint of how these principles were translated into the design for a typical learning community. The design was intended to accommodate a minimum of 150 students and seven community-based teachers as well as visiting teachers for specialist subjects such as language learning. The design included a welcoming open area (see Einstein foyer), and the total space of the community was expected to provide flexible settings and opportunities for formal and informal learning. These included not only the large open-plan areas for learning neighbourhoods, but also smaller spaces, such as the Socratic Studio with

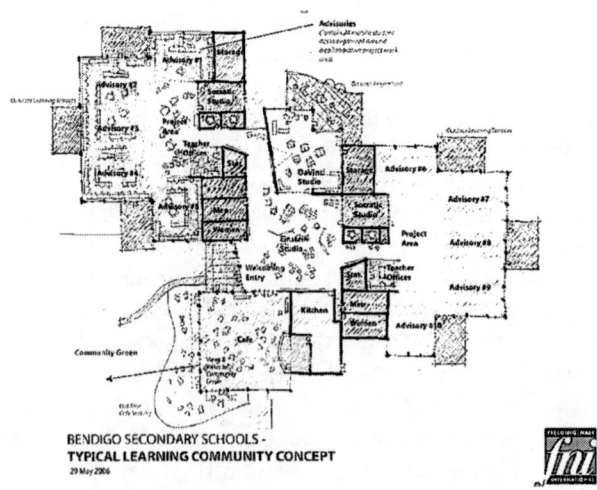

Figure 1.1. Proposed design and usage of a typical learning community.

its traditional closed classroom space, the Da Vinci Studio (the science/art areas for specific subject study), and smaller interview rooms for group-work and meetings. Teacher offices were open areas attached to neighbourhoods. Each school design also had new technology and performing arts buildings as separate learning areas.

The listed possible activities in the open areas point to the vague, aspirational aspects of the design. They did not specify precisely what the relationship between the types of seating layout and intended activities could be, including the advisory groupings. The regimentation of the indicated seating layout in some areas pointed to traditional models of the classroom as a mini-auditorium where learning was focused through a teacher out the front using a whiteboard, while other areas were presented as informal. The conceptual or practical justification for this division of space usage, and transitions between kinds of usage, was left tacit, or for teacher experimentation. The prescription that art and science classes should share the same space represented a major break with traditional practices, and implied significant capacity for professional collaboration and learning by teachers in each subject. These communities were also designed to promote potential sharing of a range of facilities with local communities and to create environments that prompted more learner freedom and creativity.

This early template points to an innocent trust that questions of structure of the syllabus, student transitions between activities, protocols of student behaviour, and expectations of student roles could be easily established through a combination of 'open' and 'closed' spaces, and shared perspectives by all participants. However, our research indicates that these new up-scaled learning communities posed many challenges around organisation of time and space, community leadership, teacher teamwork, decision-making about space use, student behaviour protocols, and actual and desirable teacher and student spheres of influence. These challenges were addressed in multiple ways, as noted in subsequent chapters.

CURRICULUM RENEWAL

While the new buildings were a major catalyst for possible changes to schooling practices, the BEP writers envisaged a new, more robust, differentiated curriculum as a crucial symbolic tool to achieve student learning and wellbeing gains. Drawing on Tomlinson (2005), Seaton (2002) and others, the BEP aimed to replace an age-based curriculum with a stage-based one, where the curriculum was differentiated to address the needs and capabilities of all learners. For Tomlinson, a curriculum is differentiated when students are given both group and individual tasks that enable learning experiences at different levels, so that all students can engage at a level and pace appropriate to them. The BEP (2005) also claimed that an effective curriculum had the following features:

– developmental needs of all students are addressed;
– higher-order thinking is integrated into all subjects;

- student perspectives and learning styles are addressed;
- students participate in negotiating aspects of content, modes of learning and assessment;
- principles of social justice and equity underpin the curriculum;
- curricular areas are integrated where appropriate;
- strong links to the community promote student independence, interdependence and self-motivation;
- strong relationships between teachers and students are developed;
- a variety of progression pathways is available to all students;
- criterion-referenced assessment methods are used to determine learner readiness for the next stage;
- curricular breadth and depth is sustained for all students.

For Seaton (2002), an effective middle years curriculum entailed a fundamental focus on learning, trans-disciplinary investigations, community development activities, and personal learning projects.

The BEP (2005, p. 18) argued that these curricular features could be achieved if students were able to personalise their learning, where students participate in planning and evaluating instruction, and where "experimentation and experience …become the basis for learning experiences". The Plan also acknowledged the developmental needs of adolescents, and that schools needed to afford students a range of opportunities to negotiate relationships, experiments with new social roles, and develop a social consciousness. Following Kubow and Kinney (2000) the Plan noted that this requires a more democratic approach to learning, where students participate actively, self-assess their efforts, set goals and reflect on learning outcomes, leading to strategic gains in new learning tasks. In place of the traditional structuring of the curriculum (fixed syllabi, age-based education, annual student progressions, and one teacher per class), the BEP proposed the development of sustainable learning communities through teaching teams and more customised approaches to individual student progress and wellbeing.

To address wellbeing needs of students, a teacher advisor program (see chapter 10) was devised whereby each teacher in a learning community was allocated as an advisor to 15-16 students and a weekly program was set up, entailing regular meetings to plan, enact and evaluate personal learning goals. This teacher was also to act as an advocate for their students in relation to general curricular and personal issues. In one school a formal developmental curriculum around social and emotional learning within a community over four years was established, and considered topics such as risk-taking, bullying, and developing skills to become an organised learner.

While these prescriptions about curricular content and methods are broadly persuasive and align with many current orthodoxies, they also represent major challenges in terms of disciplinary expertise, teacher professional knowledge about differentiation, and the ability of teachers to plan, enact and evaluate team teaching. The design and implementation of a robust stage-based curriculum where students are grouped according to academic readiness for particular curricular tasks, rather than age, poses significant structural and pedagogical challenges that we explore in subsequent chapters (see chapters 4 and 7). The BEP's prescriptions about how and why learning should be 'personalised' for all learners is at best sketchy, and understates the significant challenges for teachers in conceptualising and enacting a robust curriculum to address this dimension of learning (see chapter 3).

TEACHERS' PROFESSIONAL LEARNING

In seeking to embed a robust, differentiated curriculum within, and across, learning communities and schools, the BEP writers perceived a need for considerable professional learning for teachers. Drawing on Bransford, Brown, and Cocking (2000), Elmore (1996), and others, the BEP writers proposed that effective implementation of this curriculum would depend on increased teacher effectiveness. Following Bransford et al.'s (2000) principles of effective teaching, teachers needed to draw out and work with students' prior and current understandings, teach some subject matter in greater depth, use many examples to show multiple applications of the same concept, and integrate the teaching of metacognitive skills into the curriculum. Following Elmore (1996), teachers needed to work in teams where they continuously observed, discussed and provided feedback on their own practices, leading to peer coaching and problem-solving. Drawing on Brandt (1998), Danielson (1996), Schlechty (1997), and Wiggins and McTighe (1998), the BEP claimed that expert teaching focuses primarily on disciplinary understanding, where students wrestle with profound ideas, use what they learn in meaningful ways, and on guiding students to organise, and make sense of, what they learn and its connection to the wider world. Following Harpaz (2005), the BEP proposed that effective teaching and learning is characterised by fertile questions, intrinsic motivation, an environment that promotes active dialogue and communication, authentic problem-solving, informed feedback to both teachers and learners, and rich, positive unconditional relationships. The BEP further claimed that successful teacher professional learning is always focused on student outcomes, embedded in teacher practice, evidence-based and data-driven, collaborative, involving reflection and feedback, and supported and integrated into the culture and network of schools and regions.

Again, these prescriptions are entirely consistent with current mainstream understandings of teacher expertise. However, they imply that these principles of effective traditional classroom practices can be easily transferred to new open-plan settings, and ignore the significant challenges posed by these contexts for teachers' perceptions of sphere of influence and the necessary set of skills to be a teacher within a highly visible community. We explore this matter further in chapter 6 in terms of the emergence of new models of distributed leadership in these settings.

The practical strategies to achieve these changes during the three years of the study focused on many curricular support processes including:

- regular monthly professional support meetings for teachers from consultants on curriculum design, and effective pedagogy;
- consultant support provided by David Hopkins (2011-12) on developing model lessons and informed review of teaching and learning processes (see Hopkins, Munro and Craig, 2011);
- subject teachers across schools working to devise a shared curriculum in literacy and mathematics, and to share planning, enactment and evaluation of approaches;
- teachers within the BEP schools designated as coaches to support staff professional learning;
- consultant support for learning community leaders provided by the regional office;
- opportunities for BEP teachers to visit other schools nationally and internationally that had focused on student personalised learning plans.

FINDING PROBLEMS, NEW SOLUTIONS, AND MORE QUESTIONS

In researching the outcomes of the BEP we aimed to evaluate the effectiveness of the broad thrust of the BEP strategies through addressing the following research questions:

1. What are the individual and combined effects of the proposed strategies on students' academic efficacy, performance, and wellbeing?
2. What are the effects of these strategies on teachers' and students' practices and beliefs about effective learning?
3. What do teachers and students perceive as enablers and challenges in this educational initiative?
4. What are the theoretical and practical implications of this study for a systemic approach to addressing effective schooling for similarly disadvantaged students?

In collecting data to address the effects of these strategies we used a mixed methods approach (Green, Camilli, & Elmore, 2006; Tashakkori & Teddlie, 2010; Yin, 2008) entailing quantitative survey and student academic performance data, as well as qualitative data, including observations and participations in program activities, and interviews with principals, staff, and students in the BEP schools. We elaborate on our approach to quantitative data in the next chapter.

BOOK OVERVIEW

Our book is divided into four sections. In the first section we present a critical overview of the educational context in which the BEP was devised, justified, and enacted, its goals and methods, and its enactment strategies over three years (2011–2013). We argue that there is a strong justification for the broad scope and intentions of the Plan, but that enactment entailed significant challenges for over 250 teachers in the four schools. In chapter two we report in detail on how we developed and used quantitative research tools and methods to evaluate the impacts of the BEP strategies over this time. In chapter three we put a case for how we conceptualise personalising student learning, based on analyses of the relevant literature and our research in this study.

The second section of the book focuses on contextual adaptation by leaders and teachers in the four BEP schools, noting local differences and similarities. We report on the practical reasoning of principals and teachers as they adapted to challenges in the new settings. In chapter four we review structural issues, such as community and timetable organisation over the three years in participant schools. In chapter five we characterise virtual and actual space usage over the three years of our study, identifying enablers and constraints in this usage. In chapter six, we examine how principals and community leaders understood and practised leadership in these schools over the three years. Our analyses focus on the extent to which these understandings and practices align or diverge from accounts of school leadership in relevant literature. In chapter seven, we report on the perceptions and practical reasoning of principals and teachers as they trialled and reviewed various strategies for developing sustainable curricula. In a companion book we provide extended case study accounts of how key areas of the curriculum were taught and learnt in these settings (see Prain et al., in press). In chapter eight, we review the implications of these new settings for pre-service teacher preparation. Through analysing data from teacher-mentors and pre-service teachers we report on the new set of skills required and knowledge-changing placement models of practicum experience.

In the third section of this book, we report on our analyses of the effects on students' learning and wellbeing over the three years, drawing on quantitative and qualitative data. In chapter nine, in analysing student voice in these schools, we report on the highest and lowest student survey scales in order to ascertain students' perceptions of their readiness for voice. We report further on student perceptions of their learning environment and relationships through analyses of student interviews in the four schools. We also report on ways in which teachers are endeavouring to give students more say in their learning experience in BEP schools. In chapter ten, we report on the development of teacher advisor programs and their impact on students' relationship building, noting enablers and constraints in this process, and implications for like and other contexts. We analyse student responses to the teacher advisor program by reporting on a students-as-researchers project in one school. In chapter eleven, we draw on quantitative student survey data and interviews with teachers and students to report on student wellbeing and health.

In the final section of the book we reconsider the research questions and comment on the implications for teaching and learning in like schools. In chapter twelve, we provide a summary of findings. In the final chapter, an invited independent reviewer, Anne Edwards, responds to our research findings and points to potential future research agendas arising from this study.

BRUCE WALDRIP, PETER COX & JEONG JIN YU

2. QUANTITATIVE RESEARCH ON PERSONALISING LEARNING AND WELLBEING IN OPEN-PLAN UP-SCALED LEARNING COMMUNITIES

CHALLENGES IN RESEARCHING ATTEMPTS TO PERSONALISE LEARNING

This project aimed to evaluate attempts to personalise learning in six regional Australian schools with predominantly low SES students, including four schools with open-plan up-scaled learning communities (see chapter 1). Achieving this aim posed significant interlocking conceptual and methodological challenges. The main conceptual challenge entailed characterising what should count as personalised learning and wellbeing, and why. The main methodological problem was how to track and explain students' perceptions of teaching and learning processes, and their academic and wellbeing outcomes on these questions over three years in these new settings, taking into account salient influences.

In this chapter we report on (a) the development, validation and implementation of a survey, the Personalised Learning Experience Questionnaire (PLEQ), to monitor students' perceptions of the extent to which their learning environment was personalised, and (b) quantitative data on student attendance, wellbeing, and academic performance in English and mathematics over the three years of the study (2011–2013).

Past accounts of personalising learning have raised many unresolved questions about its reputed novelty, rationale, goals, methods, and outcomes (see Campbell, Robinson, Neelands, Hewston, & Mazzioli, 2007). This literature provided no clear conceptualisation of how personalising processes and outcomes occur, or should occur. Additionally, there were no appropriate research instruments to evaluate practices that could be claimed to enhance the likelihood of these personalising processes and outcomes. A further challenge entailed accommodating research methods to the new physical spaces in the up-scaled learning communities. Therefore, tracking possible effects on individual student perceptions and experiences of learning created further questions about which aspects of these experiences should be researched, and how (see Prain et al., in press). We also recognised that teachers and students had varying understandings of (a) what should count as student personalised learning, (b) what enables or constrains the likelihood of personalised outcomes, and (c) what practices teachers should undertake in the name of personalisation. This led to various adaptive practices in different schools (see chapter 7).

Over the three years of our study, the project researchers developed and modified our own multi-dimensional account of how learning can be personalised and enacted in the context of up-scaled learning communities in these settings (see Prain et al., 2012 and chapter 3). However, at the outset of our study, the project drew predominantly on relevant research literature on effective learning environments, including those characterised as personalised, to frame our mixed method approach. We utilised mixed methods to enable analysis of broad patterns of student responses to surveys over the three years, case study research on subject areas, and principal, teacher and student practices and beliefs in varied contexts during this time.

Past studies have explored how some personalising factors impact on learning or wellbeing. For example, Pederson and Liu (2003) found that features in the learning environment impact on student wellbeing, while Doll, Spies, Le Clair, Kurien and Foley (2010), and Velez, Sorenson, McKim, and Cano (2013) claimed a causal relationship between student self-directed readiness and learning efficacy. However, these studies and others on personalising effects examine a relatively limited number of factors to pursue limited hypothesis-testing of these factors' effects. Instead, the project sought, over three years, to monitor and analyse over 3000 students' perceptions each year of key elements in an effective learning environment, including those that contribute to personalised experiences and wellbeing. To fulfil this aim, the project devised a multi-factor instrument arising from research studies sensitised to students' perceptions of personalisation of learning and wellbeing. This instrument was more comprehensive than those used in previous studies, and enabled us to monitor changes in student perceptions. Multiple factors (initially 22), were identified as contributing to student perceptions of learning environments in low SES secondary classrooms. In the next section, the development of the instrument to monitor the outcomes of this initiative is outlined. Additionally, an emerging model is presented that shows how these factors relate to student wellbeing and academic efficacy.

In designing this instrument, we accepted the persuasive body of research that supports the BEP's (2005) strategies to improve student outcomes, including a whole-school approach (Creemers & Kyriakides, 2008), personalised learning plans (Gilbert et al., 2006; Sebba, Brown, Steward, Galton, & James, 2007; Tomlinson, 2005), and addressing regional students' needs (Onyx, Wood, Bullen, & Osburn, 2005; Taylor & Nelms, 2008). Engels, Aelterman, Van Petegem, and Schepens (2004), Kaplan and Maehr (1999), and Van Petegem, Aelterman, Van Keer, and Rosseel (2008) identified that strong teacher-student relationships, effective teaching and learning strategies, and student goal-setting are critical in promoting student academic success, engagement and wellbeing. However, identifying and addressing individual student needs within workable school structures remained a practical challenge in implementing the BEP, where student age, ability and social background may constrain the success of this approach to learning. A comprehensive participant data analysis was needed to address these matters.

CONSTRUCTING THE SURVEY INSTRUMENT

To date, little research has been conducted on school and classroom environments in which personalised learning has been explicitly attempted. The project aimed to rectify this gap in knowledge by applying the principles of learning environment research to develop a comprehensive personalised learning experience instrument. Historically, research into learning environments has been conceptualised in psycho-social terms, highlighting the origins, causes and/or outcomes of behaviour (see for example, Boy & Pine, 1988). As the concept of environment, as applied to educational settings in this literature, refers to the atmosphere, ambience, tone, or climate that pervades the particular setting it focuses on the question "what is it like to be in this environment?" In the present study, the principles of learning environment research were applied to developing a comprehensive personalised learning experience instrument. A challenge in constructing this instrument was that most instruments were designed and validated in either clinical environments or traditional classrooms.

Personalised Learning

We recognise that identifying and addressing individual student needs within workable school structures remains a practical challenge in many education systems and identifying conditions that enable effective personalised learning for this student age group remains under-researched. However, we assumed that personalised learning was more than individualised coaching, in that students participated in collective, structured activity with scaffolded support from their teachers, including modelling, guidance in goal-setting, and timely feedback (Campbell et al., 2007; see also chapter 3).

Learning Environment Research

Reviews of classroom environment research (Fraser 2007, 2012; Wubbels & Brekelman, 2005) as well as reported research on the assessment, determinants and outcomes of learning environments (Khine & Fisher, 2003; Fisher & Khine, 2006) were consulted. These studies have included comparisons of actual and preferred environments, the effects of variables on classroom environments (e.g. student gender, year, subject, and type of school), associations between classroom environment and outcomes, transition from primary to secondary school, evaluation of educational innovations, assessment of pre-service teacher education courses, differences between students' and teachers' perceptions of classrooms, using environment instruments to alter classroom life. It was envisaged that the instrument should reflect whether change has occurred over the three-year project and that results could also encourage teacher reflection to facilitate change, which would be valuable in exploring the multiplicity of factors that impact on personalised learning.

Measuring Students' Perceptions of Personalised Learning

Student views about their perceptions of selected factors were sought because students have many hours of experience in classrooms, and research shows that their perceptions are normally more conservative than the teachers' (Fraser, 1986, 1998, 2007). Research has shown that student views are not as optimistic as the teachers' perceptions and are closer than the teachers' perceptions to an outside person's observations. It was expected that the findings would stimulate teacher action to address factors where the teacher felt there was a need to maintain or modify the student perception. Such case studies would inform the broader outcomes of this study.

Over the past 40 years, many classroom environment instruments have been developed, validated and used in a range of educational settings. Some of the main instruments include the Classroom Environment Scale (CES: Moos & Trickett, 1987), the Learning Environment Inventory (LEI: Fraser, Anderson, & Walberg, 1982) and the What Is Happening In this Class? instrument (Fraser, 2012). Additionally, context-specific instruments have been used in specific settings or for specific purposes. For example, Waxman, Sparks, Stillisano, and Lee (2009) recently developed a learning environment instrument to evaluate teachers' professional development. In this study, an account of personalisation of learning informed by the literature was developed but revised during the study as explained in chapter 3. That is, the instrument was informed by the literature review and was critical in our revised understanding of personalised learning.

Designing Data Collection

Our review of the literature revealed a range of factors that can influence personalisation, but there appeared to be virtually no literature that considered the interaction among all of these factors. Results of data analysis needed to be discussed with the schools so that teachers could modify the personalising process to accord with new findings. The researchers observed classes, collected artefacts and interviewed a range of administrators, teaching staff and students to enable researchers to estimate the effectiveness of modified personalising approaches.

The research questions for this project sought a range of data and perspectives. Hence, the approach adopted was a mixed methodology approach (Plowright, 2011; Teddlie & Tashakkori, 2009) where data collection included surveys, observations, artefacts and interviews. Each form of data collection contributed to an ongoing analysis and modifications to the conduct of the research. Even in the development of the survey instrument, a mix of interviews, literature searches and analysis of past studies indicated that a mixed methodological approach was desirable.

Samples

The project was conducted in Bendigo (central Victoria) and Gippsland (eastern Victoria) and was based on the Bendigo Education Plan (BEP). The BEP was reasonably well-resourced with all schools in Bendigo being rebuilt as open-plan classrooms while the Gippsland schools were not rebuilt (see chapter one). These schools had literacy concerns and most ranked lower than the national average in terms on the Index of Community Socio-Educational Advantage (ICSEA) (My Schools 2013, www.myschools.edu.au). These schools contained more low SES students with lower literacy scores than other schools in Victoria. These lower literacy scores in national testing led us to consider a restriction on the length of the questionnaire and its readability (My Schools 2013). Australia conducts an annual standardised testing program in Years 3, 5, 7 and 9 to assess students' numeracy, reading, writing, spelling, grammar and punctuation. These tests are known locally as the National Assessment Program–Literacy and Numeracy (NAPLAN) and are administered by the Australian Curriculum, Assessment and Reporting Authority (ACARA). For these schools, the NAPLAN scores were below the state averages. See chapter 4 for further detail.

The trial sample consisted of 230 students in the two Gippsland schools. This sample was used for the initial scale development and validation. These students were not involved in any aspect of this study. Students responded to the trial form of the instrument described below. After completion of the trial, the sample involved students who were to be involved in the main study. Over the three years of the project, 7,967 students' responses were received (about 2650 students each year). The schools reported an average daily absence percentage of about 15% that means that these sample responses represent over 80% of the possible number of students.

Instrumentation

The Personalised Learning Experience Questionnaire (PLEQ) is intended to provide a comprehensive instrument designed to explore a wide range of dimensions of personalised learning, and was refined from 110 items (assigned to 22 a priori scales) to its final form of 66 items (assigned to 19 scales). In this final form, nine scales had four items and ten scales had three items.

Data Analysis

In developing this instrument, standard validation techniques were employed including reliability checks on internal consistency, discriminant validity and factor analysis. Next, MANOVA was used to study differences in PLEQ scores according to gender of student, year-level and school. In addition, univariate F- tests were used to identify scales of the PLEQ for which statistically significant differences were evident. Also, effect sizes using Cohen's d (1988) as a convenient index were computed for all statistically significant differences.

DEVELOPING THE PERSONALISED LEARNING EXPERIENCE QUESTIONNAIRE

The PLEQ was developed using an intuitive rational approach to instrument design and validation (Fraser, 1986; Hase & Goldberg, 1967). The validity of intuitive-rational scales rests partly on the subjective opinions of the investigators and other experts. Three procedural steps were followed to develop the intuitive-rational scale: (1) identification of salient dimensions through a literature review; (2) writing test items conceptually linked with each salient dimension; and, (3) field testing the questionnaire to a target group to establish internal consistency reliability and discriminant validity of each scale. In addition, factor analysis was used to assist with scale refinement.

Identification of Salient Dimensions

We wanted an instrument that explored a wide range of factors and that was relatively sensitive to highlighting these factors. Based on a review of more than fifty policy and research papers on personalised learning principles and practices, including characteristics of self-directed learning, the following tentative dimensions were deemed salient to the present instrument. Table 2.1 shows definitions of these dimensions based on the literature review.

To keep the length of the instrument to a manageable size, we chose scales that were sensitive to personalised learning. The PLEQ scales (see Waldrip et al., 2014 for details) included: Self-Directed Learning Readiness; Learning Environment; Student Engagement, (emotional, cognitive and behavioural) and; Students' Perceptions of Assessment/Assessment for Learning.

Outcome Variables

For this project, we obtained data on two outcome variables: academic efficacy and student wellbeing.

Writing of Test Items

The second step in the intuitive-rational approach to scale development required writing sets of items conceptually linked with each salient dimension. In order to limit the instrument's length, a set of five items was composed for each dimension and subjected to measurement scrutiny with a goal of having three or four per scale in the tentative instrument. Accordingly, a pool of 110 items was checked for faults and ambiguities by a group of academics with expertise in educational and psychological measurement and school assessment. In particular, consideration was given to the face validity and scale allocation of each item. These items employed a five-point Likert scale response.

Field Testing and Validation of Initial Form of the PLEQ

In line with the third step in the intuitive-rational approach to scale development, the trial PLEQ was field-tested on the sample of 230 Australian high school students

QUANTITATIVE FINDINGS

Table 2.1. Descriptive information and validation data for the initial form of the PLEQ (trial sample, N = 230).

Dimension	Description	Reliability (Coeff't α)	Discrim't Validity (Mean Correl'n)
Self Directed Learning – self-management	The extent to which students have the capacity and willingness to conduct their own education.	0.72	0.34
Self Directed Learning – desire for learning	The extent to which students have a desire for improved learning.	0.73	0.36
Self Directed Learning – self-control	The extent to which students can focus on their learning through setting and achieving goals.	0.71	0.35
Teacher Support	The extent to which the teacher helps, befriends, and is interested in students.	0.88	0.37
Personal Relevance	The extent to which there is connectedness between school science to students' out-of-school experiences and with making use of students' everyday experiences as a meaningful context for the development of students' scientific and mathematical knowledge.	0.83	0.40
Shared Control	The extent to which students are invited to share with the teacher control of the learning environment, including the articulation of learning goals, the design and management of learning activities, and the determination and application of assessment criteria.	0.90	0.35
Student Negotiation	The extent to which opportunities exist for students to explain and justify to other students their newly developing ideas, to listen attentively and reflect on the viability of other students' ideas and, subsequently, to reflect self-critically on the viability of their own ideas.	0.84	0.34

(Continued)

Table 2.1. Continued

Dimension	Description	Reliability (Coeff't α)	Discrim't Validity (Mean Correl'n)
Emotional Engagement	The extent to which students perceive their schooling as both pleasant and energising.	0.69	0.35
Cognitive Engagement	The extent to which students respond to difficult learning problems, and the level of effort they expended on these tasks.	0.75	0.36
Behavioural Engagement	The extent to which students are involved in learning and academic activities.	0.83	0.36
Assessment – Congruence with Planned Learning	The extent to which assessment tasks align with the goals, objectives and activities of the learning program.	0.82	0.42
Assessment – Authenticity	The extent to which assessment tasks feature real life situations that are relevant to the learner.	0.85	0.41
Assessment – Student Consultation	The extent to which students are consulted and informed about the forms of assessment tasks being employed.	0.78	0.33
Assessment – Transparency	The extent to which the purposes and forms of assessment tasks are well-defined and clear to the learner.	0.86	0.40
Academic Efficacy	The extent to which students believe that they can achieve.	0.86	0.41
Emotional Tone	The extent to which students feel happy about their lives.	0.76	0.37
Peer Relationships	The extent to which students perceive positive perceptions from other students.	0.82	0.29

(Continued)

Table 2.1. Continued

Dimension	Description	Reliability (Coeff't α)	Discrim't Validity (Mean Correl'n)
Affect at School	The extent to which students have a positive affect due to school.	0.88	0.34
Self-Report on Disruptive Behaviour	The extent to which students support disruptive behaviour.	0.84	-0.15
Individualisation	The extent that students perceive they have differentiated learning opportunities.	0.66	0.34
Effective Teaching and Learning	The extent to which students believe that teaching and learning in their schools are effective.	0.76	0.42
Opportunity for Personal and Social Behaviour	The extent to which students feel they can receive professional support or be involved in school committees.	0.80	0.41

described previously. The internal consistency reliability (Cronbach Coefficient α) of each scale and the discriminant validity (mean correlation of each scale with the remaining scales) were computed (Waldrip, et al., 2014).

After examining the results, some refinements were made to enhance scale validity. Initially, at least one item was removed from each scale so that the instrument could be administered within class teacher advisor time. As a consequence, the reliability was reduced for some scales. The School, and the Effective Teaching and Learning scales were deleted because of poor internal consistency reliability and conceptual overlap with other scales.

Several items were modified to enhance their face validity. While all scales had satisfactory internal consistency reliability, it was decided to economise the PLEQ's administration by reducing the number of items per scale to either three or four. The Cronbach Coefficient α for these final scales ranged from 0.67 for Wellbeing – Individualism to 0.87 for Learning Environment – Shared Control. Three scales, indicated by discriminant validity data, had overlap with other scales and were deleted: Wellbeing – Emotional Tone, Wellbeing – Affect at School, and Wellbeing – Effective Teaching and Learning.

The result of this review process was a 66-item instrument with 19 scales.

BEP Validation of the Final Form PLEQ

The team used data from the BEP study to cross-validate the final form of the PLEQ. As this sample consisted of about 2,650 students per year, exploratory factor analysis was performed on the data. A principal component factor analysis with varimax rotation revealed 17 distinct factors that extracted 69.73% of variance in scores. Fifteen of these factors corresponded exactly with 15 of the 19 a priori PLEQ scales. That is, 51 of the 66 items had loadings in excess of 0.30 on their corresponding factor. Considering the large number of factors and the potential for scale overlap, the overall factoring was satisfactory. Table 2.2 shows Cronbach Alpha (α) data for the final form of the PLEQ. All scales had coefficients above 0.68 with 12 scales having coefficients above 0.80. These coefficients suggest very sound internal consistency.

Means and standard deviations for all scales are also shown in Table 2.2. As scales had either three or four items, these statistics were computed from aggregate scale scores divided by the number of items in the respective scale. Table 2.3 shows that the reliability, means and standard deviations were remarkably consistent over the three years of the project. The consistency of means could be due to the combination of a variety of schools as disaggregated analyses showed more variation.

FINDINGS

The findings of our research are reported in two sections. In the first section we report on quantitative data on BEP schools, including results of the PLEQ and other quantitative data on school academic performance in reading and mathematics, and

QUANTITATIVE FINDINGS

Table 2.2. Validation data for the final form of the PLEQ.

Scale Name	Reliability (Coeff't α)	Mean	S.D.
SDL – self-management	0.76	3.85	0.63
SDL – desire for learning	0.80	3.53	0.76
SDL – self-control	0.77	3.96	0.65
Teacher Support	0.86	3.57	0.88
Personal Relevance	0.81	3.27	0.80
Shared Control	0.85	2.99	0.86
Student Negotiation	0.81	3.21	0.89
Emotional Engagement	0.91	3.28	0.98
Cognitive Engagement	0.78	3.66	0.75
Behavioural Engagement	0.83	3.41	0.81
Assessment – Congruence with Planned Learning	0.79	3.56	0.75
Assessment – Authenticity	0.80	3.14	0.82
Assessment – Student Consultation	0.77	2.97	0.83
Assessment – Transparency	0.82	3.52	0.79
Academic Efficacy	0.81	3.61	0.81
Peer Relationships	0.84	3.57	0.83
Self-Report on Disruptive Behaviour	0.81	2.27	1.04
Individualisation	0.72	3.02	0.75
Opportunity for Personal & Social Behaviour	0.79	3.42	0.83

Notes.

1. SDL: Self-Directed Learning
2. Scale means and standard deviations were computed after averaging aggregate scores by the number of items in that scale.
3. Main study sample $N = 7,967$ (includes the six schools surveyed)

school attendance. In the second section we report on an emerging multi-group structural equation model that explores the relationship between the factors. The results from the survey were provided to the schools in a timely collaborative manner.

Quantitative Data from the PLEQ

The averaged responses of the students from each BEP school over the three years indicate considerable stability in their responses to each scale (see

Table 2.3. Reliability, Means and Standard Deviation for three subsequent years.

Scale Name	Reliability α 2011	Reliability α 2012	Reliability α 2013	Means 2011	Means 2012	Means 2013	Standard deviation 2011	Standard deviation 2012	Standard deviation 2013
SDL – self-management	0.76	0.75	0.68	3.85	3.86	3.85	0.63	0.68	0.66
SDL – desire for learning	0.80	0.79	0.78	3.53	3.46	3.54	0.76	0.80	0.74
SDL – self-control	0.77	0.76	0.71	3.96	3.90	3.99	0.65	0.70	0.60
Teacher Support	0.86	0.88	0.87	3.57	3.52	3.56	0.58	0.94	0.89
Personal Relevance	0.81	0.82	0.82	3.27	3.17	3.20	0.80	0.85	0.84
Shared Control	0.85	0.86	0.86	2.99	2.92	2.94	0.86	0.91	0.90
Student Negotiation	0.81	0.82	0.82	3.21	3.15	3.20	0.89	0.93	0.93
Emotional Engagement	0.91	0.91	0.91	3.28	3.25	3.21	0.98	0.99	1.02
Cognitive Engagement	0.78	0.78	0.75	3.66	3.61	3.70	0.75	0.79	0.72
Behavioural Engagement	0.83	0.83	0.84	3.41	3.33	3.34	0.81	0.86	0.86
Assessment – Congruence with Planned Learning	0.79	0.81	0.78	3.56	3.57	3.60	0.75	0.79	0.73
Assessment – Authenticity	0.80	0.80	0.80	3.14	3.01	3.08	0.82	0.86	0.85
Assessment – Student Consultation	0.77	0.76	0.76	2.97	2.89	2.92	0.83	0.86	0.83
Assessment – Transparency	0.82	0.83	0.82	3.52	3.50	3.54	0.79	0.86	0.80
Academic Efficacy	0.81	0.82	0.82	3.61	3.56	3.60	0.81	0.87	0.81
Peer Relationships	0.84	0.84	0.84	3.57	3.43	3.41	0.83	0.88	0.88
Self-Report on Disruptive Behaviour	0.81	0.80	0.79	2.27	2.09	2.12	1.04	1.00	0.99
Individualisation	0.72	0.71	0.67	3.02	3.00	3.03	0.74	0.76	0.73
Opportunity for Personal and Social Development	0.79	0.81	0.78	3.43	3.45	3.48	0.83	0.86	0.82

QUANTITATIVE FINDINGS

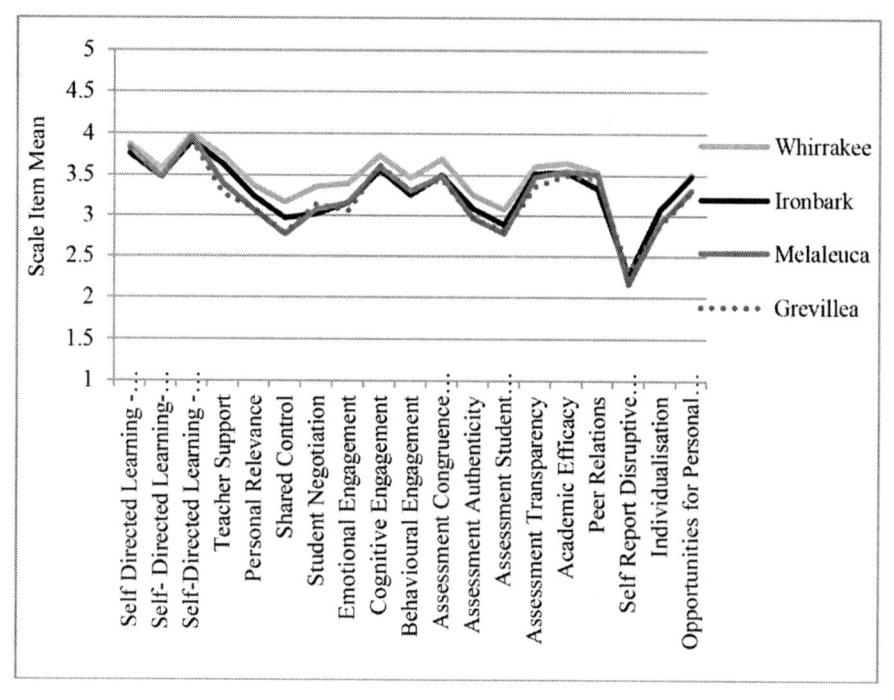

Figure 2.1. Averaged student perceptions at each BEP school (2011–2013).

Figure 2.1 and chapter 9 for more detail). A line graph has been used to provide a clearer representation of the data. While Whirrakee, the highest ICSEA school, had the most favourable student perceptions on these scales, there is a strong degree of conformity in student responses between schools, including the negative scale of Self Reporting of Disruptive Behaviour. The lack of significant positive or negative changes to students' perceptions of their learning environment over the duration of the study (see chapter 9, Figure 9.1) points to (a) the difficulty of achieving teacher-led interventions that have marked positive effects on student responses to the scales, and (b) the averaging out effect of such a large sample. As we report in subsequent quantitative data in this chapter, there were gains in academic achievement in these schools compared to similar schools in the national sample, but these gains were not mirrored in PLEQ responses. This perhaps reflects the ambitious, broad-brush scope of the PLEQ's account of contributing dimensions to personalising learning. However, as we report later in this chapter, targeted successful interventions around some scales could be developed and tracked through disaggregated analysis of the survey.

As an example of the potential value in analysing the survey data we report here on one school's year-level progressions across the three years of the study (Figure 2.2).

31

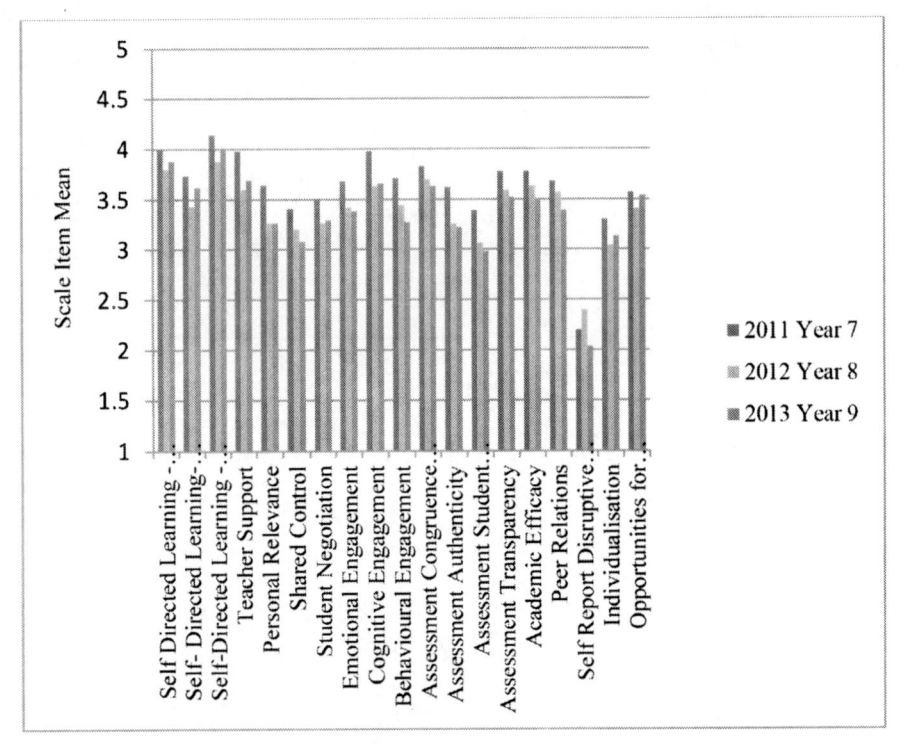

Figure 2.2. Progression of students' perceptions at Whirrakee College 2011–2013.

Table 2.4. Regression analysis with wellbeing and shared control.

	Standardised coefficient, β	t	p
Year 7, shared control	0.05	1.65	0.10
Year 10, shared control	−0.05	−1.92	0.05

Using Whirrakee College as an example, Table 2.4 shows that the typical student perceptions were less positive as they moved from Year 7 to Year 8 but, unlike traditional schools, rose as they entered their third year of secondary school. This result replicates many student attitude to school studies (see Barmby, Kind & Jones, 2008) for Years 7 and 8, but contrasts with these studies in Year 9. The Whirrakee example indicates that open-plan settings and team teaching can impact positively on older students. Whether these year-level responses can be further enhanced for all year levels in these settings remains an open but intriguing question.

QUANTITATIVE FINDINGS

The PLEQ showed a growth in most scale scores in three of the four BEP schools during the project. In addition, Table 2.4 regression analysis showed no significant contribution of shared control in Year 7 ($p< 0.10$) to wellbeing across all schools, but it was a quite significant contribution at Year 10 ($p< 0.05$). This suggests that as students mature and become more accustomed to these new open-plan settings they perceive increased opportunities for collaboration with teachers to be linked to their perceptions of wellbeing. As shown in the emerging model, see Figure 2.7, and explained later in this chapter, self-directed learning, assessment, learning environment and engagement contribute to wellbeing either directly or indirectly. It is not surprising to find strong correlation between these factors and wellbeing (average correlation is 0.64). Hence, students who perceived high levels of student wellbeing also perceive high levels of self-directed learning, assessment, learning environment and engagement and similarly students who perceived low levels of student wellbeing also perceived low levels of the contributing factors (see Table 2.5). These patterns of correlation highlight the intricate interconnectedness of influences between scales.

The Gippsland schools utilised their current facilities. Staff and students did not have the distractions of a rebuilding program and lack of recreational space. As shown in Figure 2.3, at Wattle College, 170 Year 8 students completed the PLEQ in 2011. This same cohort completed the PLEQ in Year 9 (2012) and Year 10 (2013). From analysing the PLEQ data, teachers in this school identified the need to alter student perceptions of learner engagement. In Society and Environmental Studies, up to eight teachers planned together to attempt to change student perceptions about their learning and engagement by utilising student voice and peer assessment. The students were taught in three groups in one large open-plan classroom, and while initially the teachers taught didactically, they soon modified their approach to working with students in enlarged communities by encouraging students to play a more active role in their learning.

In interviews, students reported experiencing improvement in their engagement and learning when their teachers personalised learning by incorporating opportunities for student voice during and after the learning activities and involved the students in providing peer assessment through a teacher facilitated and scaffolded learning approach. The survey data reflected positive perceptions of the learning environment

Table 2.5. Student wellbeing and perceptions of self-directed learning, assessment, learning environment and engagement.

	Assessment	Self-directed learning	Learning environment	Student engagement
High levels of wellbeing	3.74	4.22	3.72	4.00
Low levels of wellbeing	2.69	3.29	2.61	2.79

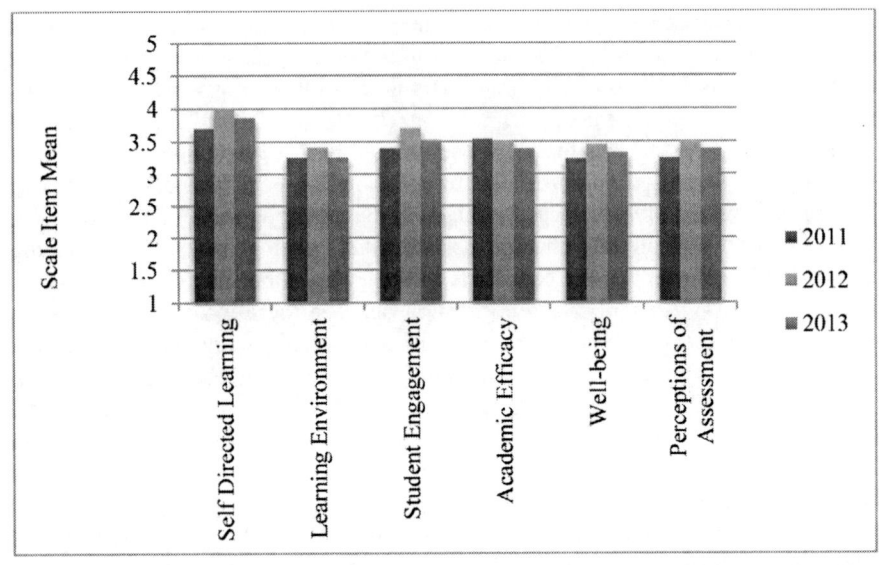

Figure 2.3. Wattle students' perceptions of scales as teaching changed from Year 8 to 10.

for Year 8 in 2011 and Year 9 in 2012 but declined for Year 10 in 2013 when teachers did not continue with the approach of addressing student voice and involvement in peer assessment.

Other Quantitative Data

We also report on student academic performance in English and mathematics over the three years of the study, focusing on reading and numeracy. In the BEP schools, the NAPLAN data for 2013 for Year 9 showed an improvement in scores from 2011–2013 (Year 7 to 9 schooling). We identified the degree of success of these schools compared to similar schools in Australia by examining the school ranking among "similar schools" as graphed in Figures 2.4 and 2.5 for Year 9 reading and numeracy respectively. Similar schools are clusters of schools that are statistically similar in educational disadvantage based on their ICSEA scores. A ranking of 1 in Figure 2.4 indicates that the school is the top performing school among similar schools and a ranking of 0 indicates the school is the lowest performing school among similar schools. This method of ranking on a scale from 0 to 1 has been employed because this method provides a common measure to compare the school ranking with similar schools.

All schools demonstrated major improvement in their relative ranking for reading. Melaleuca's results were more variable than the others but also showed a trend towards improvement. It is reasonable to suggest that these results reflect a more intensive focus on a robust differentiated curriculum in the BEP schools over this time when compared with "similar schools".

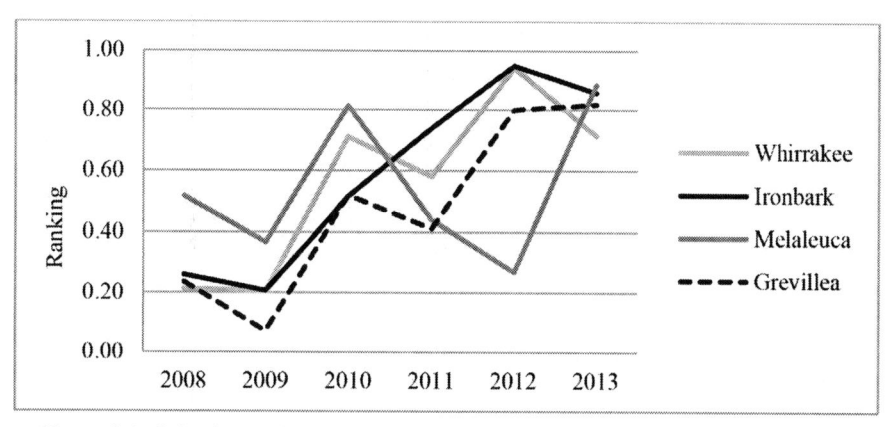

Figure 2.4. Schools' ranking among "similar schools" for Year 9 reading, 2008-2013.

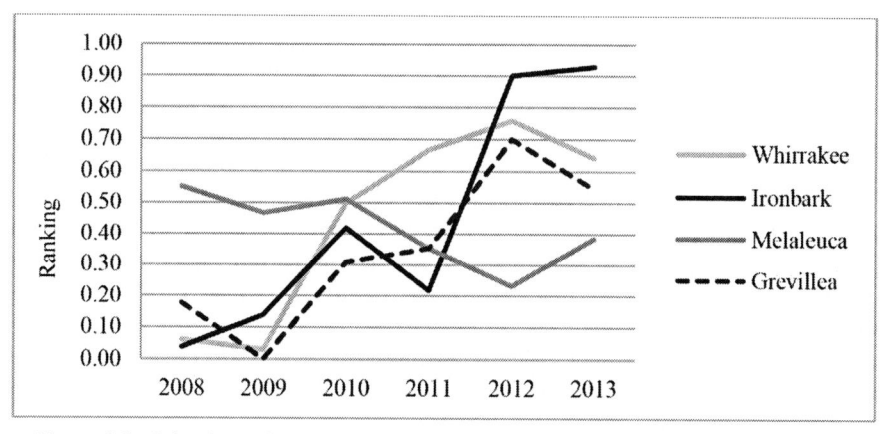

Figure 2.5. Schools' ranking among "similar schools" for Year 9 numeracy, 2008-2013

In Figure 2.5, again Melaleuca showed less improvement than other schools in numeracy perhaps reflecting the intensification of approaches in similar schools to this high stakes area of the curriculum over this period. However, the improvement in student scores at Ironbark, Grevillea and Whirrakee show major changes in rankings, and reflect significant gains. We comment further on the approach to mathematics at Ironbark in chapter 3.

The annually administered Attitudes to School Survey, commissioned by the Victorian government, was another indicator of student opinion on a range of learning and wellbeing questions, measured on Likert scales. Most measures improved, relative to state average scores, from 2010 to 2013 (Table 2.6). Here, the respective state average scores have been subtracted from each school's aggregated

Table 2.6. Changes in Attitudes to School Survey scores - school average score minus state average score for a student cohort [Year 7 (2010) to Year 10 (2013)]

School	Year 7 in 2010			Year 10 in 2013		
	Student rel'ships	Well being	Teaching & Learning	Student rel'ships	Well being	Teaching & Learning
Whirrakee	0.01	−0.29	−0.07	0.15↑	0.40↑	0.34↑
Ironbark	−0.18	−0.29	−0.21	−0.16→	−0.05→	0.08→
Melaleuca	−0.30	−0.36	−0.45	−0.26→	−0.27→	−0.17→
Grevillea	−0.23	−0.24	−0.27	−0.49↓	−0.74↓	−0.49↓

2012 Year 7 score, for Student Relations, Wellbeing and Teaching and Learning. This same calculation was done for the 2013 Year 10 scores. This was an attempt to characterise the gain of a cohort going from Year 7 to Year 10 against state average growth. The up and down arrows indicate a gain or decline of over 0.1 relative to state scores, and the horizontal arrows indicate a shift smaller than 0.1. The Student Relationship component explores aspects related to behaviour, connectedness to peers and student safety. This component was measured on a five-point Likert scale. The maximum possible rise was four on this component. Melaleuca and Ironbark had minor gains and Whirrakee showed a 0.14 gain from Year 7 in 2010 to Year 10 in 2013. Grevillea students showed a 0.26 decline during this time. The Wellbeing component was on a seven-point Likert scale. Whirrakee showed a 0.69 gain while Grevillea had a 0.50 decline. Overall, three of the schools showed an improvement as the cohort progressed from Year 7 in 2010 to Year 10 in 2013. These components will be analysed further in chapter 11. The Teaching and Learning component investigated learning confidence, school connectedness, motivation, teacher effectiveness, and the extent to which learning was stimulating. This component was measured on a five-point Likert scale. Whirrakee showed a 0.41 gain, Ironbark and Melaleuca a 0.28 gain while Grevillea had a 0.22 decline in this period.

Analysis of the school absentee data shows that there was a peak in percentage of school day absences during the transition of schools from old settings to new settings (Figure 2.6). Most of the schools were changing from traditional to new settings during 2011 with at least one school not being in the new settings until 2012. This time period was a cause of major disruptions to the schools' teaching program. A 10% value meant that students were missing for 10% of the teaching year. Regular student absences meant that students were often not in class for engagement and learning to occur. The pattern of absences varied among the BEP schools. We consider that the lower absentee rate at Whirrakee was due to the higher average SES of students than the other schools, and that the school had instituted an electronic touch-tag system for recording students' attendance.

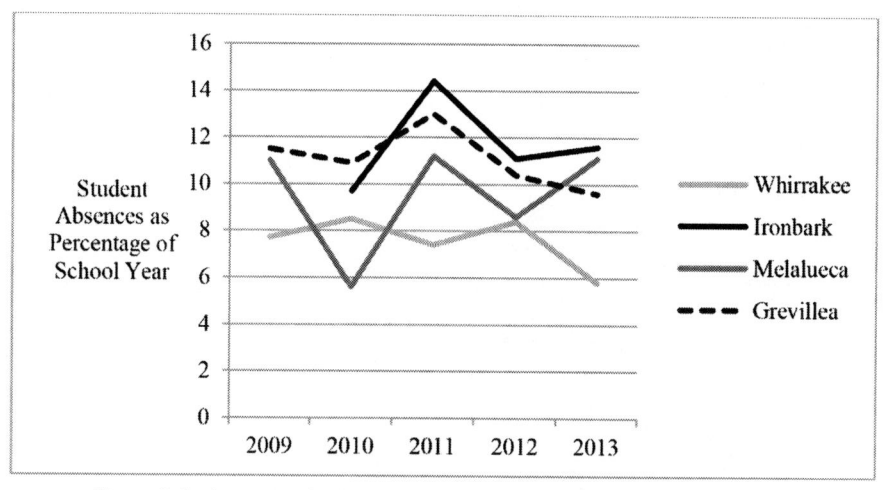

Figure 2.6. Aggregated school-level absences as percentage of school year.

EMERGENT MODEL FROM PLEQ

We analysed the PLEQ data to explore whether a workable model that explained the nature of the interaction between factors could be derived from these data. First, a measurement model was conducted to specify the relation between the latent variables and their measured indicator variables by means of multi-group confirmatory factor analysis (MGCFA) via AMOS 18.0 (Arbuckle, 2009). MGCFA is the most widely used method for testing measurement invariance. Next, a structural model was tested to specify the causal relationships among latent variables across groups (see Figure 2.7). To assess overall model fit, the following criteria were used: the χ^2 statistic, the comparative fit indices (CFI; $\geq$ .90), and the root mean squared error approximation (RMSEA; $\leq$ .08). ΔCFI and $\Delta\chi^2$ were used to investigate measurement and structural equivalence (Cheung & Rensvold, 2002; French & Finch, 2006). Full information maximum likelihood (FIML) estimation was used to accommodate missing data.

Multi-Group Structural Equation Modelling

Multi-group structural equation modelling enables testing and estimation of causal relations. AMOS utilises confirmatory modelling that allows the testing of relationships between the concepts in the model. This method can construct latent variables, that is, variables not measured directly but are estimated from several measured variables. It measures the covariance between all the items in the model. It allows evaluation of importance of each independent variable and to compare alternative models. The results of this testing indicates the extent of a fit. If it

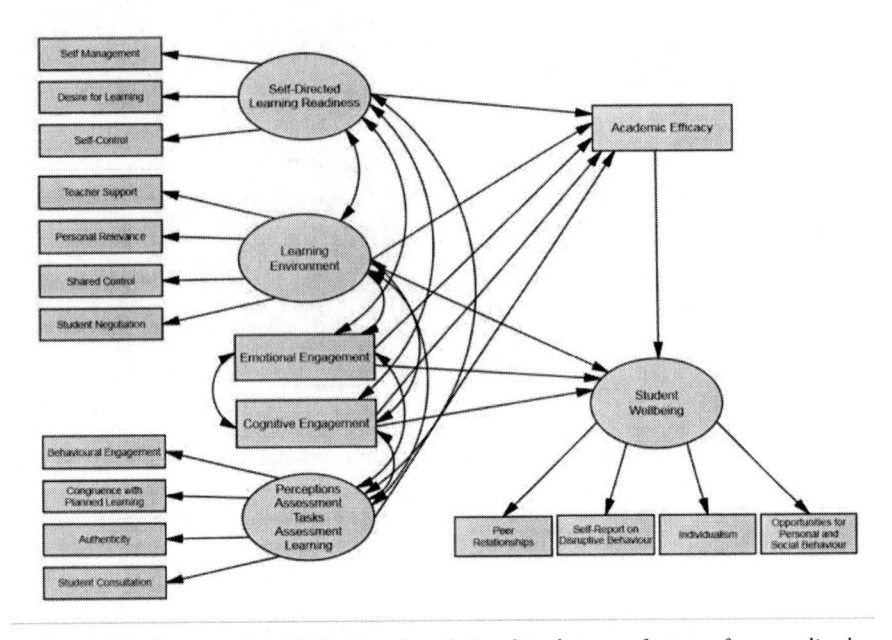

Figure 2.7. Emergent Model showing the relationships between factors of personalised learning and wellbeing.

indicates a poor fit, then the model is rejected. A poor fit can result when some items measure multiple factors or when some factors are more highly related to each other. The model is shown as path diagrams (Figure 2.7). A single headed arrow implies a direction of assumed causal influence while a double headed arrow represents covariance between the latent models. A single headed arrow assumes that the latent variable caused the observed variable.

The fit of the model was confirmed across three independent variables: calendar year, gender and year level.

Calendar year. We assessed the invariance of the measurement model across the three groups (i.e., calendar year 2011, 2012, and 2013). MGCFA was performed in the following order for tests of invariance: configural invariance, metric invariance, and scalar invariance. Configural invariance was evaluated by examining a baseline model with no invariance constraints across groups. The factor loadings caused us to drop "self-report disruptive", "peer relationships," "student negotiation," and "behavioural engagement" from consideration in the model. The resulting model showed acceptable model fit, $\chi^2(177) = 4541.54, p < .001$; CFI = .92; RMSEA = .056; 90% CI = .054, .057. In addition, all standardised factor loadings were above 0.53 ($p < .001$). The same pattern of factor loadings was found across groups, supporting configural invariance. Metric invariance was tested by making factor loadings equal across groups (i.e., calendar year 2011, 2012, and 2013). A test for scalar invariance was further conducted by constraining item intercepts to be equivalent across groups. This constrained model was a good fit with the data and suggested the full scalar invariance, $\chi^2(213) = 4644.72$, $p < .001$; CFI = .92; RMSEA = .051; 90% CI = .050, .052; $\Delta\chi^2(22) = 69.00$, $p < .001$; ΔCFI = .00. After establishing full scalar invariance, it was then tested whether latent construct means were different across the samples. Latent factor means of the calendar year 2011 group were restricted to zero, $\chi^2(205) = 4620.79$, $p < .001$; CFI = 0.92; RMSEA = .052; 90% CI = .051, .053; $\Delta\chi^2(8) = 23.93$, $p < .005$; ΔCFI = .00 and all latent means were found invariant across groups. The model showed that self-directed learning readiness, cognitive engagement, and perceptions of assessment tasks/assessment learning were all reciprocally associated with academic efficacy. Academic efficacy and learning environment were positively associated with student wellbeing. It was apparent that students were not seeing emotional engagement as being related to student wellbeing and learning. Interviews confirmed this finding in that students perceived emotional engagement as a social rather than a learning dimension. All exogenous variables (i.e., self-directed learning readiness, learning environment, emotional engagement, cognitive engagement, and perceptions of assessment tasks/assessment learning) were positively correlated with one another.

Gender. Next, multi-group analysis was performed in order to test for measurement invariance across gender. Configural invariance was tested to determine whether the factorial structure was the same for both genders. The pattern of factor loadings were the same across groups and all standardised factor loadings were above 0.49 ($p < .001$). Metric invariance was then tested by constraining the factor loadings across gender. The constrained model showed an acceptable fit. We noted that male students reported lower self-control and congruence with planned learning, but higher individualism than female students.

Finally, structural invariance across gender was tested. The baseline model showed a good fitted With the data, $\chi^2(129) = 3370.91$, $p < .001$; CFI = 0.94; RMSEA = .057; 90% CI = .056, .059. The model indicated that self-directed learning readiness, cognitive engagement, and perceptions of assessment tasks/assessment learning were all positively associated with academic efficacy. As indicated above, academic efficacy was positively related to student wellbeing. Learning environment was directly positively associated with student wellbeing.

Year level. A series of multi-group model tests were conducted to examine the measurement invariance of the factor structure across four year levels (i.e., Years 7–10). The fit indices for this model were acceptable, $\chi^2(257) = 4657.44$, $p < .001$; CFI = .92; RMSEA = .046; 90% CI = .045, .048. It was found that as students got older, they reported lower authenticity and student consultation, but higher opportunities for personal and social behaviour.

Utilisation of AMOS showed that the emerging model was confirmed when examined for each calendar year, year-level and gender impact. As described above, measurement invariance was established to examine the invariance of item intercepts, factor loadings and error variances. Next, there was a need to test for structural invariance (the invariance of the variances and the covariances of the latent variables). The model indicated that self-directed learning readiness, cognitive engagement, and perceptions of assessment tasks/assessment learning were all positively associated with academic efficacy. Academic efficacy contributed to student wellbeing. That is, the model showed that considering only a few factors (as is the case in other models) does not recognise the complex interlocking contributions of other factors. In other words, in up-scaled learning communities, a complex interactive influence of factors occurs. Therefore, to address just one variable ignores the impact of the other variables.

Because there is a complex interaction among almost all of the factors, the emergent model demonstrates that addressing personalisation of learning and wellbeing depends on a combination of factors rather than "just getting one factor right". This implies that there is a need for a coherent collaborative approach to address the needs of low socio-economic students. Implications from this emergent model are discussed in subsequent chapters.

CONCLUSIONS

In this chapter we have reported on the development, validation and implementation of a survey, the Personalised Learning Experience Questionnaire (PLEQ), to monitor students' perceptions of the extent to which their learning environment was personalised. We note that it was one of the first instruments to establish, using structural equation modelling, the complex interaction among a wide range of factors that impact on personalisation of learning, academic efficacy and student wellbeing. The PLEQ is significant in providing an instrument that enables a comprehensive evaluation by researchers and teachers of the learning environment in terms of monitoring personalised learning. Students' responses to the scales enabled teachers and researchers to:

- reflect on current student perceptions of major contributing elements to a personalised, quality learning environment;
- develop a shared language for interpreting results and appropriate responses;
- target possible pedagogical interventions to one or more scales to alter students' perceptions of how personalised they find this environment;
- track and evaluate the effect of interventions on student perceptions of the scales;
- gain a greater shared understanding of the complexity of scale interactions;
- monitor the long term learning effects of ongoing pedagogical interventions.

The emergent model indicates that there are no quick fixes, and that many of the scales interact to influence student perceptions. We also reported on and analysed quantitative data on student attendance, wellbeing, and academic performance in English and mathematics over the three years of the study (2011-2013). These results indicate the continuing challenges around influencing student attendance and also highlight the academic gains during this time. These findings are further analysed in subsequent chapters (see chapters 3 and 7).

VAUGHAN PRAIN, PETER COX, CRAIG DEED, DEBRA EDWARDS, CATHLEEN FARRELLY, MARY KEEFFE, VALERIE LOVEJOY, LUCY MOW, PETER SELLLINGS, BRUCE WALDRIP & ZALI YAGER

3. PERSONALISING LEARNING: THEORY AND ENACTMENT

PERSONALISING LEARNING

In the new up-scaled learning communities of 150-300 students in the BEP (2005), learning was to be personalised for all students. However, drawing mainly on Tomlinson (2005), the writers of the BEP were at best sketchy about the characteristics of personalised student learning experiences, their rationale, and strategies/procedures likely to promote these experiences. These authors viewed personalisation as predominantly a teacher-directed technical accomplishment around academic learning, rather than a process of optimising quality learning in academic, social, cultural and personal development terms, as suggested by Fielding (2004, 2006), Rogers (2013) and others. We concur with this broader conception, noting that over the three years of our study the teachers experimented with various curricular adaptations to enhance the likelihood of both academic and personal development processes/outcomes.

These included: team-teaching groups of 75 students to provide targeted subgroup support for a wide ability range of students in compulsory subjects like mathematics and English (see chapter 7 and Prain et al., in press); independent learning subjects where students negotiated with their teacher the goals and scope of an inquiry topic over nine weeks (see Prain et al., in press); teacher advisor (TA) programs where a teacher worked with a small group of students in a developmental curriculum in a learning community, and acted as an advocate for individual students on personal and academic matters (see chapters 9 and 10); team-teaching in Years 9 and 10 Studio Arts classes where students were supported by two teachers to develop styles and themes from personal preferences (see chapter 7 and Prain et al., in press); Year 10 students in one school undertaking a research study on the effectiveness of the TA program for Years 7 and 8 students, and reporting back to teachers; and Year 10 students in another school acting as coaching buddies for Year 8 students (see chapter 10). We draw partly on these studies and on the relevant literature around prescriptions and critical concerns to put a case for how personalising learning can be theorised and enacted in the context of the BEP schools. We begin by reviewing the emergence and reception of claims and practices about personalising learning.

V. Prain et al. (Eds.), Adapting to Teaching and Learning in Open-Plan Schools, 43–58.
© *2014 Sense Publishers. All rights reserved.*

ORIGINS, RATIONALE, ASSUMPTIONS, AND CLAIMS FOR PERSONALISING LEARNING

Educationists broadly agree that this construct, particularly in the United Kingdom, was transplanted from a policy emphasis on personalising public services, assuming that provision of quality education required experiences to be customised to address individual differences (Campbell et al., 2007; Pykett, 2010). In 2004, David Miliband, Secretary of State for Education and Skills, sought to clarify the intent and novelty of this approach by claiming that it entailed quality teaching based on meeting the individual student's learning needs. Students would not work as isolates or be left to their own devices, but rather teachers would accommodate learner differences through whole-class guidance (DfES, 2004).

Subsequent claims for this approach include socio-cultural, pedagogical, and motivational justifications, as well as appeals to its role in curricular reform (Blanchard, 2009; Drexler, 2010; Hargreaves, 2005; McLoughlin & Lee, 2010; Paludan, 2006; Sebba et al., 2007). These accounts claimed that personalised learning depends on both effective teacher differentiation of a set curriculum to address diversity of learner needs, and the development of independent learner capacities. From a combined socio-cultural/psychological/ economic perspective, Paludan (2006, p. 98) argues that personalised learning is an appropriate solution to the challenge of motivating and supporting students this century, and can lead to both personal and national economic benefits. He represents this approach as a necessary reform to the "fixed content and fixed timing" of traditional curricula. He reasonably notes that teachers are comfortable with a call for education to address individual learner needs, particularly where students are increasingly disengaged, even if the details of implementation remain vague. He suggests that student choice in "schedule and methodology" (p. 94) is easier to implement than opportunities for students to choose or devise their own subjects. From a sociocultural/pedagogical perspective, Hargreaves (2005, p. 34) asserts that personalised learning is the necessary "mass customisation" of education, already widespread in other areas, such as in health and other service provision, and in business practice. He claims that several key features are evident when learning is being successfully personalised: students are engaged in learning and schooling, they show responsibility for and independent control over their learning and behaviour, they demonstrate maturity in relating to peers and staff, and they co-design learning and teaching experiences. However, subsequent support for personalised learning has tended to remain vague about its distinctive features, representing it simply as a way to improve student motivation and learning outcomes (Department for Education & Skills, UK, (DfES), 2006; Duckworth, Akerman, MacGregor, Salter & Vorhaus, 2009; Sebba et al., 2007).

Not surprisingly, this definitional vagueness spawned various overlapping accounts of the pedagogies, environments and components reputedly required to optimise personalised learning. For Campbell et al. (2007, p. 140), the approach entails a range of pedagogies that cater for individuals, such as "cooperative learning, mentoring, valuing experiential learning, incorporating learners' personal and social experience, using ICT, and providing individual support". Various commentators broadly endorse these strategies as likely to promote personalised learning (DfES, 2006; Duckworth et al., 2009; Leadbetter, 2005; Sebba et al., 2007). Because current mainstream pedagogical practices easily fit this approach, this raises questions about what is distinctive in these teaching and learning strategies. According to Sebba and colleagues (2007) personalised learning comprises five key components: assessment for learning, effective teaching and learning (including grouping and ICT), curriculum entitlement and choice, school organisation (e.g. workforce remodelling), and relationships beyond the classroom (e.g. extended schools). The UK Department for Children, Schools and Families (DCSF) (2008) specified nine elements as features of good practice in personalised learning pedagogies. These were: high quality teaching and learning, target setting and tracking, focused assessment, intervention, pupil grouping, the learning environment, curriculum organisation, the extended curriculum, and supporting children's wider needs. The particular features of personalisation of learning are not defined, suggesting it could possibly include a return to student streaming, or much more student choice about curricular focus. From a pedagogical/economic perspective, Leadbetter (2005, p. 8) claims that personalised learning should equip children to make "choices about which subjects to study, what settings to study in, what styles of learning to employ. But choice is just a means to turn children into more engaged and motivated investors in their own education". Leadbetter's account also raises the question of how much agency or executive control should be given to, or assumed by, learners or teachers.

CRITIQUES

Accounts of personalised learning have been mainly criticised on the grounds of conceptual fuzziness (Carr, 2008; Cutler, Waine, & Brehony, 2007; Fielding, 2006; Hartley, 2009; Mahony & Hextall, 2009; Needham, 2011) and suspect ideological underpinnings and outcomes (Beach & Dovemark, 2009; Hartley, 2009; Pykett, 2009, 2010).

Hartley (2009, p. 432) claims that it dubiously combines marketing theory's interest in selfish consumerism with a nostalgic nod to child-centred education from the 1960s, and that, despite all the rhetoric, "little to do with pedagogy or with curriculum has changed". For Beach and Dovemark (2009, p. 689), this form of learning intensifies a market logic of strategic consumption for able consumers, mobilising "material and social resources in schools that support new forms of individualistic, selfish and private accumulations of education goods from public provision". They claim that the learner is cast as a rational, neoliberal individual who should become a "creative, self-reliant and discerning consumer and producer of knowledge" (Beach & Dovemark, 2009, p. 701). In other words, this model recasts education as a market for exploitation by knowledgeable consumers who operate on self-interest and informed private choice, thus continuing or exacerbating undemocratic educational disadvantage for some groups (Campbell et al., 2007; Meyer, Haywood, Sachdev, & Faraday, 2008; Pykett, 2009). Campbell and colleagues (2007, p. 138) further note that self-motivation and self-regulation are "not equally distributed" across society, and therefore this approach could increase disadvantage for some cohorts of students. For Pykett (2009, p. 393), personalisation turns questions of social justice or fairness of policy into problems about learner attributes, thus avoiding "political contestation and critical analysis". Others criticise it as a misguided alternative to more nuanced socio-cultural theories for how the needs of different learners can be understood and catered for in school (Beach & Dovemark, 2009; Campbell et al., 2007; Cutler et al., 2007; Mahony & Hextall, 2009; Pykett, 2010). Critics point to a lack of fit between a highly prescriptive curriculum and claimed freedoms for learners in personalised learning. Campbell and colleagues (2007) comment that a highly prescriptive age-based curriculum denies real scope for student choice. Cutler and colleagues (2007) and Rogers (2013) also note that personalised learning is equated with improving test results in the UK, implying that this approach to learning is as much about changing aggregated standards of performance in schools as addressing individual learner needs or goals. These researchers also note problems around questions of learner choice in the effective co-production of knowledge between learner and teacher, where both learner perspectives and teacher expertise and responsibility reputedly interact to address learning goals.

These points bring into sharp focus the question of what degree of student freedom or choice is desirable, or necessary, to personalise learning. We argue, following Moje (2007), that a socially just curriculum needs to provide access for all students to a quality mainstream curriculum, and that this implies necessary productive constraint on both the content and appropriate teaching and learning methods of the curriculum. We agree with Cutler and colleagues (2007), Mahony and Hextall, (2009) and Meyer and colleagues (2008) that there are challenges in implementing personalised learning approaches, particularly around the set of skills required of teachers, as well as teachers' beliefs about flexibility in teaching approaches and student grouping (see chapter 10). This question is particularly acute in the context of up-scaled learning communities, with their risk of individual student anonymity within a large student group. In questioning accounts of what personalised learning might mean, these critics raise reasonable questions about the extent to which students might be expected to make personal informed choices about what, how, when, where, why, with whom, and at what pace they learn.

From a philosophical perspective, Fielding (2006, p. 356) argues that an agenda of personalisation can result problematically in various negative effects, such as the manipulative subservience of individuals to 'high performance" demands, where organisational purposes override individual needs. However, he also suggests that a focus on developing individual personhood can lead to a desirable "person-centred learning community" (p. 360) with a "felt necessity of care" (p. 366). Such a community will demonstrate relationships between staff, students and parents that are "reciprocal, emergent and inclusive" (p. 364), where a "permanent provisionality" of practice is always responsive to "student voice", and where teachers and students are "working and learning together in partnership" (p. 364), as "co-enquirers and co-contributors" (p. 365). At the same time, he also acknowledges critical commentary around potential blind spots in this kind of community, where flexibility and communal purposes may oppress some members, where the call for productive relationships may fail to mask "contested realities" (p. 362), and where such a community fails to understand how it is embedded in, and dependent on, larger cultural and political contexts. We agree that any attempts to personalise learning will need to negotiate individual, group and broader cultural agendas, leading to structures and practices that enhance rather than diminish the meaningfulness of learning for individuals and groups.

OUTCOMES

Very few studies have evaluated the nature of the activities implemented as personalised learning initiatives in schools, or the impact of attempts at personalised learning on student achievement. The largest study of personalised learning in the UK to date was conducted by Sebba and colleagues (2007), who oversaw the collection of questionnaire data in 347 schools and performed in-depth case studies of thirteen schools nominated as having effectively implemented personalised learning.

When asked about the initiatives that had been implemented to reflect the school's philosophy of personalised learning, 54% of secondary schools indicated that most classes were grouped by ability, and 69% of all schools indicated that they used open-ended learning challenges, while 64% indicated that pupil autonomy and choices are encouraged at their school. A large proportion of schools also indicated that they utilised interactive whole-class teaching in order to facilitate personalised learning (Sebba et al., 2007). Targeted interventions (88%), enrichment and extension for all (77%), gifted and talented programmes (71%) and topic days/weeks (71%), were the most frequently cited curricular initiatives to achieve personalised learning (Sebba et al., 2007). New roles for support staff (72%), distributed leadership (68%) and pupil representation in policy making (63%) were the most frequently cited changes to school organisation as a result of personalised learning initiatives (Sebba et al., 2007).

Of initiatives "beyond the school" that were specific to personalised learning, partnerships with parents and the community (92%), working with other education institutions (89%) and 'the extended school' (76%) were the most frequently cited (Sebba et al., 2007). Finally, school council (89%), mentoring (77%), and advice and guidance (77%) were named as the most common personal and social development initiatives that reflected the schools' philosophy towards personalised learning. In their survey responses, most schools and teachers agreed that the implemented personalised learning strategies had "some" or "considerable" impact on student attainment and engagement at school (Sebba et al., 2007). Sebba and colleagues' study suffers from several limitations. It limited participant schools to enumerating specific strategies for implementing personalised learning from a range of strategies promoted by the UK Department of Education and Skills (DfES). Assessment of student attainment and engagement depended on teacher opinion rather than any quantitative measurement, and some participants experienced difficulty in understanding what was meant by the term "personalised learning".

Rogers (2013) claimed in his small-scale study that students rarely felt that their learning was personalised, that personal target setting was more about institutional standing than individual learning needs, and that students had little say on teaching methods. He noted the dangers in test-result data and academic learning gains becoming fetishised as schooling's only purpose at the expense of a more democratic culture. By contrast, a comprehensive curriculum should engage and develop students as individuals pursuing richer learning purposes. For Rogers (2013, p. 13) personalisation has the potential to enable social justice through redistributing goods, but authentic "democratic and trusting relationships" are crucial to this end. We share his concern for a richer account of the values, goals, processes, and outcomes of personalising learning.

CONCEPTUALISING PERSONALISED LEARNING

Our general approach draws on pragmatist perspectives on the situated and contextual nature of problem-solving, knowledge generation, values clarification, and meaning-making (Dewey, 1985; Peirce, 1931-58; Wittgenstein, 1972). From these perspectives, what personalising learning means depends on analysing the goals, values, strategies and outcomes that have occurred, or could occur, in its name. In this way we understand a pragmatist orientation to be a systematic method of inquiry that avoids a priori judgements and incorporates a reasoned collective analysis of attempted personalising practices to identify justifiable beliefs about their effects. Rather than aiming to name de-contextualised essential truths about personalising processes, we sought to identify justifiable rules for effective action in this particular setting. Open-plan settings unsettled the teachers' past habitual behaviour and perspectives on effective teaching and learning, causing them to reflect and experiment with a range of new options that were judged for effectiveness by their practicability and the degree to which they enhanced individual student learning (see chapter 7).

Researchers generally agree that personalising learning is understood as a practical way to increase the extent to which individual students find learning to be engaging and meaningful. The problem that personalised learning aims to address is a fundamental one about the characteristics of quality learning, raising larger questions about the ultimate purposes of school-based education in terms of learner knowledge, attributes, and values. As pragmatists we focus our inquiry on the particular features of the regional and school contexts to address the issue of what personalising learning could mean under these conditions. We recognise that engagement and meaningfulness as curricular effects pose heightened challenges for teaching low SES students, who are often alienated from schooling. Our inquiry therefore entails resolving practical questions assumed to have identifiable causes in these contexts, where knowledge about personalising learning is generated by logical proof and through dialogue and debate with participants.

We claim that learning is personalised when the learners are motivated to learn because they view the learning task/experience as engaging and meaningful, and as directly addressing their immediate and/or long term learning needs. Motivation for this learning may be intrinsic, extrinsic, or both (see Dweck, 2000). We claim that both kinds of motivation can occur concurrently or sequentially, and contribute to personalising learning. In this way, what learners find to be meaningful can be prompted by learner and teacher intentions and strategies, and these influences can vary over time. Learners are best placed to judge the extent to which their learning is personalised, but this process also leaves scope for teachers to make informed judgements on these matters. For their part, teachers are expected to contribute to these learner perceptions and experiences through designing curricular tasks and activities, motivating students, providing targeted teaching and timely feedback, and, where appropriate, negotiating with students their goals, tasks, and performance evaluation. Students are expected to develop more self-reliance and initiative as learners over time. The teaching experience is personalised for teachers when they bring their energy, flair, and expertise to providing meaningful learning experiences for their students (see chapter 7).

We know that this account raises further questions around what enables learner perceptions of meaningfulness, what exactly should count as meaningful and why, what responsibilities are or should be distributed between teachers and students, and who should shape curricular content and methods. Our case studies in chapter seven flesh out detailed answers to these questions, but here we summarise key aspects of our reasoning on these matters.

On the question of what contributes to student perceptions of meaningful learning, we recognise crucial complementary insights from pedagogical, cognitive, sociocultural, and psychological perspectives. From pedagogical perspectives, a robust mainstream curriculum that includes opportunities to differentiate what, how, when, where, why, with whom, and at what pace students learn, is likely to be perceived as more engaging and meaningful than a standardised curriculum. This is especially likely to be the case where there is a wide range of ability in a class. In this sense learning is likely to be meaningful when there is a good fit between individual learner needs, interests, and capacities, and the demands, or level, of the learning activities. This implies that a well-designed and differentiated curriculum increases the likelihood of student motivation.

From cognitive perspectives, learning is likely to be meaningful when learners know how to self-regulate their learning (Pintrich & de Groot, 1990). This entails constructive and intentional use of personal strategies to achieve academic and wellbeing goals (Boekaerts & Corno, 2005; Butler & Winne, 1995). Pintrich's (2004) widely adopted model of self-regulated learning (SRL) involves: (1)

forethought, planning and activation (planning and enacting behaviour such as effort and persistence); (2) monitoring (such as tracking task requirements); (3) control (such as adapting behavioural strategies to ensure task completion); and (4) reflection (such as use of self-assessing strategies achieve task requirements). For Zimmerman (2008), independent learning or self-regulated learning refers to the degree to which students are metacognitively, motivationally and behaviourally active participants in their own learning processes. In this sense learning is likely to be personalised and meaningful when students know and use a repertoire of such strategies. We acknowledge that self-regulation is developmental, and that teacher co-regulation of learning experiences usually enables this development. We also agree that learning can be personally meaningful when students with limited self-regulatory capacities are supported by this co-regulation (see Prain et al., in press). From these perspectives, the crucial element is reflection-guided action, leading to a sense of student learning mastery.

In presenting our account of personalising learning, we also wish to clarify how we see the relationship between students' personal and collective experiences. For us, learning is personalised when it promotes in learners a sense of their individual capabilities and interests. However, we regard isolationist views of personalising learning as misguided. Learners are likely to view their learning as personalised and meaningful through relational connections. From socio-cultural perspectives, meaningful learning for students also depends on successful participation in culturally valued activities (Sfard, 1998). In this sense the development of an individual identity as a person, a student of a particular subject, a class member, a group participant, or a valued learning community member depends on productive relationships with others that enable individual and group goals, and wellbeing to be achieved (see chapters 9 and 10). This is evident for example when learners contribute to such activities as large and small group discussion, debates, academic and sporting teams, group projects, musical ensembles, school community decision-making, and teamwork around small or large projects.

From psychological perspectives, learners feel that their learning is personalised if teachers demonstrate concern for, and knowledge of, students as individuals, as well as providing strategies to address their particular academic and wellbeing needs (see chapters 9 and 10). An individual learner's sense of self and personhood depends on this sense of individuation and recognition through personal achievement and through connection with others (Fielding 2004, 2006). We argue that with low SES students, this achievement and sense of connection can be enhanced by a focus on an explicit, developmental curriculum around social and emotional learning to support students becoming active, functional members of their learning community (see chapters 9 and 10).

On the question of who should decide the curriculum, we argue that in the context of highly prescriptive national and state curricula and testing regimes in high stakes subjects, teachers need to have a significant role in shaping curricular content and goals. We argue, following Moje (2007), that a socially just curriculum needs to provide access for all students to a quality mainstream curriculum, and that this implies necessary productive constraint on both the content and appropriate teaching and learning methods of the curriculum. In this we reject the view that personalising learning is inevitably a misguided return to student-centred education from the 1960s (Hartley, 2009), although we claim there is scope in some subjects for more student initiative on curricular content and methods (Prain et al., in press). In this regard learning mathematics effectively is more likely to depend on successful progression through topics/levels than learning in some personal interest-based humanities and technical subjects, although these subjects also depend on progressive skill development. More contentiously, we also argue that personalising learning can be compatible with testing regimes, in that such regimes can provide an evidential starting point for curricular design that incorporates precise differentiation of the curriculum to address learner needs. At the same time, we recognise that student academic success in subjects is not the sole indicator that learning is personalised, and that students may succeed without attaching much personal meaning to the content of this success. In terms of optimal meaningfulness, it is preferable for students to find their subject content deeply engaging. Engagement can be based on prior interest, but also on students becoming involved in a challenge that raises latent interest.

On the matter of the ideological underpinnings of personalising learning, we disagree that this form of learning necessarily equates with neoliberal consumerism (Beach and Dovemark, 2009), or inevitably increases disadvantage for low socio-economic status students (Campbell et al., 2007; Cutler et al., 2007; Pykett, 2010). Our research indicates that the ideological character of this approach emerges from the forms of its enactment rather than any inherent traits, and that it can equally serve a social justice agenda, contributing to a more democratic, trusting school culture (see Rogers, 2013). Our research also confirms that low SES students can benefit academically and socially from the approaches to personalising learning enacted in this regional setting, and that inherently this approach does not exacerbate privilege and disadvantage (see chapters 7 and 10).

Quality learning necessarily integrates psychological, epistemological, epistemic, and cultural dimensions that align with personalising learning. We claim that when students are motivated to learn, engage with appropriate tools for knowing in the topic or subject, learn how knowledge is developed in the topic or subject, and participate in culturally-valued learning experiences that are made meaningful to them, then these processes and outcomes entail quality learning over time. We well appreciate that "culturally-valued learning experiences" are deeply contested, even in the particulars of high stakes subjects such as English and mathematics, and that there are contested views about how issues around citizenship, ethnicity, class, gender, and the predicted needs, capabilities and values of future citizens should be understood and addressed (see chapter 7 and Prain et al., in press).

ENACTING PERSONALISED LEARNING

We claim that a personalised learning approach entails differences as well as similarities in the responsibilities, goals, constraints, learning needs, and roles of teachers and students. We also view personalising learning as necessarily developmental, and therefore requiring a range of teacher and learner strategies, experiences, and understandings over an extended timeframe, leading eventually to increased student capacity to contribute to, and to co-design, their curricular content and methods with their teachers.

From our perspective, the capacity for a school curriculum to enact a personalised approach to learners and learning depends on many factors, including school leadership, teacher skills and practices, and learner capacities and goals. Teachers need the expertise, time, resources, and teamwork to develop a flexible robust curriculum that is adequately structured in content, learning tasks, and adaptable classroom practices to engage all learners and address contrasting learner needs. This need not imply fixed labelling of learner capacities and long term streaming, but rather ongoing responsive flexible programming to each student's needs. We would argue that a further critical element in this approach is the "relational agency" (Edwards, 2005, 2007, 2011) among teachers, and between teachers and students, to achieve teaching and learning goals. We also suggest this relational agency operates within a "nested agency" in the development of differentiated curricula and learners' self-regulatory capacities (Prain et al., 2013). From this perspective, learning can be personalised for students when there is a productive interplay between (a) teacher expertise in identifying and addressing students' ongoing individual curricular needs, and (b) student capacity to develop, over an extended timeframe, increasing independence as learners (see Figure 3.1). The construct of "nested agency" recognises that the agency of both groups as they interact is constrained by structural, cultural, and pedagogical assumptions, regulations, and practices, including prescriptive curricula, and actual and potential roles and responsibilities of teachers and students in school settings.

RELATIONAL AND NESTED AGENCY, DIFFERENTIATED CURRICULA, AND SELF-REGULATED LEARNING

For Edwards (2005, 2007, p.4) "relational agency" refers to a capacity for professionals to work with other professionals to develop a "network of expertise" to serve shared goals, where the agency of individuals is built around distributed intelligence and diverse expertise across the group. Rather than emphasise individual action, Edwards (2007, p. 6) foregrounds "responsibility to and for others", where a shift to the relational is "an important move in the development of meshes of mutual responsibility". Edwards (2011, p. 39) does not deny the importance of individual expertise, but argues that confidence in one's own expertise in combination with recognition and understanding of the perspectives of other practitioners builds

PERSONALISING LEARNING

Constraints on Agency
Productive constraints on teachers and students as agents, including school structuring of time and space, regulations, prescriptive curricula, histories of practice, expectations on student and teacher roles

Relational Agency

Teacher/Teacher
In teams, teachers design, enact & evaluate differentiated curriculum

Teacher/Student Differentiation of the Curriculum
Variation in goal-setting, course content, tasks, teaching methods, groupings, monitoring and tracking, co-regulation of tasks, assessing

Student Self-regulated Learning
Planning, goal-setting, feedback, reflection, informed action, self-monitoring and tracking of performance, adaptive strategies, peer & self assessing

Personalized Learning Experience
Instance of integration of differentiation and self-regulation strategies by individual students

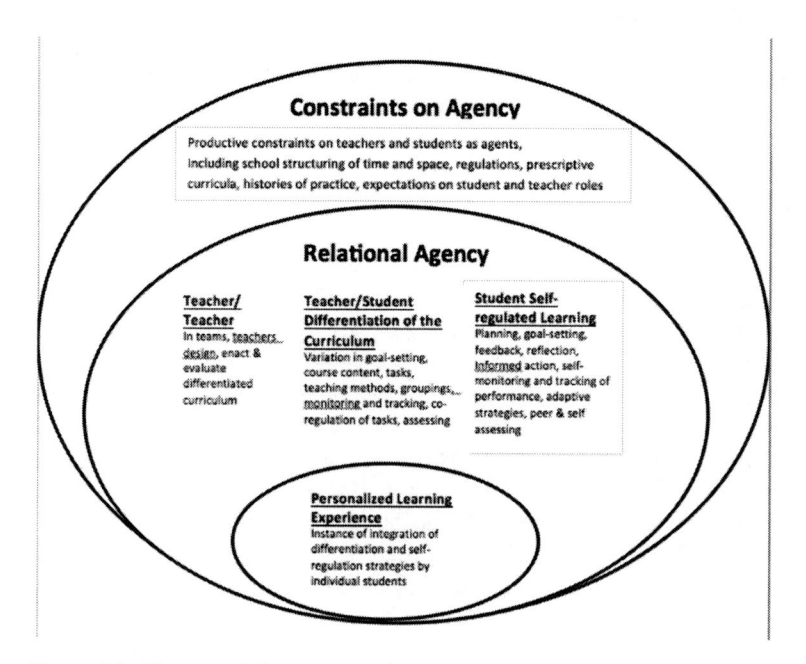

Figure 3.1. Framework for conceptualising and enacting personalised learning.

an expanding common knowledge (in this case of teacher professional needs and student curricular needs) that "mediates responsive professional action". In enacting this mutual responsibility, Edwards (2011, p. 35) notes the need for participants to (a) demarcate power in decision-making to both clarify and ensure spheres of influence, (b) focus on "the whole child in the wider context", (c) create and develop better tools for collaboration, (d) refine processes for sharing knowledge, and (e) continuously review socially-constructed boundaries to ensure that they serve shared long term goals effectively.

While this construct of relational agency is clearly applicable to teachers working in interdependent teams to design, implement, and evaluate curricula, we consider that teachers' interactions with students can be viewed similarly. From this perspective, personalised learning entails mutual responsibility among teachers, teachers and students, and among students, where teachers are responsible for designing and implementing a curriculum that (a) engages all students, (b) provides opportunities for differentiated teaching and learning that addresses group and individual student needs, and (c) motivates and develops students' capacities to become independent learners. For their part, students are responsible for their learning through participation in these curricular tasks, connected experiences, and opportunities. This also raises the fundamental question of the exact nature and scope of student expertise and agency, sphere of influence, and its exercise. While acknowledging that this agency is developmental, we argue, following Fielding (2004) and others, that students' rights and their experiential expertise as learners and learning community members should inform the culture and practices of schooling, with increasing scope for influencing the focus and methods of learning (see chapter10).

At the same time, both teacher and student agency is constrained by various factors, including prescriptive curricula, particular assessment regimes, the organisation of the curriculum, perceived and actual teacher and student roles and responsibilities in and beyond the school setting, and broader social and cultural expectations about norms for teaching and learning processes. Low SES students are also constrained typically by low aspirations, histories of modest academic achievement, and low self-efficacy that may hinder their willingness and capacity to participate in co-regulated learning (Domina & Saldana, 2011). Students have nested agency within the constraints on agency operating on teachers around their practices within school and larger education systems. Whether these constraints function productively or otherwise for both teachers and students depends on the practices that can be perceived and developed within this nested agency. We argue that well-designed curriculum differentiation, coupled with a developmental approach to learner self-regulation and growing independence, can support relational agency within these constraints.

This approach aims to motivate students and produce more effective learning by developing a curriculum that acknowledges and addresses individual differences (Stradling & Saunders, 1993; Strong, Silver & Perini, 2001; Subban, 2006; Tomlinson, 2001; Tomlinson & Kalbfleisch, 1998; Tuttle 2000). Jackson and Davis (2000) and Tomlinson (1999) claim that differentiation can occur across three dimensions: content (what students should know and be able to do, and the materials that will support them in their learning); processes (the activities that help students make sense of their learning); and products (the range of evidence students provide of their learning).

McTighe and Wiggins (2004) claim the need for a three-step planning sequence for curriculum should begin with identifying the desired results, then determining the assessment evidence, and finally planning the learning experiences that will lead to the desired results. They claim this approach "provides the structure to support flexibility in teaching and assessing, to honour the integrity of content while respecting the individuality of learners" (McTighe & Brown, 2005, p. 242). They also claim this approach preserves standards without standardisation by respecting both curriculum and learners. However, Subban (2006, pp. 942-3) notes that research on student learning outcomes for programs that attempt to differentiate learning goals, methods and assessment, according to student need, reveals only mixed success. This may further reflect the significant challenges for teachers in developing more flexible curricula, and changing to more responsive teaching styles. For their part, students need to learn how to become 'self-regulated' learners in order to motivate, monitor and manage their own learning.

In the next section we present a case study of mathematics as an example of our theoretical account in practice

MATHEMATICS CASE STUDY

Context

Prior to the implementation of a personalised, differentiated curriculum, mathematics teachers at Ironbark College worked in traditional classrooms with students of wide-ranging abilities, using age-based textbooks with no common curriculum. Over 2010–2011, the school was rebuilt with open-plan learning spaces, organised into four Years 7–10 learning communities of approximately 150 students. Each community has a junior (Years 7 and 8) and a senior (Years 9 and 10) section, physically situated at each end of the building with common space between, led by a learning community leader. The timetable is organised into five periods a day. Students meet at the start of each day with two teacher advisors in age-based groups of approximately 25 for 20 minutes. The remainder of the day is structured into four 70 minute classes. The school's policy is to prioritise English and mathematics, in line with state and regional objectives to improve learning outcomes for regional secondary students. To meet this objective, these two subjects are accorded four 70 minute lessons a week over four days.

National tests demonstrated that student performance at the college was well below national averages (see Table 3.1), while Attitudes to School Surveys revealed students were disengaged with mathematics and unmotivated. The principal sought to improve mathematics achievement scores and student motivation through employing a consultant with expertise in learner motivation and mathematics education. This consultant had extensive experience in guiding teacher professional development. She worked with the learning community leaders and teachers in a sequence of workshops that focused on improving teacher mathematics knowledge and diagnostic assessment skills to guide future learning, as suggested by Stradling

Table 3.1 Victorian NAPLAN Statistics

Victorian NAPLAN Statistics	2009 Year 7	2011 Year 9	Difference
Average Raw NAPLAN Score	497.0	541.6	44.6
Matched Cohort Raw NAPLAN Score	495.6	541.6	46.0
Victorian Average Raw NAPLAN Score	550.8	590.5	39.7
Difference A-B	−55.2	−48.9	+6.3

Source: Victorian Statistics supplied by Phillip Holmes-Smith (5/12/11); School Statistics supplied by Loddon Mallee Regional Office of the Victorian Department of Education and Early Childhood Development (DEECD)

and Saunders (1993). Through a consensual process the staff members established protocols around learning and behaviour in each community that they all agreed to reinforce consistently.

Enablers in the process included: principal enthusiasm and leadership; consultant expertise; positive staff attitudes towards adapting to change; and useful textbook resources to enable the curriculum to be differentiated. Constraints included: a lack of trained mathematics teachers; some negative staff beliefs about the degree to which they should be held accountable for student learning, given their perception of student capacity and willingness to learn; negative staff attitudes to change to team-teaching approaches in open-plan settings; and lack of a common vision.

Implementation Strategies

The consultant gathered student data from national tests, surveys and selective interviews to gain a sense of student achievement, motivation, desires, and needs, confirming the students' desire to learn and progress. She presented these data to the principal and then worked further with coordinators and mathematics teachers to improve teaching and learning in this subject. Data were then presented to staff and, through a consensual process, staff members established protocols around learning and behaviour in the community that they all agreed to reinforce consistently. The consultant then worked with the teachers to devise an effective differentiated curriculum based on use of existing textbooks. The curriculum was differentiated in practice by providing a program where (a) students were placed in groups in appropriate levels, and (b) workshops were provided with explicit teaching to support student learning. All students worked on one unit at a time but at different levels. To motivate students, and to give them a goal to work towards, the consultant devised pre-tests with the teachers. Students were given feedback on actual and expected progression levels, with post-tests confirming progress.

This co-regulated learning, through goal-setting, differentiated curriculum, formative assessment, and feedback, contributed to a sense of relational agency between the teachers and students. Teachers led small-group workshops to address individual student needs and to build skills and mathematical knowledge, while students worked with a range of stage-based resources, including ICT resources, to encourage independent learning. Providing a variety of mathematical experiences was seen as a motivating factor to meet diverse learning needs and sustain student interest. Staff members worked in teams where each had a role and responsibility for student learning, with each staff member responsible for devising a pre-test and post-test for one section of the unit. Classes were taught in blocks, so that two or three teachers grouped with a large number of students enabled flexibility for teachers and students. Staff accountability entailed staff members consistently reinforcing protocols of community behaviour. Staff members assisted students to set and periodically revisit appropriate goals, check and sign off on satisfactory completion of work, and give individual students feedback and encouragement. The mathematics

PERSONALISING LEARNING

coordinator and staff received professional development, with the consultant providing ongoing workshops and individual coaching to challenge their personal beliefs about teaching and learning, developing their expert knowledge and skills in teaching mathematics curriculum, and reinforcing key concepts and procedural knowledge. In this way, the program was informed by relational agency among the teachers, and among teachers and students, to develop an effective differentiated curriculum that was personalised to meet individual students' capacities and needs in mathematics.

Outcomes

Outcomes noted by the principal, mathematics coordinator and the consultant included an improvement in student motivation and desire to learn, evident in increased homework, more self-directed learning, and more positive Attitudes to School Survey and Personalised Learning Experience Questionnaire results. There was also increased cooperation amongst teachers, operating at higher conceptual levels, and planning together. In interviews, students claimed to be more motivated, and expressed pride in their achievement gains. Significantly, these perceived qualitative gains can be measured quantitatively as improvement in academic attainment ensued, evident in gains in national testing data that were above state average gains for 2009 to 2011, Year 7 to Year 9 (see Table 3.1 and chapter 2, Figure 2.5).

The Australian government introduced the National Assessment Program -Literacy and Numeracy (NAPLAN) tests in 2008 as a nationwide compulsory assessment of basic skills in literacy and mathematics (Australian Curriculum and Assessment Reporting Authority, 2014). NAPLAN is a simple form of data with a 'one size fits all' approach to assessing and measuring students' abilities and progress. The results place the students on a scale that compares them to all other Australian and Victorian students of their age group. The trial mathematics program has run in this school for three years (2009 – 2011). Using the school's NAPLAN (numeracy) data for Year 7 in 2009 and Year 9 in 2011, it was possible to compare directly the growth in the 2011 Year 9 cohort that has been participating in the trial mathematics program for three years (2009 – 2011).

As Table 3.1 demonstrates, the analysis of the NAPLAN (numeracy) data trends over these three years has shown that the cohort of 2011 Year 9 students who have participated in this intervention have demonstrated growth in numeracy of 46 points since Year 7 that exceeds the average growth expected in numeracy for this cohort of 39.7 points [when compared with the Victorian state-wide Year 9 (2011) NAPLAN numeracy data trend from Year 7 to Year 9]. The above expected growth is significant when the socio-economic background of these students is taken into account. This is highlighted in chapter 2, Figure 2.5, where the school is now among the top-ranked like SES schools (based on ICSEA values).

We are aware that, ultimately, students decide how personalised they find their learning, and that a Hawthorne effect from the work of the expert consultant in the new settings may explain some of the gains. However, this outcome is promising. This result of exceeding expected growth in NAPLAN (numeracy) indicates that the trial program has had a measurable effect on numeracy in this cohort, where the deficit between this cohort of Year 9 students and the Victorian state average has been reduced by 6.3 points in two years, and therefore should be considered an effective framework for teaching mathematics in this context and similar contexts. This learning outcome also concurs with Domina and Saldana's (2011) findings that an intensive focus on the mathematics curriculum benefits low SES learners.

IMPLICATIONS AND CONCLUSION

In this chapter, while acknowledging a range of reasonable concerns around past and current accounts of personalised learning, we have presented a framework to conceptualise and enact teaching and learning programs and practices in up-scaled learning communities in open-plan settings. We have argued that the core features of this approach entail strong teacher teamwork in devising, enacting and evaluating a differentiated curriculum. This approach is built around teacher expertise and mutual responsibility between teachers and students, with the long term goal of developing student self-reliance and independence in learning. Personalised learning depends on the expertise of teachers to support students' meaningful goal-setting, accompanied by the provision of an engaging curriculum that offers timely strategies and learning experiences to address student goals.

SECTION TWO

SCHOOL LEADERS AND TEACHERS: CHALLENGES IN ADAPTATION AND REASONING

PETER COX & DEBRA EDWARDS

4. RESTRUCTURING TEACHING AND LEARNING IN OPEN-PLAN SCHOOLS

RESTRUCTURING SCHOOLING

In this chapter we review structural decisions about the Bendigo Education Plan (BEP), including the physical design of buildings and the community/timetable organisation over this time (2011–2013) in the four BEP 7–10 colleges: Grevillea, Ironbark, Melaleuca and Whirrakee. We focus on the practical reasoning of the principals and teachers in organising curricula for these new settings. We briefly review the similarities and differences in the physical design and culture of the four schools to provide a broader context for this reasoning. Following the initial consultation between the architects, principals and teachers, the principals and staff members were able to develop curricula and conceptualise new ways of learning and teaching around perceived affordances in the new spaces, leading to various organisational changes over this three-year study. In tracking these changes and the reasoning around them, we were not seeking to identify optimal "best practice" structures, whether physical or organisational, given differences of scale and cultures across schools. Rather, we sought to understand attempted practices in each context, the rationale for these practices, and the challenges/benefits in each case. Related to these changes to practices, in chapter six we review how leadership was understood and distributed in each school over this time, and in chapter seven we present indicative examples of curricular adaptation in each school, noting shared and local features/successes. Our tracking demonstrates that for schools like these in predominantly low socio-economic areas, creating communities with strong teacher-student relationships can lead to improved pedagogy and student learning outcomes.

CHANGING SCHOOL DESIGNS

Prescriptions for the physical design of the new schools were claimed to align with "contemporary design principles that improve learning outcomes for students" (BEP Steering Committee 2005, p. 36). However, this alignment was more speculative than proven. Each school was to have the following design elements.

– The design should have large, flexible spaces that allow teams of teachers to work with up to 125 students using a range of approaches.

V. Prain et al. (Eds.), *Adapting to Teaching and Learning in Open-Plan Schools*, 61–78.
© 2014 Sense Publishers. All rights reserved.

- The design should maximise student access to the learning environment and so promote the ownership and use of the facilities. For example students should have open access to learning spaces, audio visual and ICT resources, and the use of the formal and informal furniture.
- Spaces must be capable of concurrent and consecutive use for multiple users and multiple purposes. Thus, these spaces need to be both formal and informal so that teacher and student centred learning is possible.
- Spaces should be inherently flexible for team and individual activities, the furniture needs to enhance this flexibility and ICT should be ubiquitous.
- The design must allow the use of the vertical dimension in the spaces, for example displaying work and materials on the walls and from the ceilings.
- The design must integrate functions so that, at all times in the day, areas for eating, circulation, formal and informal spaces, and outdoor spaces can be shared.
- Teacher and student relationships must be maximised by design features such as open staff rooms, visual connections between areas, and very few locked areas with spaces accessible to all.

These principles instantiated a growing contemporary international rhetoric around claims that new school building design should dissolve boundaries between formal and informal education (Reh, Rabenstein, & Fritzsche, 2011), provide more freedom/independence for individualised student usage (McGregor, 2004a, 2004b), and offer an attractive more open, flexible setting for up-scaled learning communities to enable team-teaching, rather than traditional cellular classes with solitary teachers (Nair & Fielding, 2005). The BEP also recognised that these new design elements would not ensure learning gains, but were viewed as a catalyst for new teaching and learning approaches.

Each school was to have four up-scaled learning communities comprising two learning neighbourhoods of 100–150 students as shown in chapter one, Figure 1.1. Each of these four communities would be located around a central community green and each learning community would be linked to one specialist area: 'Think and Inquire', 'Performance', 'Design, Creativity and Technology' or 'Health and Fitness'. Further designs indicated that within a learning community the two neighbourhoods would be linked by a breakout space (Einstein Studio) and a shared Arts/Science learning space (Da Vinci Art & Science Studio), which would all be connected to the specialist area. These prescriptions point to aspirational optimism for new generic learning tasks and innovative cross-disciplinary inquiry.

The BEP claimed that this design framework would enable:

— multi-age groupings;
— core teacher teams reflecting and learning together;
— disciplinary and inter-disciplinary teams;
— personalised learning;
— curriculum breadth and depth;

— applied and real world learning;
— learning to learn skills;
— thinking of/about/as/for learning;
— ICT as a creative tool;
— indoor-outdoor connections;
— spaces that support hands-on, real-world curriculum;
— spaces for all types of learning and all size groups.

The broad intention of this design concept was to build learning spaces able to accommodate large and small groups, including stage-based groups, and flexible configurations of groups of students and teachers, thus inherently forcing a rethink of the breadth and depth of curriculum design and approaches to teaching and learning. It was envisaged that within the larger communities there would be smaller learning communities with interdisciplinary teaching teams, as well as the more traditional teaching teams, that would lead to new and innovative ways of thinking about experiential and personalised student learning, applying learning to 'real world' situations, and creating cross-environmental connections (indoor/outdoor). This implied a radical redesign of the built environment to create the opportunity for the rethinking of performance and development cultures, the creative use of interactive communication technologies, and ways of accommodating different learning styles and needs of students.

This conceptual interaction between architectural design principles and pedagogy is not new, nor is the idea that large open-plan spaces invite new ways of thinking (see chapter 5). What was radical was the whole-scale, city-wide approach to redesigning school environments, as well as reconceptualising learning and teaching, while teachers and students were occupying the school spaces. While unintentional, this meant that the schools evolved over time and had opportunities to redesign and review ways of operating in situ.

To allay community concerns about equivalent provision/resources for each school, all schools were expected to implement the original design concept and design principles explained above. However, there was scope for local customisation of design and student groupings to address students' perceived needs and to align new buildings with each school's history and culture. While schools were constructed concurrently, from 2008–2012, the appointed architects used the design concept principles, local school input, and site constraints to develop individual school plans with their own look and feel.

OVERVIEW OF STRUCTURES, ORGANISATION AND SES OF THE BEP SCHOOLS

Table 4.1 provides student numbers for each school (2008–2013), staff/student ratios, each school's socio-economic level using ICSEA values, and socio-economic

Table 4.1 Organisational differences between BEP schools.

	Whirrakee	Ironbark	Melaleuca	Grevillea
Students (2013)	1223	553	813	619
Staff/Student Ratio (2013)	16.0	10.0	13.0	12.9
SES Level	Average	Below average	Below average	Below average
SES Distribution in lowest half	55%	86%	76%	78%
Initial learning community organisation	Each learning community houses one year level (Years 7, 8, 9 and 10 buildings). Students progress through the buildings as they move through their school years.	Four learning community buildings, each of which houses a cohort of Years 7, 8, 9 and 10 students who remain in this community for their four years at the school.	Two learning community buildings house mixed Years 7 and 8 students, separate Year 9 and Year 10 communities. Students progress through the building as they move through their school years.	Four learning community buildings, each of which houses a cohort of Years 7, 8, 9 and 10 students who remain in this community for their four years at the school.
Domains where team teaching and flexible groupings predominate	Maths, Science, Humanities, English	Maths, Science, Humanities, English	Maths, Science/Humanities (Transdisciplinary Inquiry), English, LOTE	Maths, Science, Humanities, English
Changes over time	Individual year-level communities have remained. After the first year, teaching teams were reconfigured by year level so each year level has distinct teaching teams.	Community structures have essentially remained stable with refinements to organisation and curriculum design as required.	Each community now consists of Years 7-10	Community structures have essentially remained stable with refinements to organisation and curriculum design as required

distribution in terms of the percentages of students in the lowest two quartiles. It confirms the predominantly low SES of these students, indicating that the highest SES cohort of students attended the largest school (Whirrakee College), while the lowest socio-economic cohort of students attended the smallest school (Ironbark College).

To put these socio-economic values into perspective, the ICSEA average of all Australian schools is 1000, and the proportion of students across Australia in each of the four quartiles is 25%. The quartile distribution of socio-economic groups attending each school highlights two major differences in these schools' socio-economic profiles (see Table 4.2). The first difference is that, relative to the other three schools, Whirrakee College's proportion of students from the lowest socio-economic quartile (24%) is approximately half that of the other three schools (45%, 57% and 48%). While this difference in the percentage of students from the lowest socio-economic group alters the socio-economic 'blend' at Whirrakee College, the number of students from this socio-economic group at Whirrakee College is almost as high as the numbers from the other three schools (294 vs 366, 315 and 297). The second difference is that, relative to the other three schools, Ironbark's percentage of students from the highest socio-economic quartile (3%) is approximately half that of the other two lower socio-economic schools (both 6%) while the percentage of students in the highest socio-economic quartile at both Grevillea and Melaleuca is one third that of Whirrakee's (19%). When looking at the number of students from the highest socio-economic quartile this difference is more apparent, with Ironbark having only 17 students from this quartile, compared to 37 at Grevillea, 49 at Melaleuca and 232 at Whirrakee. Thus, within Bendigo, a low socio-economic city, Whirrakee has a socio-economic distribution of students that is skewed toward the middle and higher quartiles, while Ironbark has a socio-economic distribution of students that is skewed toward the lowest quartile, with Melaleuca and Grevillea having a similar, but less extreme skew toward the lowest quartile. This variation contributed to school decisions about curricula design, to ways of ensuring student welfare, and to the structure of up-scaled learning communities.

In each school four learning community buildings formed central hubs together with specialist buildings for technology, physical education, music/performance and administration. The learning community buildings were for core curricula, such as English, humanities, mathematics and science, and also to provide a home for the management and welfare of students. The schools devised differing organisational designs for their four up-scaled learning communities based on the school vision and the perceived needs of students. Two schools were organised horizontally with one learning community for each year level while two were organised vertically with each learning community consisting of Years 7-10 students (see Table 4.1 for elaboration of school organisational differences). The rationale for these groupings is explained later in this chapter.

Table 4.2. SES distribution of students in each school (2013).

	Whirrakee				Ironbark				Melaleuca				Grevillea			
ICSEA value	1018				922				964				952			
Quartile	Bottom quarter	Middle quarters	Top quarter	Bottom quarter	Bottom quarter	Middle quarters	Top quarter	Bottom quarter	Bottom quarter	Middle quarters	Top quarter	Bottom quarter	Bottom quarter	Middle quarters	Top quarter
SES distribution	24%	31%	26%	19%	57%	29%	12%	3%	45%	31%	18%	6%	48%	30%	17%	6%
No. of students	294	379	318	232	315	160	66	17	366	252	146	49	297	186	105	37

WHIRRAKEE COLLEGE

Vision Statement: Our College is committed to ensuring every student develops the knowledge, skills and attributes needed to positively contribute to the world community as a responsible and caring citizen.

Whirrakee College's vision statement is indicative of its focus on student personal growth for social responsibility, where students are to be developed as ethical citizens capable of contributing to the broader society. This outward-looking focus is consistent with the school's culture of emphasising student academic, and co-curricular excellence, with a strong belief in the need for students to develop as independent and resilient learners in their four years at the school.

Each building has three main neighbourhood zones of 100 students (see (1) in Figure 4.1). In all four schools, the neighbourhood zones are the main teaching areas, and a home base for students where they can develop a sense of ownership and meet with their home group advisor. The furniture is flexible so that various layouts can cater for a range of learning experiences and provide areas that may be easily reconfigured for individual, small-group, and larger-group work. The teachers are

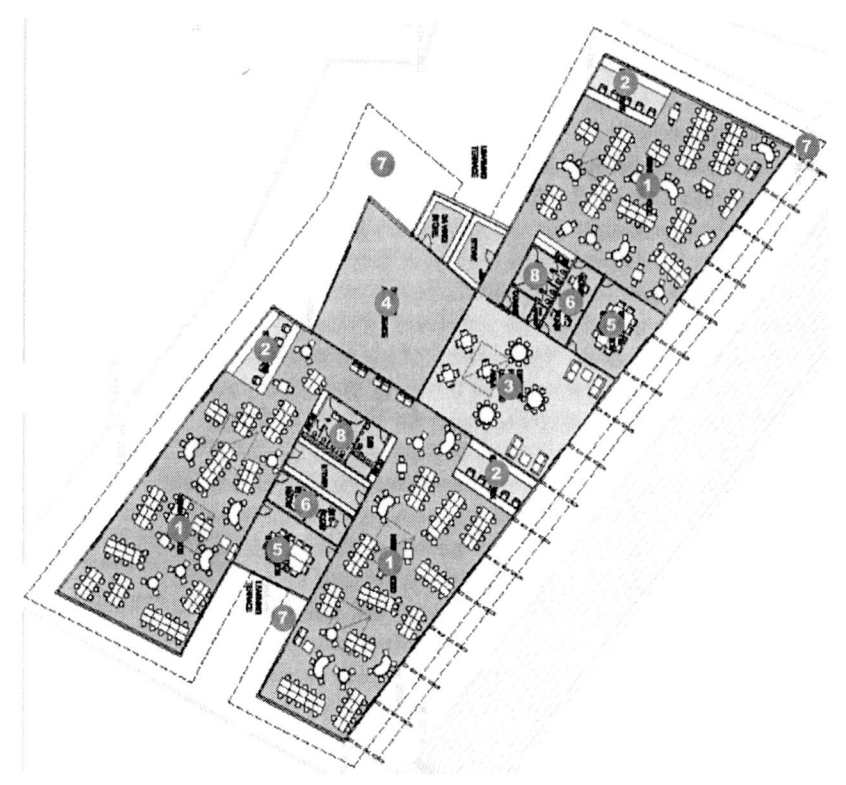

Figure 4.1. Whirrakee College community building design.

expected to work together as a team, taking collective responsibility for the student learning and welfare in their neighbourhood. In all four schools, each neighbourhood zone had a designated staff work area (2) containing teachers' desks and space where they can meet, and plan together, while also being a visible part of the learning neighbourhood and so build strong relationships with students. Staff members at Whirrakee rejected this cramped arrangement and immediately moved their desks into the second Socratic studio (5) [above (3)] that had doors opening into one of the larger community spaces and the entrance to the community. They remain in open view of students, and are still perceived by the teachers and students to be an integral part of the openness of the community. The remaining Socratic studio (5) enables focused learning such as explicit teaching, or class conferencing for a single class. The Einstein area (3) is a breakout space where students can work in small groups or individually and may also be an assembly space for larger teaching groups, this space also serves as the main entry foyer to each community. The two interview rooms for small group activities and parent/student/teacher discussions or interviews (6) were turned into two offices although they can still be used for student interviews. Outdoor learning terraces, a feature in all the BEP school plans (7), were intended to extend the learning spaces. At Whirrakee the learning terrace surrounds the entire building, and is larger near the Da Vinci studio (4), which enables classes to access outdoor space for activities. The two student toilets (8) were located internally within or beside each of the neighbourhood zones and available for both teacher and student use.

The year-level organisation of the learning communities was determined by the following considerations: (1) the size of the school was considered by the principal to make vertical groupings for teaching unworkable and unnecessary, with a wide range of ability levels present in each year level, and (2) the belief that differing developmental needs of students could be better catered for in year-level communities. "We cover a unique aspect at each year level" (Principal interview). In 2014, within the year-level communities, Whirrakee College is conducting a transition program for Year 7 students, a wellbeing focus in Year 8, community programs in Year 9, and future pathways and leadership programs for Year 10 students.

Initially in 2011, the school trialled three groups (pods) of 100 students within each year level, with four staff members team-teaching concurrently in each of the three neighbourhood zones. This arrangement was found to be difficult because of: wasted time in shifting furniture for various activities, and at the start of different subjects; lack of clarity in student expectations; staff dissatisfaction with the quality of the team-teaching, and the management and noise created by 100 students in each zone and; lack of a clear sphere of influence expected of teachers in relation to a large group of students. A further challenge in organising compulsory curricula was the distribution of staff expertise in mathematics and English within and across learning communities. The school experimented with having a group of 12 English and 12 mathematics teachers teach in Years 7 and 8 communities on a rotational basis, partly to build teacher capacity around multi-level learning. However, this approach was seen as inefficient in terms of clear staff roles in curriculum design, continuity of programming, and a lack a targeted focus on the needs of different student ability levels. This approach was changed to community based subject teams in 2012, with a focus on two ability levels for each year level.

In 2012, student groupings were modified to four pods of 75 students with three staff team-teaching. This was intended to provide more effective team-teaching and a more manageable sphere of influence for teachers (a light sphere of influence for the whole pod, and a strong sphere of influence on a smaller group of 25 students based on teacher assessment of their progress). For this four pod arrangement, two pairs of pods were timetabled at different times into these neighbourhood zones for mathematics, science, humanities and English. This organisation was viewed as a more effective use of the space and more manageable for teaching. To provide predictability and efficiency in the use of time and space, students were divided into three ability-level groupings depending on each student's ability to manage their work independently, and on their level of understanding of the content of each topic. This triad grouping was perceived as affording maximum personalisation of student learning and effective teacher teamwork because of these temporary groupings, where teachers rotated through working with the three groups for each three-week topic. Groups were flexible in that they varied according to subject and learning focus, and students contributed to the decision about the group they were placed in. Whole-pod teaching also occurred when relevant.

The triad grouping enabled variety in teaching approaches according to student need, with challenge and independent learning for the high achieving students. Within the triad arrangement, the group of "weaker" students was capped at 14 students allowing the teacher to work intensively with each individual student to differentiate their learning, and to employ concrete examples, modelling, explicit instruction and scaffolding with continuous feedback throughout the learning tasks. The group of most capable students was the largest, with up to 35 students. In these groups, the teacher negotiated the task with individuals and allowed learners to self-monitor their learning and to work independently. Where necessary, explicit instruction or whole group discussion was employed. The middle group consisted of 26 students and was run as a differentiated "mainstream" class with a blend of scaffolding, explicit instruction, and structure to develop independent learning routines.

Teachers perceived the model as affording their own professional development as well as maximising student learning. "Three of us together, I think, create much better lessons, much better learning for students than I used to by myself" (Teacher interview). While all lessons remained at 90 minutes based on the perceived workability of this fit to the space and curriculum development, the school experimented with varying the composition of subjects. For example, an investigative subject called Inquiry, combining humanities and science, was introduced in 2011. The initial rationale was to foster multi-disciplinary approaches, but teachers perceived that enrolments in Year 9 science declined because students did not recognise the science in the Inquiry subject in Years 7 and 8. As a result, Inquiry was separated into science and humanities subjects, leading to a significant gain in Year 9 science enrolments in 2014.

IRONBARK COLLEGE

Vision Statement: Challenging educational experiences in a supportive environment

Ironbark College's vision statement captures its long-standing recognition of the need to raise students' learning aspirations within a caring environment that connects with students' interests and community. The school has a well-established culture of supporting its student cohort through community connections and a focus on respect for self, the school and others while encouraging confidence, courage, persistence and teamwork. This is also evident in the strong focus on developing an effective teacher advisor (TA) program to support students personally and academically (see chapter 10).

Three years prior to moving into the new buildings, an experienced teacher, new to the school, who had been given responsibility for introducing the BEP values to the staff, noticed that staff did not get to know the students very well. He heard teachers saying how much they looked forward to the end of term when they would no longer have to deal with a particularly difficult student. This, he believed, was not helping the building of relationships in the school. When some funding was received in 2006, this teacher initiated the 'gutting' of one wing of the school by removing the walls between classrooms so that they could have an open-plan space where all the Year 7s could be taught by a team of teachers. This would remove the lottery of students having a teacher they did not get along with or one that was less skilled or experienced in teaching and classroom management.

> We thought if we could get teachers to work in teams we might be able to break some of that down and get a bit more consistency and quality teaching and teachers could learn from each other. We became very conscious that a lot of teachers were teaching the way they'd been taught and the world had changed a fair bit (Community leader).

While there was some success with this innovation, the teachers discovered that having all Year 7s in one space was problematic as there were no older students providing modelling and a mediating role. When building began on the new school the students were relocated to portable classrooms and back to the one teacher to 25 students in a single classroom structure. However, the seeds had been sown in terms of the need for good teacher-student relationships. This same leading teacher believed that:

> If we could get the ethos of small schools going where a group of staff knew those kids really well, we would establish really good relationships with kids. Because a lot of the kids in this community don't have really good relationships

with adults, (a lot of them don't have dads) they are not necessarily very trusting. I find that these kids will work for you if they trust you. So to have teachers changing kids all the time I thought was just adding to the problem, not solving it. So I was really keen to get groups of staff working with the kids over four years.

This initial experiment was the groundwork for structuring the new learning communities (see Figure 4.2). This structure afforded the younger students a range of student role models. Students as class groups were allocated to a 'virtual' community before they actually moved into the new physical location of their learning communities to begin the process of identification with a community. In addition, the sporting 'houses' were aligned with the communities. This system for organising the school sporting teams significantly contributed to the sense of identification students now have with their learning communities. No longer were students in the same class, competing for different houses. They were now in the same community and competing on behalf of that community.

Each building accommodates a cohort of students who remain in this learning community for their four years at school. One learning neighbourhood holds Year 7 and 8 students while the other holds the Year 9 and 10 students (1). This two-neighbourhood design is a common feature in three of the four schools. In each neighbourhood there is a designated staff work area (2), an enclosed classroom with flexible walls called the Socratic studio (5), an interview room (6), outdoor learning terraces (7), and toilets (8). An Einstein area (3) and a Da Vinci studio (4) (art and science) is shared between the neighbourhoods.

The Principal and staff members supported the Years 7–10 organisation of the communities because: this structure was perceived to support student long term connectedness to communities; it could offer the flexibility to introduce stage-based learning as envisaged by the BEP; and staff believed it encouraged "cross-fertilisation of culture and ideas" among older and younger students. In this low

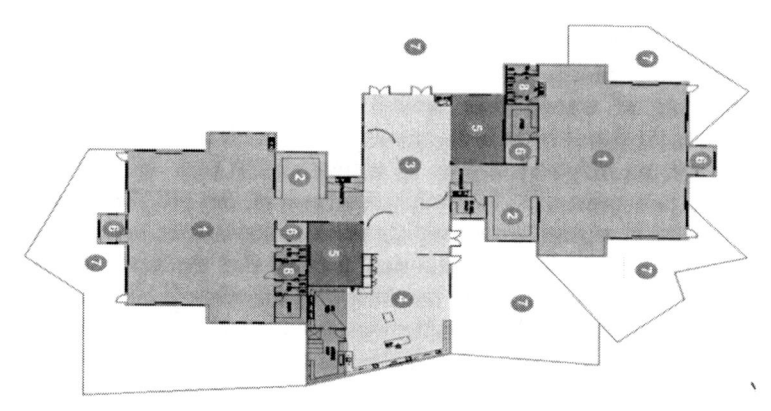

Figure 4. 2. Ironbark College building community design.

SES school, building positive peer relationships and relationships among staff and students was the top priority. A strong TA program was perceived to be vital to establish relationships that would underpin academic achievement by encouraging self-development and confidence in all students (Principal interview). An initial curricular rationale for this approach has been augmented by more recent perceptions of the benefits of mentoring. For the Principal, "the culture it creates amongst even Year 7 students feeling comfortable to have real relationships with Year 10 students and being supported by them that's where the significant growth has been". He further claims that "Year 9 and 10 students have significant opportunities for leadership in their own community because there are a substantial number of students that are younger than them, and look up to them, and need nurturing, support, coaching, and mentoring."

Student interviews support this with students perceiving that the multi-year-level communities created a space where they can work alongside younger and older students and build relationships that were less likely in a more traditional setting (see chapter 9). From this perspective, according to the Principal and the school vision statement, positive relationships among students are foundational to learning, "and if you don't sort out that aspect of your school first then you are building on a foundation of sand that won't last very long". He further considered that "everything is based around the relationships between students within a year level, the relationships between students in different year levels, and the relationships between students and their teachers." He added "I do not think that applies to all schools but it certainly applies to schools that have lower socio-economic status". A former principal commented that the communities have become "families" and that "the mixture in age has a calming effect" (Principal interview). "We hoped that by having a TA program we'd be supporting our students better and we'd be engaging teachers specifically with the cohort they'd stay with and support through 7-10 schooling". Student and teacher interviews support this perception of connectedness. Students in particular commented on their familiarity with other year levels and the consequent reduction in potential conflict (see chapters 9 and 10).

The school initially allocated the timetable in the new settings into 6 by 50 minute classes following past practices. However, this approach was seen as inefficient, disruptive because of wasted time around transitions between classes, and unnecessary given the shared space in the new settings between teachers and students. The timetable was reconfigured to 4 by 70 minute classes each day, to optimise learning, and this arrangement has been maintained over the last two years. Teachers have had to develop new practices to break up sessions into shorter, more engaging segments to hold students' interest. The staff decided that the most productive learning occurred in the mornings and therefore only one class is conducted after lunch, with school ending at 3.05 pm rather than the normal 3.20 pm. While there were some elective subject choices for students in the old settings, teachers now recognised the potential for student independent, self-managed projects in these new settings. For example, one girl intending to be an architect undertook an independent study on house design and produced a set of house plans. Core subjects were blocked in Years 9 and 10 across the school to enable team-teaching across communities and to introduce more elective options in the unblocked time.

As at Whirrakee College, teachers attempted to introduce inquiry-based multi-disciplinary subject options in 2011; however, pressure to increase academic performance in high stakes subjects such as English, maths and science led to more allocated time for these subjects, at the expense of cross-curricular inquiry and development. While stage-based programs were considered desirable, the curriculum tended to be age-based because of: problems in available expertise in both full-time and part-time teachers to contribute to such a program; timetable constraints in blocking subject specialisms across and within learning communities; and pressure to improve academic performance in English and mathematics. These factors encouraged teachers to revert to traditional year-level groupings. For some teachers the increasing consolidation of identity in each learning community posed challenges for fragmentation of the larger school ethos. By contrast, other teachers welcomed this intensified connectedness at the learning community level. Shared protocols and cross-community teaching were seen as ameliorating this tendency while preserving the advantages of well-linked communities.

The open-plan settings not only affected options around teachers organising time and space to enact the curriculum but also altered their sphere of influence at Ironbark College. Teachers felt both connected to, and responsible for, all students in their community in a light sphere of influence, but also experienced more intensity in relationships with the students in their TA classes and those for whom they completed subject assessments.

GREVILLEA COLLEGE

Vision Statement: Respect. Integrity. Personal Excellence

Grevillea's vision statement indicates its priority to foster students' personal attributes as a basis for academic success, and acknowledges the necessity to focus on developing these attributes with a predominantly low socio-economic cohort.

This school's design was similar to Ironbark's (see Figure 4.3) based on the same rationale around connectedness and building strong relationships between students, and between students and teachers. Like Ironbark, the physical design of each community incorporated a wide range of physical settings for small and large group work with designated areas for activities such as TA groups. To optimise the attractiveness of the Einstein area (3), teachers incorporated informal lounge settings for flexible group work, independent learning and a student meeting place. In each learning neighbourhood (1), there was a designated staff work area (2), a Socratic studio (5), an interview room (6), student toilets (8), and outdoor learning terraces (7). The Da Vinci studio (4) and the Einstein area (3) were centrally located with the community leader's office and additional toilets near the main entrance. To enhance the physical environment of the school, architects included a grass covered central

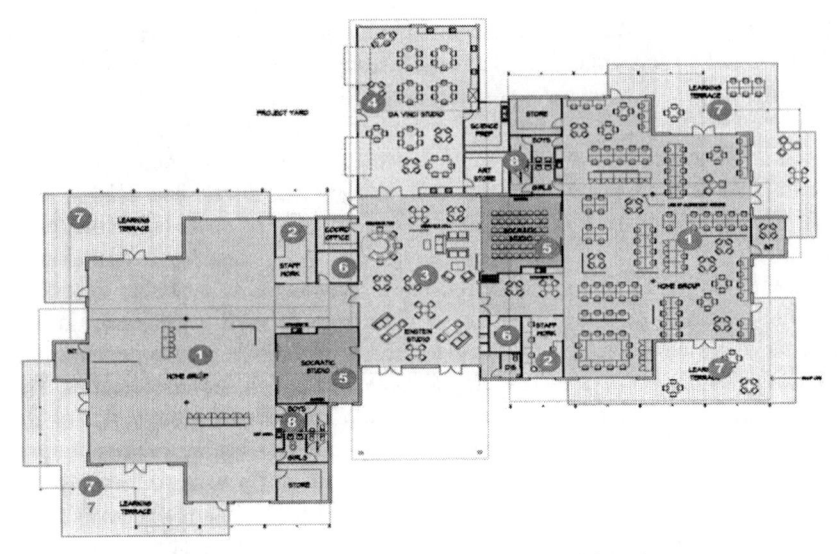

Figure 4.3. Grevillea College community building design.

hill as a natural amphitheatre extending the built and outdoor performance area. This area has proved to be a very popular meeting place for students.

Students are arranged into two neighbourhoods, on a year-by-year basis, to maintain strong connections with same-age peers. Each neighbourhood houses a mixed cohort of three or four groups of students from Years 7 to 10, and in any one year the mix of year levels in a neighbourhood can vary depending on the configuration of class numbers at each year level. For example, in 2014, one particular community had two Year 7 groups, two Year 8 groups, one Year 9 group, and one Year 10 group. For timetabling of core subjects and electives they function as one community to maximise opportunity to personalise learning for students in key academic areas. The neighbourhoods are used for TA groups and other subjects designed to develop student resilience, wellbeing, leadership and connections with same-age peers and the wider community. Groupings of students into neighbourhoods are determined by the learning community leaders each year and, for the example above, where there were two Year 7 and two Year 8 groups and only one Year 9 and one Year 10 group in the community, the neighbourhood groups both had a Year 7 and a Year 8 group and one group of either Year 9 or Year 10 students. This afforded leadership responsibilities to both the Year 9 and the Year 10 groups.

The students remain in one building, but can move on a yearly basis between the two neighbourhoods within this building, as they progress through the four years of schooling. The rationale for this organisation was to achieve "a cross-section of students within each of the learning communities" rather than "just have a very mature, calm Year 10 learning community, whilst at the developmental stages at

Years 7 and 8 you might have students who are a little bit more exuberant" (learning community leader). It was envisaged that this organisation afforded "modelling of behaviour [and] allows peer support from the older students to the younger students" (learning community leader).

As at Ironbark College, this model was viewed as supporting wellbeing and connectedness through building long term relationships between staff and students. As noted by the Principal, Year 7 students "get to know their teachers really well. They come in at Year 7 and we say, "This is your space for four years". While some Year 7 students did feel separated from other Year 7 students, as indicated in the Attitudes to School Survey, a Year 7 camp was designed to retain a sense of Year 7 identity across communities.

Learning sessions are divided into four 70 minute classes per day and core subjects (maths and English) are blocked in each learning neighbourhood and given extra time to enable stage-based teaching and learning. A specialised trade training centre was included in the new school to enhance increased pathways for Years 9 and 10 students as recommended by the BEP (BEP Steering Committee 2005).

MELALEUCA COLLEGE

Vision Statement: Personalised learning, one child at a time

Melaleuca College's vision statement highlights a focus on the individual student's needs, moving from a strong knowledge and skill base in the early years to increasing choice, independence, and inquiry at Years 9 and 10.

This school's design for the four community buildings was initially based on junior and senior year levels with two of the buildings housing mixed Years 7 and 8 students, while the third building housed Year 9 and the fourth building housed Year 10 students. The rationale for grouping Years 7 and 8 students in one community for two years was to develop strong teacher-student relationships and to focus on explicit teaching of knowledge and skills before moving to year-level communities that allowed greater subject choice with maturity. Each building had two learning neighbourhoods (see (1) in Figure 4.4), with a designated open staff work area (2), a pair of interview rooms (6), a series of learning terraces (7), and student toilets (8). The Socratic studios (5) were readily accessible from both neighbourhoods as was the Einstein area (3) and the Da Vinci studio (4).

As described in the other three schools: the Einstein area (3) functions as a breakout space, assembly space for larger groups, and as the main entry foyer; the Da Vinci studio is a shared arts and science specialist facility with a connection to outdoor space (7); and the Socratic studios (5) enable focused learning such as explicit teaching, or class conferencing.

Originally the school had planned to have four vertical (Years 7-10) learning communities but the Principal explained that, after consultation, it was considered that the parent community, student body and teachers were not ready to implement the type of teaching and learning required in a vertical arrangement. Rather than

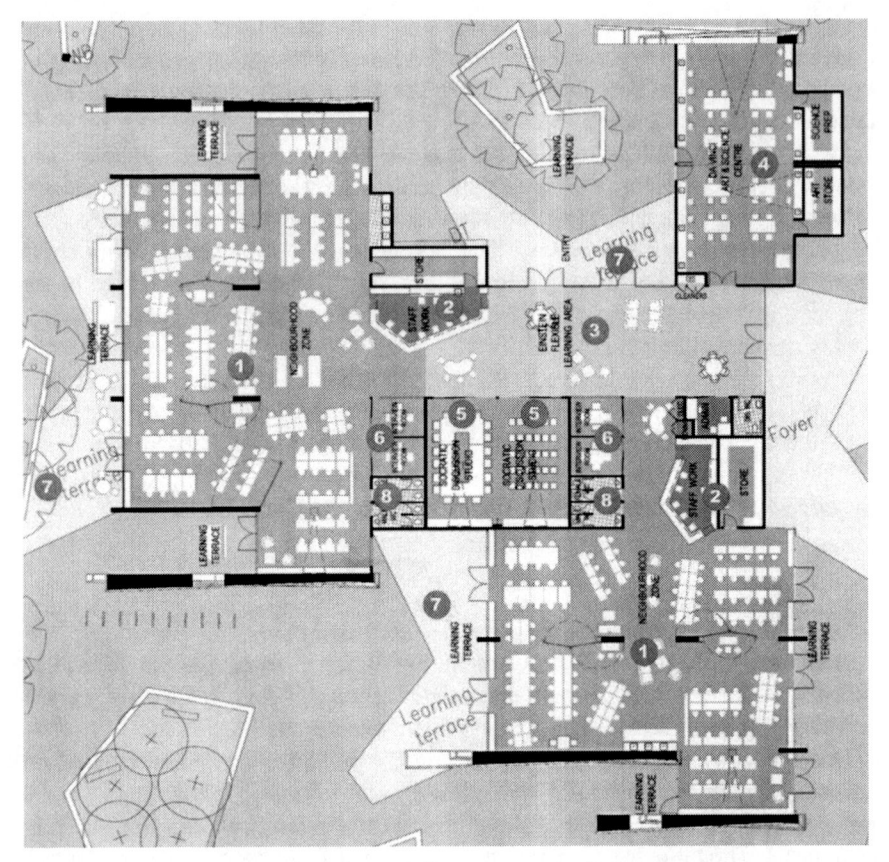

Figure 4.4. Melaleuca College community building design.

increase student mentoring and interaction, he considered that "in reality you would have had a Year 7 English class in one corner, a Year 8 science class over there, and a Year 9, with a whole lot of cross noise happening". He claimed that Year 7s and 8s were "at a similar point of development" cognitively and emotionally with Year 8s able to provide some leadership. This also fitted the school's focus on developing a strong student academic knowledge and skill "toolkit" in preparation for more independent learning in later years. By contrast, he considered that Year 9 students were developmentally ready to occupy their own building. Also, "we wanted to say there are still a number of parts of the curriculum that were compulsory for Year 7 and 8 students, but as students move to Year 9 there became much more freedom and choice". He saw Year 10 as a step towards post-compulsory schooling and wanted to offer subject choices to prepare students for greater independence. Hence, the mixed vertical/horizontal year-level community structure.

At Melaleuca personalisation of student learning has been built into the assessment design as well as the community and timetable structures. The timetable structure affords opportunity for teacher collaboration in teaching subjects and student arrangement according to interest and need. Three classes of the same subject are scheduled at the same time in the same space for English, science, maths, humanities, physical education (PE), languages other than English (LOTE) and design and creativity to enable teachers to have a more authentic collaboration around curriculum, and teaching and learning experiences:

> I think teachers and students are seeing how the buildings can be used to collaborate and how they can be used to regroup students and provide a much better learning environment. For example, with our Year 7 English, there are three classes timetabled at the one time in the space and there's nothing else happening in that space. This allows for flexibility and movement of students and collaboration of teachers. (Principal)

After this initial approach had been established and had operated for a year, problems were identified with the combined Years 7 and 8 areas around concern for respect for the environment. As a result of this perceived problem, the school decided to separate the mixed Years 7 and 8 communities and move to separate Year 7 and Year 8 neighbourhoods in 2011. In 2012 they were then moved into separate buildings. The reasoning driving this restructuring of the Year 7 and Year 8 communities was a desire to provide a smooth transition to the Year 7s and reduce student disconnectedness:

> To replicate the safe and secure environment of primary school, particularly for the Year 7s and have an area where they felt safe that it was their own so that they were not feeling unsure or intimidated by other students or by the size of the school. (Assistant Principal)

This change had unexpected consequences, with the Year 7 community lacking clear positive student role models. Concern with this issue and further consultation with other schools led to a decision at the start of 2014 to move to a vertical structure (see chapter 11 for more detail). As the Assistant Principal explained, the move to the Year 7-10 vertical structure was "so that kids would have more opportunities for student leadership and to get to know the other kids in the school through a more community-based approach from Years 7 through to 10".

This new model has been perceived to be working well in creating a positive ethos within the school. The Assistant Principal perceived this to be due to:

> lots of cross-age mentoring going on between Year 7s and 10s because it can happen within the community... The junior kids are seeing good role modelling displayed by the senior kids in terms of their classroom work ethic... We have had visitors come to the school who have been here for many years and have seen a whole range of different stages that the school has been through and they have said that it is by far the most work-productive, quiet, school that they have seen– it has been great.

IMPLICATIONS

This chapter has highlighted the key dimensions principals and leadership teams considered in organising the communities in these open-plan settings. Parallel to developing a workable culture, leaders had to consider effective use of time, space, physical resources, student groupings and desirable and actual subject choices. This practical reasoning was influenced by past professional knowledge and experience, teacher disciplinary expertise, available staff profiles, including full and part-time teachers at each school, trial and error in experimenting with different structures, and recognition of marked developmental differences in student ability and interests across and within year levels. The reasoning was also influenced by perceptions of SES profiles of students and past culture within the traditional settings, external accountability pressures on improved academic performance in high stakes subjects, and responsibility for the wellbeing of students.

Temporal organisation of the curriculum spanned micro, meso and macro considerations. At the micro level there was relative agreement across the schools that 70-90 minute classes effectively utilised the scope for deeper learning in these settings, with high stakes subjects prioritised. At the meso level of topics and subjects, all schools tended to preserve traditional term-based organisation in order to provide curricula variety and choice for students. Allocation of 100 minutes per week for TA programs in some schools indicated prioritising social and emotional learning and teacher-student relationships within the daily school agenda. At the macro level, community organisation retained age-based development largely for administrative convenience.

Adapting to the new open-plan spaces entailed both negative and positive influences. On the negative side problems around student mobility, limited access to particular resources, noise, distraction and shared spaces were addressed by planning, enactment and review of a robust curriculum and appropriate student protocols (see chapters 3, 7, 9, 11). As noted, leaders' reasoning about student groupings in each school was influenced by staff profiles, and pragmatic considerations around student and staff capabilities. Stage-based subject groupings only occurred in electives in Years 9 and 10 because of challenges around timetable manageability and staff profiles. However, other cross-age groupings were encouraged in peer tutoring, buddy systems, TA activities, sporting 'houses', and whole community meetings.

Over and above these influential elements, staff sought to address the compelling need for student connectedness and identity in these new settings and to provide workable programs that addressed a significant variety in student ability levels.

DEBRA EDWARDS, CRAIG DEED & ANTHONY EDWARDS

5. LEARNING IN TECHNOLOGICALLY-MEDIATED SPACES IN OPEN-PLAN SETTINGS

PRODUCTIVE DISRUPTIONS

Networked learning environments disrupt the constitution of the conventional classroom. As part of the BEP each student was issued with a personal notebook computer, the assumption being that new technologies offered foundation possibilities for innovative teaching and learning. Here, we argue that these new virtual learning options can be generative in terms of teacher and student agency, depending on the usage/social practices that are enabled (Deed & Lesko, in press).

In this chapter we define agency in relation to teaching and learning in virtual learning spaces. Our line of reasoning is that both virtual learning spaces and open-plan settings offer affordances for personalising learning, agency, social learning, student autonomy, and collective intelligence. We present an outline of literature about the affordances of such spaces, then, within this framework, outline three case studies of teachers and students perceiving, and responding to, these possibilities. The construct of agency is defined as contextually dependent, effortful teaching and learning actions, grounded in context, that are both individual and relational.

Educators are beginning to recognise that the highly personalised and multi-dimensional experiences that Web 2.0 affords have significant implications for learning and teaching in schools. They also recognise that much activity in the virtual world is communal and interactive in nature. Texting, voice chat, wikis, blogs and, in particular, virtual worlds with avatars, have the potential to provide rich immersive learning experiences. These Web 2.0 experiences are transforming ideas about how education can be organised, and how learning occurs, in both formal and informal settings. These disruptive ideas have led to rekindled interest in notions of optimal, blended learning communities beyond face-to-face contact. Yet, while this virtual networking provides a heightened sense of agency and control for learners, and thus power to think and act differently, these interactions are often mired in complexity and uncertainty about outcomes.

This may be even more so when contrasted with the enclosed physical learning environments in most schools. While the technological tools that mediate virtual communities can be informal or formal, and open or closed, in terms of purpose, structure, surveillance and outcome, they are usually deployed within a classroom space. However, the affordances and constraints of informal social networking,

V. Prain et al. (Eds.), *Adapting to Teaching and Learning in Open-Plan Schools*, 79–93.
© 2014 Sense Publishers. All rights reserved.

and the experiences, perspectives and capacity of users, remain largely hidden and under-utilised in these settings.

In this chapter we consider how schools are extending the notion of open-plan learning space from a physical to a virtual context. The concept of virtual learning spaces fits neatly with the conceptualisation of the open-plan physical environment affording ways to think and act differently about learning. Virtual spaces can be fixed and transitory, spontaneous and planned, affording opportunity for students to build on the skills and knowledge they have learnt and utilised outside the formal classroom, and to take up opportunities for new learning. While other chapters plot the reasoning and activity of teachers differentiating the curriculum (see chapter 7) here we take the view that students are also co-owners of this process.

We employ a sociological perspective to examine the pervasive and disruptive influence of technology on formal and informal learning structures using the concept of student and teacher agency. Agency, understood initially as the capacity for individuals to act differently to shape structures (Giddens, 1984), is now broadened to include relational capacities between individuals and within groups around personal and shared goals (Barton & Tan, 2010; Goulart & Roth, 2010). The largely informal and diverse social networking experiences of modern students is potentially a "radical disjuncture of an unpredictable kind which ... threaten[s] or destroy[s] the certitudes of institutionalised routines" (Giddens, 1984, p. 60). In contemporary schools, students use social networking skills to disrupt and subvert sanctioned learning processes through informal idea and experience sharing, peer support and collusion.

The thwarting of student individual and collective agency in traditional educational settings has been a recurrent theme in progressive education from the 1960s onwards (Illich, 1971). This alternative philosophy of more learner-driven learning has been largely constrained by systemic structural educational boundaries, including the need to formally control, measure, and report individual student learning, and the physical limitations of buildings and timetables.

The anticipated freedoms of differentiated agency were largely incompatible with formulaic practices of the industrial-age classroom. However, for some educators, modern technologies, particularly those deployed as diverse, global networking tools, pose new possibilities for student-centred learning, differentiated instruction, open-plan learning spaces, and personalising learning. This question of agency is examined here in terms of the capacity of students to enact these possibilities and their teachers to grasp the potential of student technologically- mediated agency and increased sphere of influence against the inertia of industrial-age, classroom-based education.

TECHNOLOGICAL AFFORDANCES IN OPEN-PLAN LEARNING ENVIRONMENTS

The principal affordance of working in open learning environments is that students can access/participate in the collective intelligence distributed across the resources and participants of the shared networks. Drawing on an idea originally derived from the natural world, in the form of beehives or ant communities, Levy (1997) defined collective intelligence as a type of widely distributed and dynamic intellectual capacity enabled through Web 2.0 participation. Collective intelligence remains ill-defined, in that what and how contributing aspects of expertise are sought, understood, mobilised, and shared, remain an emergent area of study. However, successful participation is easy to recognise in the interactive business practices of Amazon for example, and used in wikis and blogs, hyper-linking, Rich Site Summary (RSS) and Google (O'Reilly, 2007). It remains important to explore this emerging concept as a means to improve understanding of student knowledge-building, co-operation, and dissemination in contemporary learning environments.

Lee and Lan (2007), and others, make the claim that knowledge emerging through web-based interaction challenges the notion of top-down, one-way expertise readily evident in the traditional classroom. Expertise is thought of as distributed across multiple-user understandings, intentions, and capacities to access relevant resources and strategies available online via formal and informal means. Interaction between novices and 'mentoring' experts provides experience and practice in development and use of contextual language, building knowledge deemed useful and relevant by practitioners within defined contexts, and learning strategies. Instead of the predictable traditional role of the teacher as expert learning coach, networked participants explore, negotiate, and swap roles depending on purposes.

Table 5.1 provides a speculative overview of some primary elements of open-plan learning environments afforded by technology, as compared to more traditional classroom environments (based on previous work reported in Deed & Edwards, 2013).

Table 5.1. A comparison of traditional and virtual learning environment characteristics.

Traditional classroom environment	Open-plan/virtual learning environment
Centrality of teacher expertise to prescribe and critique student efforts	Distributed expertise within and beyond the classroom, unpredictable pathways, sources, exchanges
Teacher formal control, structured, hyper-designed	A mix of formal and informal pathways, less clarity in design, pathways, knowledge gains
Guided and discipline-based reasoning processes	Individual students and groups locate, interpret, interact with, share, and analyse/evaluate sources and relational interactions and feedback
Paper-based tasks and assessment	Multi-modal shared texts, informal online interactions, social learning
Procedural and expert-directed lessons within set time and space e.g. classroom	Individuals/groups of students varying degree and context of their efforts

While an open-plan learning environment may be conceived of as an extension of the traditional classroom, it also affords opportunities for newly imagined ways of learning that have previously been considered the domain of virtual environments. In practice, it is difficult to simply identify a traditional classroom, because there are many educational settings that can be identified as progressive or innovative in their pedagogical approaches, independent of features of the physical setting. This somewhat reductive comparison is offered as a basis for continuing dialogue concerning conceptual differences in learning environments.

Our comparative table shows that the open-plan and virtual classroom increases opportunities for student independence and 'unsupervised' networking practices. In open-plan and virtual classrooms, each individual/student group determines the pace, character, degree of contribution/collaboration, and questioning or learning from their interactions. Unlike the traditional classroom, there are fewer fixed and final points of expert authority/feedback, depending on the topic and learner intentions.

Open-plan and virtual learning environments can be conducive to what Engeström and Sanino (2010) have characterised as expansive learning. Engeström, Brown, Christopher, and Gregory (1997) argue that the driving influence in expansive learning is disturbance, unexpected events and a lack of co-ordination. The following three case studies provide examples of designing and refining learning tasks that attempt to take advantage of the affordances of open-plan physical and virtual learning environments. Each case study is based on interviews with key participants, observation, and artefact analysis over at least two terms.

CASE STUDY 1: SELF-DIRECTED LEARNING AT MELALEUCA COLLEGE

This case study demonstrates, over time, a lessening of teacher control, and increased use of the technological affordances. This manifests in contradictory ways. For example, when Lauren (the teacher) decided to increase her control over the planning and assessment process while simultaneously allowing students more freedom of movement, she also considered how her role changed towards facilitation rather than prescription.

The self-directed learning (SDL) class was a Year 10 elective subject at Melaleuca College. The SDL class provided students with freedom to select and study a topic of interest. They had to choose their topic, plan, research, deliver and evaluate their learning in a school term, assuming that such a subject encouraged students to be more self-reliant learners.

A teacher framework was provided, in the form of a course overview, a timeline for completion, advice on planning, and presentation and assessment criteria. SDL promoted self and peer assessment of the final presentation. This was considered by the teacher as complementary to the generative authorisations of open-plan physical and virtual space, and the learning preferences and approaches of neo-millennial students.

The enactment of the SDL class was the responsibility of Lauren, a newly graduated teacher. Lauren had no prior experience of working in open-plan learning environments, or in the use of technologically-mediated learning. Nevertheless, she took up the challenge, following some orienting conversations with teachers who had previously taken the subject. Lauren perceived her role in the SDL class as providing opportunities for students, and her, to learn skills in personalised and autonomous learning, and different approaches to assessment. She anticipated that her role would be to act as a facilitator rather than a traditional teacher, although she expressed uncertainty about how to make the transition from traditional to new approaches to teaching. Lauren doubted her own knowledge and was unsure how she would blend direct teaching with supporting and motivating students. She was aware that each student provided a different challenge, and that some would not be ready to embrace sustained autonomous learning, perhaps even seeing the subject as an opportunity to avoid learning. Yet Lauren did not want to be perceived as providing explicit control and direction. This would prove a difficult balance to achieve.

The physical space for the SDL class was a semi-enclosed rectangular corner of the learning environment with walls on three sides and one side open to the rest of the learning area. Banks of computers were centrally located in a circle and student lockers served as space dividers in the learning environment. Lauren arranged tables and chairs in a large rectangle. Students each had a laptop computer and this provided potential to sit in a range of spaces. However, Lauren initially controlled movement within the learning space, as she was unsure about her students' capacity to manage their own learning. This attempt at a provisional boundary to the physical space for student work is typical of many transitional classes in these new settings where teachers feel the need for a defined, if permeable, physical sphere of influence over student effort.

The first time Lauren took this class over nine weeks most students managed to identify research, produce and present a topic. All students undertook online research projects. Apart from the demonstration of agency in their choices of topic, Lauren perceived limitations to their independent work, including use of few or obvious websites, lack of distinction in the quality of sources of information, little use of other sources such as books or interviews with experts, and lack of imagination about ways to present their projects. Because students were continually online they were easily distracted. Lauren found it difficult to know how to encourage students to work rather than socialise. As students were in charge of their own learning, she felt they needed to find out for themselves the consequences of lack of effort. A major issue for the teacher was that there were no external consequences for non-completion of the project. Lauren decided to focus her attention on developing supportive relationships. She believed that this mutual respect should be a feature of SDL and she therefore encouraged an informal atmosphere, allowing free discussion among students. Lauren positioned herself centrally and encouraged the students to approach her when requiring assistance rather than seeking them out or checking up on them. Building trust and raising student expectations are traditional teacher skills, but she felt that the increased informality in her relationship with the students in this setting was a positive factor in guiding and supporting successful student-directed learning.

In the following two iterations of SDL, Lauren continually modified her approach. She was concerned about the lack of effort from several students, and a general lack of capacity to plan, monitor and adapt learning approaches. She increased the requirements of the planning part of SDL, making goal-setting and timelines more explicit. More importantly, Lauren added a teacher assessment sheet to the peer and self-assessment sheets. This was an example of co-regulation of learning, rather than complete self-regulation. On the other hand, as her experience with SDL increased, she allowed students more freedom over their use of the physical space. Some students remained close to Lauren's immediate sphere of influence, but others moved beyond this. Students intermingled with those from other classes or worked on their laptops in the informal community space.

Computers are frequently based in open-plan classrooms, usually at designated learning stations. Students also have mobile technology including laptops, tablets and smart-phones. Although an ill-defined and emerging concept, mobile learning environments usually refer to those created by an individual or group to achieve a learning purpose through the use of mobile technology (Collinson, 1999; Solvberg & Rismark, 2012). Mobile technology can be characterised as personal, user-centred, mobile, networked, ubiquitous, and durable. These afford new conceptions of learning as personalised, learner-centred, situated, collaborative, and ubiquitous (Collinson, 1999; Sharples, Taylor, & Vavoula, 2010). The SDL example demonstrates student agency as they simultaneously negotiate the construction of knowledge and the creation of their own temporary learning space (Collinson, 1999). The learning space, both physical and virtual, and the process of learning are integrated.

Although SDL provided a new and different way of teaching and learning, sustained motivation continued to be a problem for some students, as often attributed to low SES students. As the term progressed, the teacher became increasingly concerned that students wasted class time, working on projects at home. Lauren's concern was how she should mark students who did competent presentations showing evidence of research that she herself had not monitored directly at any stage in their production. Therefore, she considered that it was valuable for students to demonstrate their understanding by re-representing their work verbally to her and their peers.

After taking SDL for three iterations, Lauren commented that she was surprised by the high quality of the students' work, in particular the way they used multimodal media to represent and communicate ideas. As a result, Lauren transferred some of the SDL techniques to her other, more traditional, classes.

CASE STUDY 2: A GAME DESIGN PROJECT AT GREVILLEA COLLEGE

In this cross-curricular unit at Grevillea College, an English teacher and an ICT teacher teamed to make linkages between their subject areas. Years 9 and 10 programming students were expected to create an educational game to enhance Year 10 literacy through a game design project. Students were expected to identify the core elements of game-making, including creating a quality storyline and mastering the use of story-writing, creating rules and levels.

Ten male students were enrolled in the project from Years 9 and 10. The Year 10 students had already completed two semester blocks of programming while the Year 9 students were new to this subject. Thus, only the Year 10 students were able to begin the process of game making. The ICT teacher's aim was to encourage teamwork by allocating different roles and responsibilities to each student in order that "the students get to understand how a business situation would operate, how they'd have to work with people in different fields and how all these people impact on the end result".

Various disruptions affected the unit including the ICT teacher leaving this community to become an acting leader of another community. Interruptions to classes in term two for camps and work experience resulted in irregular attendance by some students, impacting on the continuity of skill building and teamwork and ultimately the quality of the game developed. Finally, the timetable changed at the end of semester, which meant that the ICT teacher no longer had the same cohort of students in term three. The programming class attracted twenty-five students in term three. Only one of these students had previously been involved in developing the game.

At this point the teacher modified his expectations and the class organisation to suit the circumstances. As most of the twenty-five students (again all boys) were not ready for game creation, but were still learning the basic features of computer programming, the teacher chose three students, two Year 10 students and one Year 9 student, who had prior programming knowledge, to complete the game. While other students focused on workshops to build their skills, these three students worked together on developing their game. While building the ability of his students to work in teams was an important priority for the teacher, he had to modify this expectation. At the beginning of term the three students were allocated different roles according to their strengths. "One has good communication skills and seems able to direct a group, one is quite creative in . . . being able to see the way a game operates, and how to implement (it) and the third is more of a task master. He is given a task and can complete the necessary work". The students developed and refined a game concept working together, and then individually produced a game level.

In view of the constraints outlined earlier, completing the literacy focus of the game proved a challenge. The English students were not involved in developing the game narrative or the English based grammatical information that provided the game's educational focus. The difficulty in playing the game from a player perspective depended on the player's visual acuity in navigating the maze of each level, and the ability to anticipate obstacles and manual dexterity. Despite its limitations, the ICT teacher believed this experiment could potentially be expanded to offer an engaging and challenging way to teach new skills.

The teachers involved had designed this project in an attempt to draw upon the affordances of the flexible learning spaces and a games-based pedagogy that would provide an engaging means to differentiate the activity. The English teacher, in particular, was prepared to treat the project as a learning experience, commenting "Hopefully (the project) will enable me to look at things in different ways as well... We'll learn as we go. We learn by doing."

The ICT teacher wanted more expertise in 'new' ways to teach, new understanding of how games are developed, and how to guide student knowledge and skill development, problem-solving, and teamwork.

The ICT teacher considered that this student practice in self-reliance was crucial if students were to "self-direct their own learning, ask questions when necessary but also find answers if the teacher is unavailable". He found the experience of game creation a valuable learning experience. He believed his students developed the ability to learn the complex thinking associated with programming language, to problem solve in a self-directed way by working together, and using online trouble shooting sites, and to be creative in coming up with a good idea to engage the user. Researchers observed that the students demonstrated persistence in problem-solving in a self-directed way, by trial and error, using online support or peer support. They were able to work to a deadline to produce a coherent finished game.

While this case shows how teacher knowledge is situated and refined in practice, it also demonstrates the challenges for teachers and students. In particular, although the project was engaging for students, they were expected to quickly learn and apply high-level skills of programming, and problem solving within a cross-curricular environment. The question of exerting agency over a new environment was located in the teacher's capacity to adapt to circumstances and context, while students had to apply a range of skills related to autonomy and self-regulation.

CASE STUDY 3: THE DASHBOARD AT WHIRRAKEE COLLEGE

The dashboard is a digital system designed to "capture data about learner activities and visualise these data to support awareness, reflection, sense-making, and impact" (Verbert, Duval, Klerkx, Govaerts, & Santos, 2013). Learning dashboards in school have evolved from being the digital visual display of a database for organising information to be used as an early warning system for alerting teachers and students to a student's lack of progress with learning or behavior, to having multiple functions. Such digital systems have been given the name 'dashboard' because, like a car dashboard that displays information about the different components of the car and provides early warning of any malfunction, they display information about the different components of a student's learning. In schools, learning dashboards have been used to develop and monitor student learning goals and strategies for learning. Such a digital system can be designed to allow access to this information for students, teachers and parents. Verbert et al. (2013) identify a variety of dashboards currently in use internationally that reinforce face-to-face, virtual and blended learning. While

TECHNOLOGY IN OPEN-PLAN SETTINGS

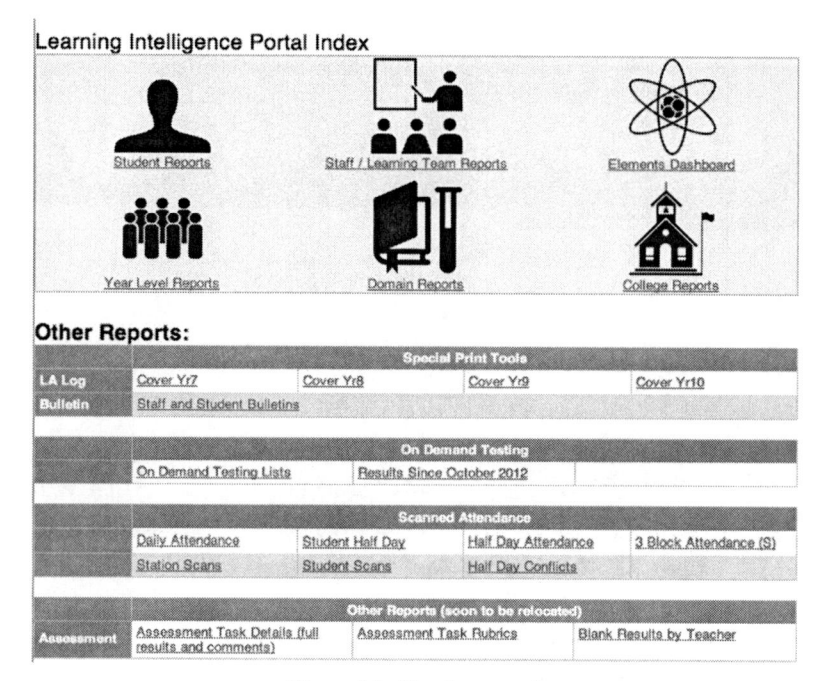

Figure 5.1. Teacher portal.

these all monitor student learning activities and assessment, Verbert et al. (2013) and others, (Mårell-Olsson, 2012, Britzman, 1991 and Kress & van Leuwen, 2001), also note the potential of such digital technology for making learning visible to students and teachers in ways that have not previously been available.

The Whirrakee College dashboard draws on Web 2.0 technology to create a virtual space that supports the development of student self-regulation of their learning in physical open-plan learning environments. The dashboard at Whirrakee College developed from teacher concern that the existing systems for monitoring student learning in a traditional classroom with one teacher were not sufficiently robust for the new open-plan and team-teaching environments. Coupled with this was a desire to facilitate independent learners who had contributed to personalising their own learning. The dashboard at Whirrakee College organises information about individual student learning and progress in one place so that multiple people may have instant access to that information via the internet. The information provided also assists with student, teacher and school-wide goal-setting.

While the dashboard is a tool for recording goals and may facilitate goal-setting (Figure 5.2) through the designed prompts provided to students, its key value is in the affordance offered to students of making their learning over time visible to themselves and others. In the traditional classroom, student assessment, and the record keeping involved, is the domain of the teacher. In contrast, the dashboard is a

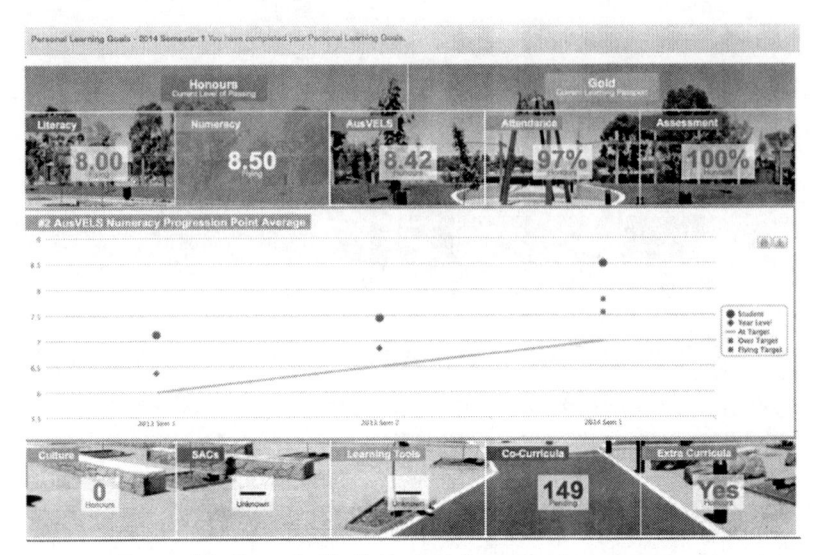

Figure 5.2. Record of individual student progress in numeracy.

technological tool whereby students can personally monitor their learning progress in collaboration with the teacher.

The school intranet is linked to the dashboard with students and teachers having access to a portable computer device twenty-four hours, seven days a week. While students, teachers and parents have different interfaces, there are also interconnected public and private spaces on the dashboard, affording varied opportunities for personalising learning. Differentiating entry to the dashboard for students, parent/carers and teachers maintains the traditional quarantining and selective sharing of information. However, it may also be argued that this is important in ensuring student wellbeing and trust. Students and parent/carers can only see their own and their child's learning record and progress (Figure 5.3), while teachers have access to all student information (Figure 5.4).

Teacher action, however, is made visible to other teachers through the information that they and the students enter, in accordance with the greater visibility afforded by open-plan settings. This disrupts the traditional closed teacher-student interactions around assessment and monitoring of learning. Teachers are able to use this real time information about student progress to inform the learning conversations they have with students and the learning activities they design to personalise student learning. Students are also able to have current information about their own learning and progress, potentially increasing student agency in contributing to, and taking responsibility for, their own learning in these conversations and learning experiences. The challenge for teachers is in reconceptualising their role from that of assessor responsible for the monitoring of learning, to a more collaborative role with the student, where both take responsibility for the monitoring of learning aims, experiences, and

TECHNOLOGY IN OPEN-PLAN SETTINGS

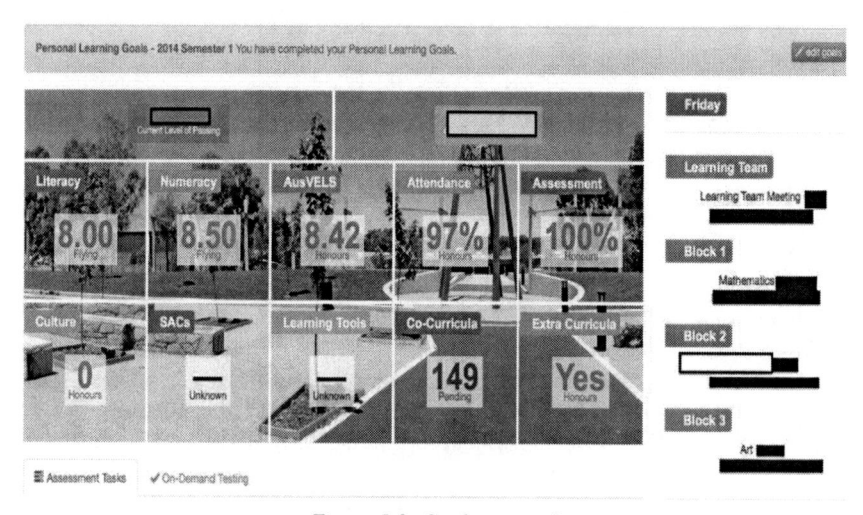

Figure 5.3. Student portal.

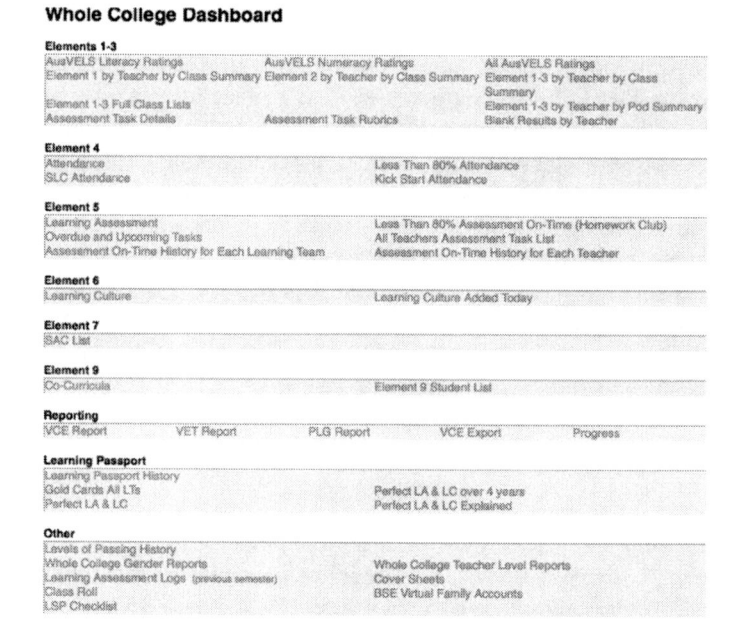

Figure 5.4. Teacher view of all student data.

outcomes. The dashboard allows the student access to information that previously was held by the teacher. Therefore, students arrive at the conversation with existing knowledge about their own learning, enabling them to be informed participants in the decision-making process. Thus, students and teachers collaboratively construct

89

individual learning goals, rather than simply exchanging information. Collaborative construction of student goals affords students opportunity for agency in their own learning that they did not previously have in the teacher-determined goals.

The potential of the dashboard for recording student strategy use and providing a space for collaborative, networked learning has to date largely been under-utilised at Whirrakee College. As noted in the first case study, student perceptions of the affordances offered by the technology were often influenced by their use of multiple forms of media, and their social and active learning in virtual environments, outside the classroom. As with other facets of the open-plan classroom design, the dashboard is evolving as the affordances offered are recognised and enacted by students and teachers.

The initial student and teacher perceptions of the affordances offered by the dashboard were governed by the college and focused on the reporting of student learning outcomes. Given that the college has initiated and developed the dashboard, and has control of the platform design and student access, this is not surprising. At present, the dashboard is perceived by students and teachers predominantly as a technological tool that offers a means of making visible a student's own learning process and outcomes. It does this through the recording and monitoring of student learning within an open, yet boundaried, digital environment rather than as an open space for student interactive learning. However, using the dashboard has prompted teachers to consider additional purposes, such as a space for creative collaborative learning. In addition, there is potential for the dashboard to act as a repository for multi-modal artefacts demonstrating learning outcomes in new ways, or old ways repurposed, such as a virtual gallery. Collaboration is already occurring among teachers who are using the dashboard as a space for collaboratively designing and sharing student learning activities, as well as a repository for the artefacts produced from this collaboration (Prain et al., in press). The potential exists in the dashboard for such a collaborative virtual space to also be used by students and students and teachers to interact to construct knowledge, thus addressing the challenge of boundaries, and allowing greater agency for students.

USING AFFORDANCES OF OPEN-PLAN AND VIRTUAL LEARNING ENVIRONMENTS

Prior to analysing the possibilities for agency in virtual learning environments, as demonstrated in the case studies, it is worth commenting on the similarities and differences between open-plan and virtual space. Both open-plan and virtual space challenge conventional teaching and learning roles, routines, and relationships. We see this as a potential modification of the authority and formality vested in the conventional enclosed classroom. This point hinges on conceptions of physical, cultural and social boundaries. The same routines can be enacted in any educational space; it is how the boundaries are perceived as either affording or constraining certain activities that is the driver of any transformative teaching or learning activity.

While virtual learning space may be conducive to more autonomous and social learning, there are dangers in idealising these approaches, and in assuming that students and teachers want to transgress normalised school routines.

These case studies highlight the complexity of characterising and enacting student and teacher agency as well as relational agency between the two participant groups. The studies indicate that this agency includes not only an individual student's power to make strategic and reasoned choices about current and future actions, but also participation in relational agency with others, including the teacher, on shared or negotiated goals. The capacity of students to enact this agency is constrained and enabled by habit, reason, and imagination. Refined versions of agency are required and enacted by both teacher and students in open-plan and virtual space.

The three case studies provide examples of how Web 2.0 technology may afford opportunity in virtual learning environments for exercising increased student agency. Here we have conceptualised agency as the development, practice and application of skills required for effective participation in learning, whether individual or shared, and in particular learning decisions and interactions mediated by technology. Teacher agency, as outlined in our case studies, is less clearly routinised in technologically-mediated open-plan settings when contrasted with roles in traditional settings. There is scope for a more precise sphere of influence with individual students (because of the tracking affordances of the dashboard), and a more diverse sphere of influence across a larger community and/or neighbourhood of learners. Student agency, in open-plan and virtual learning environments, as explicated here through our study, involves building cognitive depth to the sense of autonomy, and valuing different experiences within a frame of reasoned and justified knowledge construction.

Agency in open-plan learning environments concerns imaginative personal and mutual action, drawing on the generalised capacities of learning established in more traditional contexts. The virtual nature of Web 2.0 spaces and digital platforms such as the dashboard can be represented as a set of potential connections and interactions with unknown and geographically distant insiders or outsiders, where the system only exists as the sum of an individual's/group's actions as they go online, search, visit, post, bookmark, join networks, and create artefacts. Students potentially create their own learning space as they make decisions about connectivity and interactivity. Each action emerges from individual agency within a networked practice to achieve a purpose.

The learning environments in the case study schools are both physical and virtual spaces. The virtual open learning environment only exists when it is pieced together and traversed by agents as solo or sharing travellers. It does not remain in a physical place; it is a virtual set of dots that are joined temporarily as part of a cognitive leap through virtual time and space. An indicator of the difference in agency between traditional and technologically-mediated, open-plan learning environments can be gained by comparing the artefacts in each. In technologically- mediated open learning environments, conventional academic outputs continue to include written essays where the reference list and in-text arguments, evidence and reasoning, provide the cognitive pathway. However, these new learning environments also permit the production of a wider range of artefacts including transcripts and multimodal forms of interaction and production such as text messages, emails, videos, photos, and blog postings, along with semantic data recording website and page visits and preferences. Importantly, artefacts may also include collaboratively and socially constructed student and teacher outputs as well as individual outputs informed by accessing expertise and information external to the physical classroom. Agency is thus realised as a dynamic and relational interplay between the student and others, including access and use of their own and others' resources, the design and program affordances of the technology used, and the contextual grounding/ purpose/judgement of the activity.

Based on the review of literature and the case studies, we have identified a number of indicators of agency in open-plan and virtual learning environments:

- a view of knowledge as distributed and collective;
- a critical view of conditions for knowledge construction;
- immersive engagement in different learning experiences;
- effective use of Web 2.0 social networking tools;
- representation and communication of ideas through interactive use of multimodal resources;
- engaging with diverse perspectives;
- global awareness and intercultural competence;
- managing contestability through application of higher-order questioning and reasoning strategies;
- an understanding of the meaning and characteristics of expertise;
- adaptation to affordances of different learning environments;
- engaging in collaboratively constructed meaning-making and knowledge as well as information sharing.

Semiotic agility is a key component of agency, defined as the use of a variety of representational modes/sign systems to interpret/construct and share understandings. Deliberately seeking outside ideas and diverse perspectives will require the use of diverse semiotic modes. While this may be workable at the simple cognitive level, such as descriptive accounts and basic sharing of images and text, academic disciplinary knowledge is also influenced by these modal affordances in frequently nuanced, specialised and complex ways (see Lemke, 2014).

CONCLUSION

We began this chapter by referring to virtual and open-plan learning environments as a productive disruption. By this we meant the disjuncture between traditional enclosed classrooms and open-plan or virtual learning spaces. Through the case studies we identified the necessary shift, not only in context, but in agency: the relationships, interactions, tools and language of both students and teachers, possible in open-plan and virtual learning spaces.

Agency, to us, is primarily about a capacity for individuals, in this case students and teachers, to act in ways that contribute to new learning. As well as the relational capacities between individuals and within groups to enact personal and shared learning goals. When educators speak about wanting independent learners, they are referring to a desire for students to be agentic, and actively participating in the direction of, if not totally taking control of their learning. As outlined in earlier chapters this was one of the key drivers of, the Bendigo Education Plan. Learning in any environment is about engagement and disengagement as a dynamic reaction to time and space, simultaneously real, virtual and imagined, and mediated through old and/or new technologies. The self-directed learning class and the digital dashboard are examples of how adding a virtual learning environment to the open-plan learning environment may be productively disruptive in its placing of responsibility for learning on both teacher and student. Agency of the student (and also the teacher) infers an ability to cope with the increasing contestability and uncertainty evident in open-plan and virtual learning spaces that may foster new ways of thinking about personalising learning in contemporary secondary schools.

Both teachers and students need to cope with non-algorithmic conversational pathways, uncertainty about meaning, applicability and questioning, as part of reasoned analysis and evaluation. They need to deal with potential conflict of perspectives and cultural boundary-crossing in both digital and physical open learning environments. The up-scaled learning communities in the BEP schools prompt these new accounts of student and staff agency.

MARY KEEFFE

6. DISTRIBUTING LEADERSHIP IN OPEN-PLAN SCHOOLS

INTRODUCTION

While there is an extensive literature justifying different leadership models in traditional schools, the new up-scaled learning communities posed many challenges and complexities about how leadership should be understood and enacted, and by whom, and on what bases. These challenges included how leadership of learning should be orchestrated within and across learning communities. Should each learning community be understood as a self-determining educational entity? What should be the roles of staff and students in contributing to the evolution of this community purpose and reviewing its processes and structures? Older hierarchical models of centrist control seemed a poor fit for the new arrangements and for the increased reality of shared roles and responsibilities for community members. In this chapter we review the literature on past models of leadership in traditional schools to frame the reasoning and practices of staff in engaging with questions of distributing leadership for learning in the new settings, noting that these settings inevitably acted as catalysts for emerging new leadership roles and foci. This did not result in a uniformity of structures and processes across each school, but entailed adaptive local strategies based on school cultures and leadership initiatives in each college. Over the three years of the study different rationales and structures evolved. In analysing these new adaptive practices we were interested in the following research questions:

1. In what ways, and to what extent, did leadership practices and rationales in these schools differ from those espoused in past models in traditional settings?
2. How was teacher capacity-building around distributed leadership attempted in the BEP schools?
3. What organisational processes and structures were attempted to enable teachers to become effective leaders?
4. What student roles were envisaged as part of distributed leadership?

This chapter is structured around headings that explore these four questions.

OLD AND NEW VERSIONS OF SCHOOL LEADERSHIP

Hierarchical top-down models of school leadership based on organisational efficiency rather than values negotiation (see Simon, 1976) have been contested in recent decades. As noted by Leithwood, Mascall, and Strauss (2009), the sheer complexity of the principal's role and its broad range of responsibilities render highly centrist models at best inappropriate, at worst unworkable. Single person leadership models are also challenged by more democratic notions of leadership, entailing more 'flattened' power structures, in which individuals are listened to and treated with respect, and collaborative decision-making processes engage all stakeholders (Woods, 2004). These processes apply to students as well as teachers. Bush and Gamage (2001), advocated a more responsive personalised learning approach that foregrounded the importance of individual students rather than compliance with systemic and authoritative requirements.

However, Woods and Gronn (2009), claimed that broad democratic ideals of a civic society, such as equal representation, are not easily transposed to organisations such as schools, and a more focused idea of democratic rights and roles is required. Despite the lack of clear definitions of organisational democracy (Holmes & Gutierrezz de Pineres, 2006), several authors have tried to elaborate on signs of more democratic school leadership and governance styles (Andrews et al., 2011; Bernstein, 1996; Halpin, 1998; Sergiovanni, 2000; Slee, 2001). These researchers claim that such schools have decision-making processes more responsive to the educational needs of diverse student populations. More recently, democratic notions of voice and agency imply that including students' opinions in this decision-making increases student engagement with learning. (Keeffe & Andrews, 2011; Rudduck & Fielding, 2006). Other authors more specifically state that collaborative processes are an essential characteristic of democratic governance arguing that these processes motivate stakeholders to participate and contribute towards shared goals in energetic and constructive ways (Green & Etheridge, 2001; Habermas, 1987; Skrtic & Sailor, 1996).

Networked, distributed, or parallel leadership structures endorse teachers as leaders and decision-makers in their own right. Teacher leadership is viewed as central to the work of Andrews et al. (2011), who describe the concepts of parallelism and mutualism. Parallelism places teachers as strategic equals to the principal leader on questions of curriculum organisation and developing the ethos of the school, while mutualism couches the relationship in terms of respect and trust. Teacher leadership values the diverse perspectives of teachers, students, and the community, to resolve difficulties in collaborative and respectful ways to facilitate school success for all students. Thus, the democratic processes of collaboratively determining core school purposes become more important than the influential role of an individual teacher or student leader. This is consistent, in part, with Katzenmayer and Moller's (1996) early perception that teacher leaders are the unrealised key to social reform in schools and society.

These insights imply that the following elements are needed to structure and enact distributed leadership: more democratic forms of decision-making, teachers as leaders, collaboration and responsiveness, student leadership, accountability, capacity-building, and quality learning outcomes. In his original explanation of distributed leadership, Gronn (1999), acknowledged the complex and yet unrealistic expectations of the role of a single, hierarchical leader, and preferred a model in which organisational structures magnified the influence of a network of decision-makers. Heterarchical responses, according to Gronn, give leaders the flexibility to respond in creative ways to the unique challenges that are part of daily life in many schools. Examples of heterarchical leadership from our study of the four BEP schools include groups of teachers sharing ideas and resources to resolve problems of curriculum differentiation, students contributing to resolving challenges of learning community organisation, and welfare officers responding to a spate of substance abuse in the school. These situational responses are all forms of leadership actions that are not determined by traditional status or control. Gronn also recognised that a hierarchical core of linear leadership responsibilities was necessary to provide consistency and coherence. He saw the creativity and responsiveness of heterarchical leaders as complementary to the more linear approach determined by a leadership hierarchy. Distributed leadership is therefore a hybrid of a democratic or team approach with a leadership style (charismatic, transformational, instrumental etc.) that suits the accountability processes of the principal. In this sense, distributed leadership is not an abdication of responsibility by principals, but a more nuanced approach to decision-making within structures understood by all members of the school community. Distributed leadership is thus understood as an ongoing, shared social practice to serve shared goals.

All four BEP principals adopted approaches that fit Gronn's (1999) hybridised model. In line with broader accountability requirements, they had to focus on raising teaching and learning standards in a context where their schools' academic performance is constantly measured against others, and enrolments (and therefore numbers of teaching staff) depend upon establishing and preserving good reputations. Consistent with Gronn's notion of shared responsibilities, the principals perceived themselves as responsible for guiding and managing public and parent perceptions of the coherence and workability of the new school structures. In this sense they had to justify the educational value of the new settings within and beyond the school, and build a positive culture around new practices. They saw themselves as ultimately responsible for the organisational structures that should enable quality teaching and learning. They accepted that a distributed form of leadership was a necessity in each school. The scale and complexity of learning communities and their separation from one another required devolution of leadership, the need for collective quality leadership on learning in each community supported this devolution, and the development of a sense of belonging and connectedness in these settings that could only be achieved through shared responsibilities and participatory decision-making in each community. They understood that networked, layered approaches to leadership, including a shared whole-school vision, were crucial to successful educational outcomes. They saw that each learning community needed to be autonomous in some areas to optimise buy-in by participants. This hybridised form of distributed leadership implied the need for parallel leadership among staff members (Andrews et al., (2011). As noted by one principal in justifying the necessity of devolution of leadership on learning to community leaders:

> I would quite confidently say all these people [community leaders] would have a much higher level of technical knowledge in those areas than I would. I have to have confidence that they are keeping up to date with that. I rely on their advice to make some of those big-picture decisions.

Another principal commented that if schools "break a larger school down into more direct relationships and accountability then the learning group becomes a critical part of that structure". A third principal claimed that "you have to have a successful organisational culture that the teaching and learning sits on top of and then you will get high performance out of your students which is the whole reason these four walls exist". These comments highlight the complex nature of enacting hybridised leadership. The principals are accountable for upholding the reputation of the school but rely deeply on partnerships within and across the learning communities to build local and collective effort and develop productive innovations. The fourth principal claimed that all learning community leaders are part of the school leadership team that meets regularly to discuss the strategic plan, and direction and priorities for the school.

TEACHER CAPACITY-BUILDING

Capacity-building was attempted through (a) establishing a collective staff and student agreement on school values and goals, (b) use of internal and external coaches to support teacher and leadership professional development, and (c) extended consultation around the goals and outcomes of these processes. Establishing collective agreement about the mission and desired ethos of the schools was undertaken through extensive meetings both before and after the schools were built, including inputs from staff and students. Coaching support was provided by designated teachers in each school on curricular matters as well as external consultation on effective curricular practices (see chapter 3).

Community leaders were also supported through regional office consultation on how to be an effective learning leader. In each school this capacity-building was focused on learning and how to be a leader of learning, whether as a community or curriculum leader, staff member or student (see chapters 3, 9, and 10). For example, at Grevillea College, capacity-building processes included organisation of meetings of staff within and across learning communities to share emerging wisdom on topical issues such as effective use of ICT and interactive whiteboards. Though attendance at such meetings was voluntary, the principal expressed delight at the participation and professional learning witnessed in these meetings. All staff members were encouraged to contribute to these conversations about learning in the new settings.

In the first two years, a leadership coach was involved with the community and neighbourhood leaders in two schools. She claimed her greatest challenge was to:

> develop teacher/leader confidence in terms of shared responsibilities. I wanted to help them feel confident about their own expectations so they could model to others and insist on standards of professional behaviour to improve attitudes towards students and learning.

The first phase of community leadership involved regular mentoring and capacity-building from district advisors and school administration in regular meetings. Some topics were professionally complex and included role clarification, conflict resolution, boundaries, and referral, while others were structural and related to timetables, lesson structures, and assessments.

Some community leaders also needed one-on-one mentoring for personal skills such as good listening, communication, and assertion. To build capacity in the personnel skills required to address, support, and challenge a range of daily issues, the community leaders practiced role-play responses where their colleagues and mentors gave them feedback. Contentious issues raised by teachers, parents and students were discussed and trialled before implementing a range of strategies in the community context. The new responsibilities to mentor staff were structured in terms of student advocacy in the neighbourhood settings and were regarded as a positive professional challenge, a welcome way to build capacity with teacher colleagues, and to create meaningful relationships.

ORGANISATIONAL PROCESSES AND STRUCTURES TO DISTRIBUTE LEADERSHIP

Community Leadership Structures, Roles and Challenges

Processes, structures and roles evolved over the three years of the study, with multiple inputs from participants. As the four learning communities at each school were divided into two or three neighbourhoods, the learning community leaders appointed to each community were also supported by neighbourhood leaders. These leaders exercised considerable autonomy in their communities. At Grevillea College, for instance, two community leaders were appointed to each of the four Years 7-10 communities, where their role initially entailed multiple functions. One community leader at Grevillea saw her role as fourfold. She was expected to organise the use of space to make sure the community functioned smoothly, support staff in student management, recognise student needs and advocate for students. She was also expected to be a communication conduit between the school leadership and staff in the community. In this context, all teachers in each community met every two weeks to discuss matters of community organisation, smooth functioning of the timetable, setting of protocols, student management, and use of space in their learning community. Students were also invited to solve problems on the functioning of their community. To assure accountability, meetings were conducted formally, with a published set agenda, a chair person, and a minute taker to ensure records were kept of meeting decisions. One learning community leader, after working in this role for two years, commented that the skills required of him were:

> people skills, emotional intelligence, time management, organisational skills, learning how to communicate ideas clearly in disagreeing with people comfortably and reasonably. You have to care and be passionate and be prepared for conversations around teaching and learning.

In a parallel version of the principal's role, this community leader saw that negotiating expectations with staff, providing fresh ideas and informed response to suggestions by others, and coping with differences were crucial to his leadership role. The daily shared space enabled these more democratic processes to be enacted.

At Melaleuca College the principal found a major challenge in broadening leadership in the school was that some staff expected leadership to be the principal's responsibility rather than theirs. Furthermore, he was concerned that initiatives in team teaching and innovative curriculum, though occurring in some communities, were not broadly accepted or practised. He believed these challenges demonstrated that staff needed support in developing leadership skills and confidence in experimenting with new ways of teaching and learning. He saw his own role as removing the impediments to successful teaching and learning in the school by addressing perceived management problems and began by fostering boundaried communication among staff. He claimed that distributing leadership required all staff members to "understand the lines of communication, that there are forums for staff to have input into the health and wellbeing of the organisation". He noted that there needed to be a strategic structure of leaders across learning communities, "so that everyone has the trust that the school is well managed", and where inputs from staff and students can be discussed. He considered that "people have got to have their say but you can't have open staff forums". He saw a major need to change teacher classroom methods to a more collegial, team-teaching approach and believed that teachers needed encouragement to be innovative:

> Although we're getting people to behave in different ways, the research tells us that once they behave in different ways their values and beliefs will change to fall in line with that. It's a painstaking process.

At the same time he saw that building leadership about learning at this school was a combined responsibility of staff, including subject leaders and coaches. "It's as much about all of those people being on the same page philosophically as each other as it is about the way they go about leading". He considered that internal and external coaching around pedagogy was crucial to academic gains over the three years.

At Whirrakee College, the principal focused strongly on accountability for student academic performance, including ongoing analyses of this performance. This entailed ongoing discussion with community and curricular leaders on strategies for improvement, including support for enrichment programs for students (see chapter 7). His democratic approach to leadership in this area was evident in the take-up of one teacher's suggestion of how to structure learning experiences in each learning community using temporary, flexible groupings of students by ability (see chapter 4). In this way all staff members were encouraged to own, share, and contribute to the distributed expertise in learning at the school.

At Ironbark College, the principal recognised that the first priority in introducing distributed leadership was to create a new sense of shared responsibility and empowerment among teachers. As noted by Andrews et al. (2011), a school-wide approach was needed to build teachers' confidence in their own professional knowledge. In the first instance, the teachers had to review their expectations about student capacity for success and their acceptance of student disengagement at their school. Discussions about family and student expectations of success were contextualised in the broader community experiences of unemployment, poverty, incarceration rates, and mental health and wellbeing issues. Through ongoing meetings within and across communities, staff members accepted that these students needed a responsive school culture with a personalised approach to learning, combined with raised expectations about what the students could achieve. The next phase involved developing an organisational structure that enacted active participation in decision-making about staff and student roles in creating respectful, inclusive community cultures focused on learning and wellbeing.

Learning community leaders had a community liaison role that linked school administration and the neighbourhoods within each learning community (see chapter 4). The community leader also had a significant curriculum role in the school. By transferring this leadership role to the learning community leader from the traditionally accepted model of a whole-school curriculum coordinator, schools were prioritising the leading of teaching and learning as a major role for community leaders. Four curriculum priorities were identified and re-negotiated every three years at Ironbark College. In one year of the study, the curriculum priorities included teacher advisor co-ordination, transition (career and learning pathways), vocational education, and information technology. The community leaders were autonomous in their communities, and were expected to inform the staff of changes in the field, promote and monitor innovative curriculum approaches, and remain accountable for the quality of teaching and learning in that area.

Learning community and neighbourhood leaders worked together, both within, and across learning communities as members of the school leadership team, to support and complement each other in terms of their skills, and responses to student welfare, curriculum, and administration. They also modelled the values and processes to all other teachers in the learning community and mentored teachers in conducting respectful, clear, and assertive conversations with students and parents.

One neighbourhood leader described the complex range of people skills required:

> Wow! Lots of people skills. First of all you have to be a good people person. You need to be able to read and understand staff and be able to stand your ground when a staff member is trying to do something that is not according to our protocols, or not appropriate, or not good teaching practice, but at the same time, not put them offside in such a way that you can't work together.

To give them a level of credibility in organisational curriculum issues, the community leaders were responsible for procedural actions to refer students to wellbeing coordinators or to support personnel. The principal commented that this approach "distributes responsibility through many different themes within the school, rather than levels of job".

Teacher Leadership in Student Management and Advocacy

Successful distributed leadership in BEP schools broadened as teachers, through mentoring and support, embraced the implications of shared responsibilities. The most convincing change occurred as the teachers became more confident in their interactions with students and parents. Following Greeno (2006), agency here is not a fixed personality trait or attribute; rather, it is the ability to participate and contribute to various situations. That is, the leadership is embedded in social practices, and understood by all participants. The quality of collaborative relationships between colleagues, teachers and students changed as each school improved the level of active participation by all teachers.

Active participation in leadership was centred in the role of teacher advisor (TA). This role was extended by the BEP (see chapter 1) from the role of form teacher in traditional schools so that each teacher took responsibility for the learning and wellbeing of a specific group of between twelve students (Ironbark and Grevillea) and twenty-five students (Whirrakee and Melaleuca), and to advocate for their educational needs. The Ironbark principal regards the teacher advisor role as "the hub of our distributed leadership model. Our whole system comes back to the teacher advisor."

This section focuses on an exemplar teacher advisor program at one of the four BEP colleges. At Ironbark College, the teacher advisor (TA) spends twenty minutes per day with a group of about 12 students. The program at Ironbark is more formally structured than the other schools, and implemented to foster learning skills and build sustainable relationships. TAs are responsible for a TA curriculum that makes learning skills explicit, guides students through curriculum choices, negotiates learning plans and goals, analyses contentious life contexts, and provides a forum for relationships based on mutual respect and advocacy. As they stay with their group throughout the four years of the students' Years 7-10 education, the TA's relationship with those students is personal and committed. Some teachers initially struggled as they engaged with the responsibility of the teacher advisor role. The aim of the TA program was to build student agency in problem-solving and decision-making about contentious living and learning topics, through frank discussions, group coaching, peer support and individual advocacy. The social and emotional development of students was an unfamiliar notion that unsettled some teachers, who saw it as being an area outside their expertise. Lipponen and Kumpulainen (2011) suggest that teachers who are not agentic in their own personal or professional lives will not be able to develop confidence in personal decision-making in students. They claim that social and dialogic spaces are required to build agency for both and that the processes involved should be made explicit to some extent so that each can learn about their roles in life, learning and the community in a safe and nurturing environment.

The structured curriculum of learning activities was developed and made compulsory to provide support for, and build confidence in teachers, and so that all teachers and students would be actively involved. Without the structures it was found that TA time easily degenerated into chat sessions. In interviews, teachers claimed that the advocacy role of caring for students and contacting parents was the most challenging, yet rewarding, part of their role. TAs build personal and respectful relationships with families, and play an important part in making the school environment responsive to the complex needs of students who often struggle with life and learning challenges. The comfort and confidence that teachers described in the advocacy role was morally consistent with their initial intention to provide personalised learning for students from challenging backgrounds.

However, some teachers did not feel the same level of confidence during discussions about contentious topics, particularly when they concerned important life choices. Their life experience did not extend to some issues raised by students and they felt vulnerable in the way they managed such conversations. One teacher commented, "I am glad I have a background in psychology. You really need it sometimes when these kids bring up shocking situations from their lives or from what they have seen on the internet. You have to help them make sense of it all."

The reciprocal nature of the relationships in the TA group provided a level of reliable security in reflection and decision-making for students. One student appreciated the relationship he had established with his TA teacher. "We have Mrs. G. She knows us all really well and we all like her. She knows when I am having trouble with something. She just knows as soon as I walk into the room and I can trust her when I talk to her."

Traditional forms of leadership are challenged by the TA leadership structure. Decisions do not always have to be at the strategic level to have a significant influence on students and the way they make decisions. A kind thought, a trusted relationship, and peer support are valuable experiences for adolescent students. A level of distributed leadership that is rarely discussed in the literature involves teachers leading students in life and learning choices, and students leading teachers and peers in connecting learning with the drama, trauma and excitement of their

Table 6.1 Teachers' changed perceptions in the teacher advisor role.

Teacher Advisor Duties	2007	2012
Administrative Duties	50%	20%
Wellbeing Role	35%	40%
Planning for learning	10%	40%
Community Links	0%	0%
Behaviour Management	5%	5%

own lives. Teachers advise, counsel, support and lead students towards quality of life choices when there are structures and decision-making processes within the school to facilitate these actions.

At Ironbark, teachers' perspectives of the change in the nature of TA duties were monitored in a survey of all teachers in the school over six years. Table 6.1 shows a significant reduction in administrative duties and increases in wellbeing and planning for learning over time, suggesting that shared responsibilities for decision-making and a greater focus on students' wellbeing and learning are experienced as more constructive approaches in a TA program.

STUDENT ROLES IN DISTRIBUTED LEADERSHIP

For reformists in this field, student voice and student leadership are the ultimate indices of desirable distributed leadership in schools. Our study highlights the challenges and tensions for principals and teachers in seeking to develop and harness collective expertise and responsibility in all school community members, including students. What student agency could become and how it could contribute to the quality of school experiences and learning remain open questions. Deep understanding of leadership depends on the evolution of participant values, roles, and practices within structures for shared decision-making and review. As noted in our study, this evolution entails a complex acquisition of new understandings, capacities, and opportunities for all participants, and depends on a shared vision of mutual responsibility and reciprocal learning. Hart (1997), Fielding (2008), Smyth (2006), Keeffe and Andrews (2011) connect student perspectives about their understanding of agency with their own schooling experience (whether negative or positive) and their engagement with learning.

Students at BEP schools generally continue to play traditionally accepted roles in student leadership. Leadership structures for students include the School Captains who represent the student body of the school at community functions, Junior and Senior Community Captains who represent the students in their communities and the Students' Representative Council (SRC) in each school which comprises student representatives from each year level. Matters raised by the SRC generally focus on fundraising for student facilities and local charities, and social events for students.

However there are signs that schools are recognising the leadership potential of their students and are beginning to involve more students in other less traditional ways. All Year 10 students at Whirrakee College who do not have an official leadership role are encouraged in leadership by playing an active mentoring role with younger students in liaison with the TA teacher in TA sessions (see chapter 9).

Grevillea College has implemented a formal avenue for student leadership that attempts to reach the broader student population. Students are encouraged to feed ideas on community improvement through a student representative in their TA group who reports to a student voice committee. In one community when staff identify a community challenge or concern, students are invited to suggest solutions. An example was that staff were concerned that students were late coming to their first class of the day after the TA meeting. Several student suggestions to remedy the problem were discussed at the community staff meeting. From listening to the students the teachers gained a better understanding of the reasons for the students' apparent carelessness about time. Students wanted a chance to talk to their friends in the mornings but were not allowed to enter the community building before the bell. For some, chatting to friends is prioritised over organisation. They go to advisory without their books and have to return to their lockers after advisory. However, no changeover time is allowed between TA and the first class. The decision was made to introduce measures responsive to student suggestions on a trial basis that the students would be responsible for monitoring. First, the community building would be open to students earlier and students permitted to sit in their teacher advisory class and talk quietly to their friends. Second, students who were remaining in their community for the first and second period of the day would be required only to take books for the first session to advisory. The community leaders would take a request for a five-minute changeover between periods one and two to the leadership team.

Beaty (2013) examines the contradiction that while teacher expertise is required to develop student agency (in the TA group for example), the constraints imposed on the outcomes of agency itself may hinder that development. The TA groups were formed to encourage collaborative decision-making with students, yet, one primary function of all schooling must be to assist students to make decisions themselves. The emergent and problem-solving approach of the learning activities in the TA group at Ironbark College was designed to provide a safe and supportive structure where students could reflect on the issues in their own lives and make confident and constructive decisions. It is expected that the improved, more democratic staff-student relationships in BEP schools will, in time, lead to greater leadership roles for students.

CONCLUSION

In this chapter we have claimed that the new settings prompted productive challenges for staff members to conceptualise and enact effective school leadership, with signs of generative approaches to distributing this leadership in each school. Principals increasingly understand their responsibility not only as maintaining a positive school culture but providing the seamless management that underpins the main purpose of the school – to provide an excellent standard of teaching and learning. The community structure of the BEP schools has resulted in distributed leadership structures as responsibility for teaching and learning is devolved to community and neighbourhood leaders while teachers in turn play a greater role in student management and advocacy. The extent to which students have been able to take up leadership roles remains less clear, but we pursue this topic in more detail in chapters 9, 10 and 11.

VALERIE LOVEJOY, LUCY MOW, DEBRA EDWARDS,
BRUCE WALDRIP & VAUGHAN PRAIN

7. ADAPTING TO TEACHING IN OPEN-PLAN UP-SCALED LEARNING COMMUNITIES

REDESIGNING SCHOOLING

So it's open, they learn from each other ... teachers are really prepared to be honest about their own teaching practice and look at things they can do in order to change. (Principal)

You need problem-solving skills, patience and people management skills. You've got to be able to value others and feel valued yourself. There's no freeloading. You've got to really carry your own weight and contribute to the team. And there's no hiding. (English teacher)

These comments reflect positive staff perceptions of adapting to the new settings in the BEP schools. However, for some other staff members the new settings entailed excessive noise, increased student distraction, loss of intimacy and structure, threats to traditional practices, exposure to the gaze and critique of colleagues, and demands for new team and individual skills. In this chapter we identify staff perceptions and practices around the challenges and opportunities arising from the settings in terms of perceived affordances, relational agency among participants, changing spheres of influence for teachers and students, attempts to personalise learning, and activity system dynamics in the new settings (see chapter 3). We also characterise observed changes to teaching and learning processes, as well as enablers and constraints to these changes.

STAFF PERCEPTIONS OF CHALLENGES, ACTION
POSSIBILITIES AND CONSTRAINTS

Participant teachers and principals identified many challenges, but a major one was the question of the adequacy and developmental coherence of current curricular content and teaching methods within and across communities and across year levels. As noted in chapter 4, the increased visibility of teaching in the communities, and the external and internal pressure to improve student academic performance in state and national tests, prompted diverse curricular review and change. This led to new demands on teacher planning and review time, some teacher and student resistance to change, and perceptions by some teachers of lack of adequate support in time and resources to embed successful new practices. A further main challenge related to teacher and student perceptions about appropriate behaviour in these settings, including problems of increased noise and student distraction, lack of privacy for all participants, and the need for appropriate protocols for student movement in and between communities to prevent disruption and thoroughfare effects. Both concerns highlighted the need for more, not less, structure in curricular organisation. As noted in chapter 4, over the three years of the study, these challenges were addressed variously within, and across, learning communities.

These settings were a catalyst for change (see themes in Table 7.1). Increased visibility in each learning community prompted teachers to develop new, more intensive and focused collaboration, to re-structure the curriculum into block timetabling and shared teaching, leading to more informal interactions and closer relationships between teachers and students, as noted in chapter 5. Immediate responsibility for a class in progress shifted attention to the broader workability of parallel classes and groupings. Teachers recognised that this broader sphere of influence necessitated more structure for planning and activities within learning neighbourhoods and communities, in order to meet their own and students' ongoing wellbeing needs. These up-scaled learning communities also generated new, complex, and diverse, participant interactions. Some teachers found it challenging to respond to the new professional opportunities, and to adapt to the alteration of their sphere of influence. In Table 7.1 we identify several key themes in teacher perceptions of factors that enabled or constrained learning and wellbeing in these contexts over the three years of the study.

Teacher Adaptive Practices

The four schools experimented with block timetabling of core compulsory subjects, such as English and mathematics, in the open-plan settings with practices affected by the availability of specialist teachers within and across learning communities, as noted in chapter 5. The large foyer in each learning community, designated the Einstein Studio in original planning templates (see chapters 1 and 4), was used for diverse activities, including specialist subject teaching, independent student work, and more informal discussions within and outside official subject timetabling. In some schools this area was set up with lounge suites to create an informal learning/ meeting space. Interview rooms functioned as multi-purpose areas, including teacher planning meetings and small-group student project work. The combined art/science spaces, called Da Vinci studios, were also used as breakout spaces to accommodate teaching and learning needs.

Some teachers struggled to see that these new affordances, including more space for class activities and more informal groupings, might outweigh constraints of increased noise, distraction, and potential loss of personal connection with their students. These issues were addressed in some schools by teachers enforcing

Table 7.1. *Teachers' Perceptions of Action Possibilities and Constraints.*

Themes	Action Possibilities/Affordances	Potential constraints
Teacher collaboration	More collaboration, team teaching, resource sharing, communication, and professional learning in visible classrooms.	Learning community leaders unprepared/unfamiliar/unwilling to take on responsibilities, lack of time for planning together for team teaching and professional learning.
Curriculum innovation	Opportunities for innovative practices in teaching and learning, and introduction of a flexible curriculum to address needs of individual students.	Commitment and readiness of teachers to adapt to change from traditional practices in individual classrooms. Lack of agreement around teacher sphere of influence and mindset.
Relationships	Respectful, harmonious relationships among students and between students and staff, and greater feelings of connectedness through relaxing formal boundaries around designated staff/student spaces. Underpinned by common set of protocols around respect and trust, reinforced by all teachers.	Poor fit between environment and needs of some students and teachers, loss of personal connection and intimacy, stress or distraction from background noise and movement, increased opportunities for socialising impinge on quality of learning. Intensification of teacher roles leading to lack of respite and loss of private space for reflection.
Organisation of time and space	New structures and methods of organisation to maximise support of teaching and learning in new spaces.	Immediate practical difficulties in fulfilling needs for timetable reorganisation such as block timetabling, time for team planning and teacher release for professional learning. Longer term departmental and school leadership vision constrained by traditional expectations regarding school structures and organisation.
Modification of learning environment	Teacher and student input into modification/redesign of learning environment to suit local contexts and school values/culture.	Financial constraints make ongoing large-scale redesign of learning spaces difficult.

protocols on student behaviour, and by teachers negotiating the use of potentially disruptive resources and/or activities such as videos and physical games in the open-plan settings. Concerns that students with special needs, as well as younger students, were easily distracted were addressed through the use of designated closed classroom spaces for these students, and transitional programs for younger students, where they worked mainly with one or two teachers in home groups for the first six months before moving to larger group-work.

We provide some examples of general, as well as distinctive, adaptation features in the following case studies of English, studio arts and mathematics in four schools. Each of the four case studies highlights the effects of shifting teacher spheres of influence and diversifying student and teacher roles to facilitate greater agency amongst both teachers and students. The case studies also indicate the diverse ways that teachers in the new settings adapted their teaching and learning practices across the curriculum over the course of three years. We cover this adaptation in more detail elsewhere (see Prain et al., in press), but here we intend to show some illustrative examples that indicate the range of experimentation and the reasoning behind teacher action.

Our first two case studies report on Year 8 English interventions at Whirrakee and Melaleuca Colleges. The first case study explores the enactment of collaborative small-group work within a reasoning-based curriculum designed for a cohort of medium- to high-ability student as part of a film studies unit. The second example explores student and teacher experiences of a team-teaching approach to English in the context of a unit of work on persuasive language that was co-taught by two teachers with a group of 50 students.

CASE STUDY ONE: ENGLISH ENRICHMENT AT WHIRRAKEE COLLEGE

This unit, focused on film studies, involved collaboration between a researcher and an experienced Year 8 English teacher who was also Year 8 Coordinator. At the time of the project in 2013, the teacher was working with students in a relatively high-ability grouping as part of an organisational model that had been adopted by the college in the interests of catering to diverse student needs (see chapter 4). The unit, which took an inquiry oriented, reasoning-based and collaborative approach to the study of film, aimed to address concerns that students in this grouping were not being sufficiently challenged. By diversifying the range of experiences and epistemic roles on offer to students, it was theorised that there would be greater cognitive gain and increased student engagement with film texts.

In keeping with the reasoning focus of the unit, students were cast from the outset as 'film detectives'. The title of the unit, along with initial framing activities, suggested that students would assume roles as active inquirers who would be responsible for articulating and substantiating their own responses to visual texts by making predictions, forming hypotheses, and using available evidence to support claims in a process akin to induction. In keeping with contemporary views about interpreting film texts (Wharton and Grant, 2005; Anderson and Jefferson, 2009; Stafford, 2011), the students were expected to read film language by responding to visual and aural clues and interpreting the use of sound, editing, cinematography, and mise-en-scène, to support claims about intent and meaning. The unit comprised three key elements, including initial framing activities, a collaborative reasoning activity, and a scene analysis designed to demonstrate individuals' capacity to reason effectively about moving-image texts. The initial framing activities were conducted in the open-plan classroom in two separately timetabled groups (35-40 students per group) while two other stage-based groups continued their work in the space, supported by the two other staff.

The activities were designed to orient students to the thinking dispositions that are generative in film study. They included a class discussion and brainstorm around the concept of 'film detectives', a pre-test that required students to infer and induce meaning from a film still, and a task that required students to annotate stills from a film trailer, using visual and aural clues to support claims about setting, genre and theme. These activities sought to prioritise effective reasoning above 'right-answers' and to orient students to thinking dispositions that would require them to formulate, test, and evaluate claims about the meanings conveyed by multi-modal texts. The teacher-participant involved in the study reflected an epistemological view that was consistent with this kind of thinking, commenting in interviews that her role was "to get students to question what they are doing and then explain to me why". However, she also expressed concerns that high-ability English students were not being sufficiently challenged, a concern she attributed to: problems with scheduled and unscheduled absences, compounded by time constraints and curricular demands; the size of the cohort and the diversity of abilities within the grouping, including the fact that disruptive students were regularly moved to the group as a behavioural management strategy; and the tendency of high-achieving students to be concerned with "teacher-pleasing", rather than "going where their intellect takes them".

The atmosphere of the teaching and learning space in which the unit took place was generally relaxed and comfortable (see chapter 11 for a discussion of wellbeing factors). It was apparent that the routines, structures, and expectations that had been adopted in response to the affordances of the space, had generated a sense of community responsibility and respectfulness that was, for the most part, evident in students' behaviour. The model of teaching and learning that had been adopted by Whirrakee College (see chapter 4) required teachers to work closely together in the classroom, usually in teams of three, while curriculum planning was distributed amongst a larger team of six. While the default model was for each teacher to assume responsibility for one of three ability groupings during a unit of work, it was clear that the space engendered a need for close consideration of the interplay between the groups, especially in terms of behaviour, but also in relation to curriculum enactment and timing, as well as considerate use of resources. In terms of the film studies unit, this meant that film viewings were synchronised to minimise the potential for visual, physical, and auditory disruption to other groups in the space, necessitating considerable planning and, in effect, limiting the capacity for repeated, or spontaneous, shared viewings of scenes and sequences. While the professional support, co-teaching opportunities and broader sphere of influence were obvious gains for professional practice (see Table 7.1), the awareness of other groups within the space, along with the sense of responsibility to others, also constrained opportunities for rich curricular practices, including instances of discussion and small-group work which were perceived to be potentially distracting and difficult to manage with larger cohorts. In her reflections on the unit of work, the teacher participant regularly returned to this sense of interplay and mutual responsibility among the three groups, suggesting, in her final interview, that she had realised that her teaching is "centred around getting the whole room okay", a characteristic she attributed partly to her leadership role but which was broadly evident in teacher behaviour.

In this context, the teacher was also anxious about conducting small-group tasks in the open-plan space and managing direct instruction because of (a) perceived potential for a diminished sphere of influence over participant student behaviour, and (b) concerns about how such an activity might increase noise distractions for other students and teachers. Informed by work on the use of exploratory talk in English and other subject areas (Barnes and Todd, 1977; Mercer, 2008; Sutherland, 2013), the initial draft of the curriculum featured several collaborative activities. However, a range of factors, including those mentioned above, impacted negatively on the teacher's perception of her capacity to manage small-group tasks in the open-plan setting, prompting her to use the nearby Da Vinci art/science studio for such tasks. In this space, which was arranged in a traditional configuration with desks in rows facing a whiteboard, students completed two small-group activities, one collaborative in nature and the other cooperative. While constrained by their lack of experience with exploratory talk, the students perceived the small-group collaborative task as highly beneficial for their learning:

> So we have different opinions and we can expand and go 'above and beyond' as they say, with each-other's work, so like, we can go from this really simple idea and we just keep putting ideas and more ideas 'cause we're all different and we have different minds and so we can just think of a really good plan.

Students valued the opportunity to encounter different perspectives and build on ideas, noting that such exposure helped them to improve their answers by drawing on input from others. In this way, they developed a sense of relational agency as learners. Several students also noted the reduced wait-time (Alvermann et al., 1996) afforded through small-group activities, in contrast to their larger class-size discussions. This points to the need for flexible arrangements in open-plan settings, where continuous high-ability groupings of 30-40 students with one teacher may slow, restrict or discourage rapid and/or lively exchanges of student contributions. The teacher's decision to move away from the open-plan classroom to a more traditional classroom for small-group activities reflects, in part, the affordance of varied spaces for specialised uses. The teacher reflected that, in some ways, this movement into a different space also signalled a particular kind of learning for the students who thought "'so this is where we discuss and we get things out and we move things around in our heads'...it was like that idea that this is our collaborative time and then in the pod is our work time, our [time for] sitting down, getting something down on paper and putting our ideas down rather than fleshing it out in that different room." However, movement out of the open-plan classroom was seen to have a detrimental effect on other students, with higher-ability and more independent students expected to model appropriate behaviour and "set the tone" for the whole room. This, in turn, limited scope for students to be absent from the setting for prolonged or regular periods of time. In this way, the up-scaled learning communities can prompt a conservative approach about perceived high- and low-risk activities.

The final component of the curriculum involved a scene analysis that required students to make a series of reasoned claims about the opening scene of their feature film, using visual and aural evidence. Students were removed from the open-plan classroom to enable this viewing to take place without interference to other groups. The teacher brought a portable digital projector into the Da Vinci studio to facilitate this viewing. It should be noted that the fixed features of the open-plan design, including the placement of large windows on either side of whiteboards in most rooms, made quality screening of visual materials extremely difficult. This could be ameliorated by the installation of curtains. However, opportunities to bring soft furnishings into the space were limited by financial constraints (see Table 7.1) and concerns about durability. After an introductory activity, designed to familiarise students with filmic techniques, students watched the opening scene from the film as a class. Students took detailed notes about what they 'saw' and 'heard' as the opening scene was screened, so that they would have a record of details that they could then use to support a claim (see Table 7.2).

The aim of this activity was to put students in charge of deciphering and understanding the ways in which meanings are shaped by the composition of moving-image texts. Whereas in previous years the teacher had "walked the students through" the opening scene, this time she deliberately held back, allowing students to construct their own responses. Studies have pointed to the need for teachers to withhold their personal viewpoints and knowledge to offer genuine invitations to students to be active in the process of constructing knowledge (Johnston, Woodside-Jiron, & Day, 2000). In keeping with these views, the teacher in our study explained, "I'm probably not being as explicit because I want them to start being more powerful, for them to find it themselves", a belief which she also made explicit to students.

Students found the task challenging but exciting. In the interviews, and in their written reflections on the unit, many described a 'light-bulb' moment in terms of their understanding of the constructed nature of films. This case study identifies the impacts of an extended sphere of influence on one teacher's capacity to diversify learning experiences for a high-ability student cohort in English. In this context, small-group work, coupled with an orientation towards reasoning, was seen to be highly beneficial for students' learning but difficult to manage in open-plan settings

Table 7.2. Student reasoning about film language.

Claim	Soundtrack	Cinematography	Editing	Mise-en-scene
Set in South Africa	Music (in the credits – sound bridge), South African accents and people chanting 'MANDELA'.	Long shot (difference between white and black people, across the road).	Cuts between black and white faces/people and cuts to stock footage (sepia).	Clothes (black, white and green), difference between fences and props.
Rugby team	The dialogue between team mates indicates that it is a rugby team, grunts from the scrum, coach telling them what to do.	Panning (used to show where all the players) and zoom in/out of the scrum and what the players are doing.	Cross-cut/parallel editing (used to show different players and go from the coach to the players.)	Costumes (the players are wearing white and green tops which are the South African colours). Setting (they are on a rugby field which has stands and goal posts)
Nelson Mandela coming out of jail and being a free man	Dialogue (reporters trying to speak to Mandela and), Voiceover (the news reporters asking questions and telling everyone what is happening)	Close-up (used to show people voting for Mandela and also a close up on Mandela saying his oath and talking to South Africa), Long-shot showing all the South African people lining up to vote for the first time	Cuts between Nelson and the citizens of South Africa voting and cheering for Nelson.	Props to show people voting and costumes show the importance of Nelson and the people around him and the difference between black and white South Africans (white people wearing up market clothes and black people wearing rags)

(*Continued*)

Table 7.2. (Continued)

Claim	Soundtrack	Cinematography	Editing	Mise-en-scene
Riots between the white and black people	Little kids screaming because they are scared, Voiceovers (from news reports explaining what's been happening)	Close-ups (used to show the emotion on the kids' faces), Long-shot to show all the injured/dead people and how South Africa has changed.	Flashback (shows the riots and how the country changed when Nelson was sent to prison and freed)	Props (lots of people holding guns and knives), Setting shows smashed glass in shop windows.

unless other groups in the space are engaged in similar tasks. Teacher decision-making in this context reflected both the perceived needs of particular student groups and the broader interests of a learning community in action.

CASE STUDY TWO: COLLABORATIVE TEACHING AT MELALEUCA COLLEGE

At this college two English teachers, Cynthia and Carole, team-taught a group of 50 Year 8 students in a learning community as a local initiative, responding to our invitation to try new practices. In concert with three university researchers from our project, they developed a unit on persuasion to be taught in term four of 2012. The class took place in a large open-plan learning neighbourhood, where 50 students occupied an area that could have fitted 100 students. Despite the simultaneous timetabling of their two English classes, the teachers had not previously team-taught, claiming their students preferred their own English teacher. The teachers agreed to trial team teaching, to attempt to differentiate the learning tasks for the unit, and, with the assistance of the researchers, to trial small-group work once a week.

The teachers developed a nine-week unit that aimed to familiarise students with persuasive language and techniques to be applied to creating their own persuasive texts. Teachers typically led a 15-minute introduction to the day's theme, sharing responsibility for introducing and leading discussion. This whole-group activity was intended to focus all students' attention on tasks, explain the aims of the session, and review past learning. Visual stimuli used to engage students included snippets from advertisements, original poetry, and teacher-student role-plays. Whole group participation was encouraged in answering questions. Following the introduction, students worked individually, in pairs, or small groups, on their assignments for 45 minutes. Classes concluded with a ten-minute teacher-led summary session for the whole group.

In one 70-minute session a week, after the introduction, the class broke into five mixed gender and mixed ability groups of up to ten students, facilitated by the teachers and the three researchers. In these sessions, for the first four weeks students read and discussed a range of persuasive texts, including advertisements, letters to the editor and essays. Working with familiar material, such as logo identification, stimulated the students' awareness of the subliminal power of visual design. Students analysed the language in persuasive texts, practised recognising persuasive techniques, and wrote a range of brief responses.

During the second half of the term students prepared for formal debating in their mixed gender small groups. In groups of six to eight, students presented a debate to the class on a controversial topic that the group had chosen by discussion and negotiation within their small group with the teacher as facilitator. The teachers also introduced a form of peer assessment for both the essay presentation and the debate, by asking particular individual students to comment on the quality of the presentation. These students received a formatted sheet, completed it during the presentation and handed it to the presenter after the debate. This was completed in conjunction with the teachers' comments.

Teacher and Student Perceptions

After team teaching the unit, the teachers saw merit in this approach. They had enjoyed working together because it had allowed them to share ideas and knowledge and give mutual support. To their surprise the students adjusted quickly to the larger group with two teachers. The teachers thought their different strengths were advantageous; Cynthia with her greater experience, and Carole with her "earthy passion and links with the kids". Combining their classes made for continuity if one was absent. The teachers in this class exercised relational agency (see Prain et al., 2013; Edwards, 2011) by clarifying their spheres of influence, refining their processes for sharing knowledge, and creating collaborative tools (see also Green and Beavis, 2013). Critical factors in successful team-teaching, according to these two teachers, were a respectful professional relationship, time spent planning and reflecting together, shared values of building relationships with students, and clear consistent expectations of behaviour and progress.

The teachers perceived that the open-plan setting facilitated flexible student learning experiences. They used the extra space for embodied learning activities such as line debates, role-plays, and quizzes involving student movement and physical engagement. The once-a-week small-group sessions were judged to have novelty value, allowing a different way to learn, engaging reluctant students, and providing opportunities for reserved students to share their ideas. Groups had been carefully constructed on friendships and a mix of abilities. However, flexibility was allowed as some co-dependent students had difficulty being separated from friends. The success of group sessions was judged to be an effect of the presence of researchers who were also appreciated as 'critical friends', allowing deeper sharing and reflection. The teachers thought that such small group activities without added classroom support would be difficult to organise in a two-person team. Perceived constraints included a lack of scheduled planning time for team-teaching, lack of reliable technological and material resources, and a lack of control over external distractions and interruptions.

We interviewed ten students who offered diverse reactions to learning in these settings. Although they had enjoyed the type and range of activities in the persuasion unit, their perceptions of the most valuable activities varied considerably. They had all found the team-teaching experience valuable. Their least favoured experience was whole-class activities either because it was too easy to shirk participation, or because they felt threatened by their visibility in such a group. A common fear was oral presentations to the whole group. Small group rehearsal before presentations greatly alleviated this fear. Apart from a few students who preferred to work alone or with one friend, most enjoyed the small group work for the opportunity to learn from others' views and for mutual peer support. Some found that working with each other had helped them to make new friends. Learning in open-plan settings gave the students a sense of freedom, relaxation and sociability. Most found the atmosphere of many classes working within the space productive though some students commented that the noise and distraction of others walking through or using central computer pods affected their concentration. The interviews confirm Gislason's (2009) suggestion that open spaces foster a sense of community among students that outweighs disadvantages such as distractions or noise.

The teachers were timetabled together, but there was no time allowance for planning, professional up-skilling in team teaching, or optimal combinations of classes to enable curricular differentiation according to ability. The positive effects of school design depend on school commitment to organisational support and staff commitment to team teaching and collaboration (Gislason, 2009). Had the participant researchers not been present to enable small groups, at least three classes would need to be timetabled together to allow more flexible student groupings. The space makes it eminently possible for three or four classes to be simultaneously timetabled, but realising this affordance depended on both staffing and other timetable priorities. The teachers perceived that a lack of whiteboards, glare from uncurtained windows, and the unreliability of technological resources, interfered with realising the full potential of an up-scaled learning community. Solving other challenges such as disruption from external movement was a matter of establishing broader protocols of respect in the learning environment (see Table 7.1).

These case studies of English in two settings highlight the necessity of teacher teamwork and a highly structured curriculum to enable effective teaching and learning in small groups in these settings. In the English class at Melaleuca College the teachers made a first attempt to adapt to team teaching and to differentiate the curriculum, allowing students a greater sphere of influence in peer learning.

CASE STUDY THREE: STUDIO ARTS AT MELALEUCA COLLEGE

This case study reports on a 2012 project in studio arts that involved teachers using the increased space and visibility, and the capacity to vary time and space usage flexibly, to engage students, personalise learning (see Keeffe, Lovejoy, Spencer-Jones, & Prain, 2013) and guide and nurture students' creativity (Loi & Dillon, 2006). Two teachers team-taught this subject to a group of 50 Years 9 and 10 students in the open-plan Da Vinci art/science studio in 2012. By introducing students to a range of modes and mediums and allowing freedom of choice, the teachers encouraged all students to discover their creative talents. Student work was self-directed, with teachers responding to queries rather than initiating discussion. The students drew on each teacher's individual strengths for assistance in different areas, while the teachers routinely circulated to answer questions, discuss ideas, demonstrate techniques, assist individual students as they practised different techniques, provide timely feedback, and facilitate student research inquiries (see Figure 7.1 for an example of teacher-assisted shading practice).

In addition to teacher and peer support, resources included internet access on personal computers for expert advice, and ready access to art books. In positioning students for future art studies, some formal teaching through art appreciation workshops was conducted once a week at the start of class for half an hour, when students were introduced to famous art works in different media. Teachers contextualised these works and introduced appropriate technical terms. Students were invited to study the artwork in detail and then complete appreciation worksheets, giving personal responses. Workshops were restricted to small groups of student invitees as needs arose. For example, researchers observed a workshop on pencil drawing in which students practised drawing light and shade in folds of curtains.

Agency was reflected in the students' positive responses to the degree of choice, freedom and responsibility vested in them. At the end of the term, students reflected on their achievement against their initial individual goals. Students also kept an art journal to record ideas and reflect on developing artwork. They chose who they

Figure 7.1. Practising pencil drawing, cross-hatching and shading. Page from student workbook.

would sit with in class, with most students sitting in shared-interest groups while working with a particular medium. Some chose to sit with friends and others worked alone. If they wished, students listened to music using earphones. They were free to move around the classroom and access materials from the adjoining storeroom. They were responsible for maintaining and caring for all equipment and returning it to the storeroom after class. Researchers observed that these tasks were routinely performed without needing teacher reminders.

Working together relationally, teachers spent time after class discussing challenges facing individual students, planning workshops, and preparing to address curricular requirements and student needs. They found the affordances of the open-plan classroom included opportunities for student choice, freedom of movement, team-teaching, peer tutoring, and precise curricular differentiation. They also considered that the open-plan classroom improved the quality of learning, with one teacher noting that, "having light airy rooms is fantastic…it works so much better than it used to". They claimed that their students were more attentive, motivated, self-reliant, and more connected to peers and teachers. While other subject areas entail contrasting challenges and opportunities for incorporating these types of goals and practices into the curriculum, this case study highlights possibilities for personalised, differentiated learning that all participants found rewarding. The teachers found that the difference between the old teacher-directed course with set tasks and their new way of teaching resulted in high quality work of the students' own choice: "The students make their choices, they live with their choices and they do really well with them".

This case study highlights the potential for personalising learning in a practical subject through teacher cooperative teamwork and relational agency between the teachers as student facilitators/motivators. Both teachers and students benefitted from increased collaboration afforded by the setting, leading to a productive expansion of participant sphere of influence.

CASE STUDY FOUR: MATHEMATICS AT WARATAH COLLEGE

We report here on curriculum innovation in a non-BEP, low SES, regional school that was included in our study for comparative purposes. This school, Waratah College, based on its initial experience of two teachers in different subjects working together to ensure a common strategy to learning, decided to explore the viability of all Year 7 and Year 8 teachers adopting a common approach across core subjects. Following discussions with the research team, these teachers wanted to increase learning personalisation. This school had not been performing well in the national testing regime, NAPLAN, in the area of numeracy. Figure 7.2 shows where the school ranked with other similar schools before the project commenced in 2011 and the changes in ranking as they implemented the teaching approaches described in Figure 7.2. A score of zero indicates the lowest ranking and a score of one indicates the top based curriculum, then all the learning felicities demonstrated in this class can be up-scaled and augmented, with increasing scope for a larger group of staff members and students to contribute to ongoing curriculum renewal.

IMPLICATIONS

This chapter highlights both significant challenges, and attempted teacher adaptations, to curricular enactment in the new settings. Despite the many challenges of adaptation to up-scaled learning communities, these case studies show that teachers have developed innovative practices in personalising learning for their students. The open-plan settings have encouraged teachers to envisage new ways to develop curricula that challenge and inspire students to take responsibility for their learning on their journey to learning independence. A common theme of our case studies is that up-scaled learning communities create greater opportunities to vary interactions, allowing a more fruitful exchange of ideas among students and teachers. Additionally, extending the range of resources that students draw on, and giving them greater control over these resources, and the knowledge they gather, encourages the development of students into independent, creative learners, and flexible problem solvers. Quantitative and qualitative evidence demonstrate that, depending on teacher and student perceptions and practices, these new settings can contribute to enhanced participant learning.

CRAIG DEED, PETER COX & DEBRA EDWARDS

8. PREPARING PRE-SERVICE TEACHERS FOR OPEN- PLAN UP-SCALED LEARNING COMMUNITIES

PREPARING FOR COMPLEXITY

Clark (1988, p. 9) noted that teaching is "complex, uncertain, and peppered with dilemmas." More than two decades later, perhaps this comment could be made even more emphatically (Santoro, Reid, Mayer, & Singh, 2013). How best then to prepare pre-service teachers for the differences inherent in the nuanced and multi-faceted work of teaching in open-plan learning communities? We would argue that novice teachers require preparatory experiences that afford productive participation in the culture, narrative, and community of practice of being a teacher. This chapter draws from current critical perspectives on teacher education, and ecological accounts of influences on teachers' and pre-service teachers' adaptive and interactive practices in the settings (see Greeno, 1994).

Teacher graduates are often perceived to have inadequate capacity to enable them to adapt to the diversity of contemporary learning environments and diverse student populations (Darling-Hammond, 2006; Zeichner, 2006). One means of addressing these criticisms is to improve the cohesion of preparatory experiences through building productive partnerships between university and school-based learning (Eames & Coll, 2010; Grossman & McDonald, 2008; Koc, 2011). In addition, consideration needs to be given to recent changes to the shape, form, and activities of schools and education.

Emerging technological, architectural, and sociological concepts related to the openness have influenced both the physical organisation of contemporary school buildings, and authorised a diverse set of approaches to teaching and learning (Barrett & Zhang, 2009; Deed & Lesko, in press; Gifford, 2007; Mahony, Hextall, & Richardson, 2011). As a consequence of these influences, modern school architecture in Australia and the United Kingdom favours large open-plan buildings which afford innovative educational practices (Leiringer & Cardellino, 2011). Openness also incorporates teacher and student use of virtual space through computer-supported learning environments and Web 2.0 technology (Cabitza & Simone, 2012).

Although new buildings and mobile learning technology are an obvious element of transformational change in schools, multiple factors impact on the teaching and learning equation. Teachers must adapt to new learning contexts through dynamic interpretations of how best to enact local versions of abstract concepts like personalised learning (Alterator & Deed, 2013; Deed, Lesko, & Lovejoy, 2014; Zou, 2011). This chapter contributes to ongoing discussion concerning how to reposition teacher education in response to contemporary changes to educational space and pedagogy.

The Theory-Practice Gap

University learning is usually characterised as formal, abstract, theoretical, and unrelated to the reality of classroom work (Hammerness, 2006; Korthagen & Kessels, 1999). For instance, university lecturers may focus on theories of learning, while pre-service teachers may not be able to imagine how to apply these ideas in what appears to be a complex and noisy classroom. Yet, pre-service teachers may be more concerned with questions of what and when (enacting practice) rather than with questions of how or why (critically analysing practice).

Pre-service teachers are students at university, yet are expected to be a teacher on practicum. These are alternate narratives: one concerned with abstracting and representing rules and models; the other with intentional action and reaction. Further, the theoretical narrative positions university expertise external to the classroom, outside the practice of teaching activity (Korthagen, Loughran, & Russell, 2006). Not surprisingly, this often leads to a perceived gap between encountering abstract ideas about learning and applying these when teaching (Calderhead & Shorrock, 1997).

Teaching practice is situated in the classroom. Classroom survival is the primary concern of pre-service teachers and they tend to look to experienced teachers, or mentors, for practical tips and strategies. Teacher mentoring involves an orientation to the school and classroom, passing on practical knowledge of 'what works' by modelling and supporting the practicing of teaching strategies, including approaches to classroom management. Mentors also have a supervisory role, providing feedback and formal evaluation (Koc, 2011). Yet, while mentors have considerable practical knowledge and contextual expertise, they may also have limited or uncritical ideas about how teacher knowledge is developed or its contribution to adaptive practice (Putnam & Borko, 2000; Zeichner, 2010).

In addition, isolated workplace experiences are often insufficient to afford breadth and depth of learning (Billett, 2009). Preparatory experiences must therefore be designed so that knowledge about teaching and learning is not situated within one person or classroom but distributed over, and between, a range of contexts and experiences, including both university and school (Zeichner, 2010).

Integration, Coherence and Expertise

It is worth considering how each theoretical and practical experience constitutes different pieces of the preparatory puzzle. As noted by Billett (2009), universities and schools each afford variable kinds of experiences leading to different but compatible learning opportunities.

Teacher educators are increasingly intent on improving the coherence of university and school-based learning experiences (Billett, 2009; Gallimore, Ermeling, Saunders, & Goldenberg, 2009). Coherence, within and between university and school-based learning, is one generally agreed principle of quality teacher preparation (Adler, Ball, Krainer, Lin, & Novotna, 2005; Darling-Hammond, 2010; Hammerness, 2006; Korthagen & Kessels, 1999; Zeichner, 2010). The extent of coherence between theoretical and practical components of a pre-service teacher preparation program impacts significantly on pre-service teachers' capacity to integrate knowledge and perspectives (Allen, 2009; Harlen, Holroyd, & Byrne, 1995; Jung & Tonso, 2006). A potentially significant way to build coherence is the design of mutual university and school experiences to develop pre-service teachers' "repertoire of practice - along with the knowledge to know when to use different strategies for different purposes" (Darling-Hammond, 2006, p. 304).

While coherence is characterised as a common framework between the university and school experience, it is pre-service teachers that have to engage with the "invitation to change" afforded by each unique learning experience and to actively integrate these into teacher practical knowledge (Billett, 2009, p. 835). The process of integration is not a simple or linear process (Putnam & Borko, 2000). Several strategies have been suggested to address this complexity, focusing on creating productive contextual learning experiences, building coherence between university and school placements, and using a frame of moving from novice to expert teacher (Deed, Cox, & Prain, 2011). This requires, as an underpinning, a meaningful relationship between teacher educators, teacher-mentors and pre-service teachers (Korthagen et al., 2006). The use of teacher inquiry into their own practice is explicated here as one effective method to achieve coherence between, and integration of, university and school-based knowledge and perspectives.

Coherence and integration can be enhanced though a shared discourse community involving pre-service teachers, mentors and teacher educators (Putnam & Borko, 2000). This implies a need to prepare pre-service teachers as classroom investigators and collaborators in order to draw on separate sets of practical knowledge that are then collated and refined by individuals to their own context (Darling-Hammond, 2006). This involves making sense of contextual challenges and new experiences that emerge during practicum and drawing upon different, including theoretical, perspectives to gain insights into implications for teaching practice (Korthagen et al., 2006). This also entails working closely with peers, rather than seeing classroom-based learning as an isolated and intensely personal experience (Korthagen et al., 2006).

Coherence and integration are concerned with developing pre-service teacher practical knowledge. Elbaz (1981) defined a teacher's practical knowledge as the complex set of knowledge that teachers draw upon and reconstitute in their day-to-day practice. Ottesen (2007) and others have made the claim that the process of making sense of practice is relentlessly reflexive. Connelly and Clandinin (1988) conceptualised teacher knowledge as personal, emerging from past experience, and informing current and future practice. Clandinin (1985) argued that teaching practical knowledge is neither entirely theoretical nor simply practical. Rather, it is a contextually grounded dynamic blend of formal and informal knowledge (Hoekstra & Korthagen, 2011). In this way, knowledge for teaching becomes individually situated (Verloop, Van Driel, & Meijer, 2001). This would appear to be consistent with Darling-Hammond's (2010) reference to "wisdom of practice", learning, applying and refining concepts and strategies in-practice.

A common theme is that teacher knowledge provides a basis for making sense of and translating experience into subsequent action. Therefore, one means of examining university and school-based preparatory mechanisms is how these act, in complementary ways, to frame the development and refinement of pre-service teachers' teaching practical knowledge. Ellstrom (2001) suggests this requires intentional and formalised actions for coherence and integration, including common framing of planning and critical reflection processes. Importantly, pedagogical approaches learnt at university need to be applied during professional experience, and subsequently reflected on in both school and university settings (Billett, 2009). This locates practicum as a central learning experience, while making sense of the experience requires consideration of diverse (complementary and contradictory) theoretical and practical perspectives (Pridham, Deed, & Cox, 2013).

A powerful lens for conceptualising changes in pre-service teacher practical knowledge is the conceptualising of novice to expert teachers. Experts differ from novices in terms of the knowledge they apply to problems, efficiency of problem-solving, and their insight (Sternberg & Horvath, 1995). Knowledge is made up of general and practical teaching knowledge, as well as pedagogical content knowledge. Efficiency refers to the automatic use of well-learned skills and an ability to effectively plan, monitor, and adapt problem-solving approaches. Insight results in more creative re-definition of a problem and reaching ingenious, novel, yet appropriate solutions. In general, experts take a more planned, complete, and complex view of problems, generating alternative solutions; novices have a more immediate, restricted, and solution-oriented view. This approach is evident in the comment made by Sternberg and Horvath (1995, p.13) that "true experts seek progressively to complicate the picture, continually working on the leading edge of their own knowledge and skill."

Building Expertise through Inquiry

If integration and coherence are applied to the development of expertise it may be characterised as "learning to practice in practice, with expert guidance" (Darling-Hammond, 2010, p. 40). Developing expertise involves pre-service teachers controlling their own learning through in-practice inquiry: defining local problems and devising responses; drawing upon current stocks of practical knowledge and being prepared to teach in ways markedly different to the ways in which they were and have taught (Hargreaves, 2003; Sachs, 2003; Schon, 1983). Kelly (2006, p. 509) comments that expertise is the "constant and iterative engagement in constructing and reconstructing professional knowledge using various perspectives including teacher research with the aim of conceptualising and addressing problems."

This is not to suggest that problems examined during an in-practice inquiry process can be definitively resolved. It is a reasonable starting point to ensure pre-service teachers explore a range of beliefs, values and knowledge, and seek out and engage with alternative perspectives (Louie, Drevdahl, Purdy, & Stackman, 2003). Inevitably, changes in understanding lead to further questions, leading Hammer and Schifter to comment (2001, p.456) "(inquiry) provides not an empirical finding but an analytical lens, an intellectual resource for thinking."

Pre-service teacher inquiry into their own practice contributes to a capacity to adapt to different contexts and experiences, involving constant reflective monitoring and reinvestment of learnt professional practical knowledge and skills (Matthew & Sternberg, 2009). This implies a view that expertise is developed though the relationship between an individual pre-service teacher's practical knowledge and specific contexts, moments, challenges, and reflection (Schon, 1983).

A key element of the inquiry process is that pre-service teachers "make problematic their own knowledge and practice" (Cochran-Smith & Lytle, 1999, p. 273). The investigation of practice is one means of making sense of the "uncertainty, uniqueness, conflict and confusion" of new and emerging learning environments (Cherry, 2005, p. 311). Personal, collegial, and critical reflection is a key component of pre-service teacher inquiry. Loughran (2002) makes the point that the framing and reframing of a problem is a "crucial" part of knowing about teaching. Reflecting on experience has the potential to change or clarify understanding, leading to reasoning about possible options and consequences (Boud, Keogh, & Walker, 1985).

As noted in the introduction, teaching is complex and becoming even more so with the introduction of flexible learning space and time (Alterator & Deed, 2013). Pre-service teacher inquiry involves a mindful awareness of current experience, opportunities and problems, and the reflective element makes "conscious and explicit the dynamic interplay between thinking and action" (Leitch & Day, 2000, p. 181). The reflective processes of sharing understandings about local problems, accessing multiple perspectives, and raising doubts and uncertainties about possible solutions, are the base elements of pre-service teacher inquiry (Grangeat & Gray, 2008; Yost, Sentner, & Forlenza-Bailey, 2000).

PRE-SERVICE CASE STUDY

This case study includes the four junior secondary Bendigo Education Plan (BEP) schools. Over the period 2011-2013, a total of seventy pre-service teachers were placed in these schools. Each school was characterised by their open-plan settings and a pedagogical approach that emphasised personalised learning. These dual changes to space and pedagogy meant a change in schools' expectations about the knowledge and skills required of pre-service teachers and new graduates. In response to these concerns a practicum project was initiated. The aims of this project were to: build a productive partnership between La Trobe University and the local school cluster; develop a framework supporting flexible practicum pathways and models; and integrate university and school-based learning through the practicum experience. The project was funded by the Victorian Department of Education and Early Childhood Development's School Centres for Teaching Excellence initiative.

Project Outline

The initial 2011 iteration involved a group of 25 pre-service teachers spending up to 30 days on school placement, using a two-day a week immersion model. Pre-service teachers were placed in multi-disciplinary teams in school learning communities. Each of the four schools accepted teams of 6-7 pre-service teachers. A key element of the new practicum model was that the pre-service teachers and mentors became co-teachers. This approach was consistent with the notion of team teaching prevalent within the open-plan learning environment. Each team had to, in addition to their disciplinary teaching, combine to take part in a pre-service teacher inquiry project. A university based coordinator was appointed to liaise with schools, visit each school on a weekly basis, and support, monitor and assess the pre-service teachers.

A further group of 30 pre-service teachers participated in 2012. The second iteration was modified in response to three major issues identified in 2011: mentors and pre-service teachers struggled with the extended part-time nature of the immersion model; there was a perception that pre-service teachers were underprepared for the school-based teaching and learning models employed in the new learning spaces; and recognition that mentors lacked skills to consistently work effectively with pre-service teachers.

In response to these issues the two-day a week model was retained but commenced later in the school year. The community and multi-disciplinary components were retained, as was the university coordinator. More emphasis was placed on effective communication, planning and review processes to mediate the difficulties of the part-time model of placement. In addition, an expert mentor was selected by each school, based on an assessment of experience and capacity, in order to build mentor skills. These expert mentors created closer links between the university and school-based experiences by delivering lectures in the university program on topics such as differentiating the curriculum, personalising learning, working in team-based environments, teaching and learning in open-plan learning environments, and interdisciplinary teaching.

In 2013 changes were made to all secondary practicum placements: a 25 day practicum using a four-day a week model, preceded by three weeks of two days a week for observation and planning, was introduced in order to retain the extended nature of the immersion experience. This model was the result of a survey of schools in the region, which preferred a longer practicum placement, but also wanted to retain a model close to the current block mode. Multi-disciplinary teams were placed in learning communities, although some single-disciplinary teams were also deployed. Expert mentors and the university coordinator were no longer funded, although there was a residual level of expertise spread across the schools that participated in the project. These included an emphasis on contemporary pedagogical approaches being used in local schools, and application of a broader definition of teaching as part of the university practicum assessment. Key features of the pre-service teacher inquiry project formed the basis for a core practicum-related subject. Ongoing changes to the teacher preparation program were influenced by the open channels of communication forged during the project between participating schools and the university.

FINDINGS

Over the period 2011-2013 the mentors of pre-service teachers were invited to complete an online evaluation of the practicum in the flexible learning spaces following the departure of their pre-service teacher. The number of completed surveys is shown in Table 8.1.

To explore the knowledge and skills that mentors believed that pre-service teachers required to complete a practicum in the new learning spaces the data were analysed using thematic analysis. The three years of data were aggregated as a set of 47 responses.

The survey questions asked: for the recent practicum conducted in the new flexible learning spaces, what additional knowledge and skills do you think are required to effectively: be a pre-service teacher (35 responses – Table 8.2); work in teams (35 responses – Table 8.3); utilise flexible learning spaces (31 responses – Table 8.4); and, use ICT (31 responses – Table 8.5).

Additional Knowledge and Skills Required to be a Pre-service Teacher

The theme of knowledge of school protocols, teaching space, school and lesson structures, mentioned by 40% of the mentors (see Table 8.2), related to the need for pre-practicum orientation visits at the school to obtain first-hand experience in the way these new flexible learning spaces operated and related student behaviour protocols. This knowledge is considered essential for the pre-service teachers to have prior to their practicum if they are to operate effectively in their practicum.

A day prior to starting at the school to be familiar so ready to go on first day. (Mentor, 2012)

Table 8.1. Number of completed teacher-mentor surveys over the period 2011–2013.

	2011	2012	2013	Total
Number of respondents	19	14	15	47

Table 8.2. Major themes for the question related to additional knowledge and skills required for pre-service teachers to be effective in flexible learning spaces.

Theme	Number (and percentage) of respondents
Knowledge of school protocols, teaching spaces, school and lesson structures (by pre-visit orientation)	14 (40%)
Knowledge in, and availability for, preparation and planning	9 (26%)
Skills in flexibility, creativity, open-minded, initiative	9 (26%)
Knowledge and skills in management issues for large groups	7 (20%)
Skills in team teaching	7 (20%)

The second additional skill required by pre-service teachers is the knowledge and availability for planning and preparation with the team of mentors. The third skill is somewhat difficult to teach – that of flexibility, creativity, open-mindedness and initiative. These mentor beliefs are shown in the following quote:

> Be flexible - come on days that suit the program (if the set days don't!) and be prepared to jump in and do stuff on short notice. (Mentor, 2011)

Additional Knowledge and Skills Required to Effectively Work in Teams

The overwhelming, and perhaps predictable, response to this question was that the mentors wanted the pre-service teachers to have developed skills in team teaching, and to a lesser extent knowledge of team teaching. It is challenging for the university to incorporate this skill development into early pre-service teacher training and assessment. As was found in the results presented in Table 8.3, the mentors believed that pre-service teachers require a professional disposition that includes flexibility and open-mindedness.

> Need to be able to work as a team member. (Mentor, 2013)

> How to plan together, how to present together, how to reflect together and how to give and receive feedback from each other. (Mentor, 2013)

Additional Knowledge and Skills Required to Effectively Utilise Flexible Learning Spaces

The thematised mentors' responses in Table 8.4 indicated that the most frequent additional knowledge required of the pre-service teachers was effective ways to use the flexible learning spaces, followed by effective teaching and learning strategies. This is exemplified by comments such as:

Table 8.3. Major themes for the question related to additional knowledge and skills required for pre-service teachers to be effective in working in teams within flexible learning spaces.

Theme	Number (and percentage) of respondents
Skills in team teaching	17 (49%)
Knowledge of team teaching	8 (23%)
Flexible, open-minded, willing to be mentored	5 (14%)
Available for planning and preparation meetings	4 (11%)
Able to teach across a range of methods	2 (6%)

Table 8.4. Major themes for the question related to additional knowledge and skills required for pre-service teachers to effectively utilise flexible learning spaces.

Theme	Number (and percentage) of respondents
Knowledge of effective ways to use, and to arrange space within, flexible learning spaces	9 (29%)
Knowledge of effective teaching and learning strategies	7 (23%)
Initial pre-visits to gain practical knowledge of flexible learning spaces	5 (16%)
Knowledge of school protocols in flexible learning spaces	3 (10%)
Knowledge and skills in differentiation and personalised learning	3 (10%)
Skills in appropriate use of voice	3 (10%)

Knowledge of different learning styles and activity ideas. Maybe have discussed use of flexible learning spaces in university classes so students have some idea of where to start and how to use them effectively. (Mentor, 2011)

As has been discussed, the mentors considered the pre-practicum orientation visits to be essential for the pre-service teachers to gain practical knowledge of these new flexible learning spaces.

Visit the college prior and observe them in action so as not cold to the practice. (Mentor, 2013)

Additional Knowledge and Skills Required to Effectively Use ICT

The overwhelming response (65%) to this question (see Table 8.5) was that mentors expected the pre-service teachers to be competent with ICT prior to the

Table 8.5. *Major themes for the question related to additional knowledge and skills required for pre-service teachers to effectively use ICT.*

Theme	Number (and percentage) of respondents
Competent to meaningfully use ICT	20 (65%)
– smart boards	(10)
– aware of ICT use in method area	(4)
– Ultranet	(4)
– Netbooks	(4)
– blogs and wikis	(2)
Pre-practicum visits to become aware of available technologies and be provided passwords etc.	7 (23%)
Skills to explain ICT use to students	3 (10%)
Knowledge of ICT issues/problems in the classroom	2 (6%)

practicum; the range of sub skills mentioned indicated that there were a wide range of expectations but half of those mentors were in agreement that the competent use of smart boards was required (32%). The next most common theme reinforces the need for a coordinated approach to pre-practicum visits so that the pre-practicum orientation visits cover all essential elements of the school's ICT program:

> Visit college prior. Go through the ICT used at the school. Allow the school to log them on, etc. (Mentor, 2013)

> Evidence of competency in the use of ICT is imperative...... data projectors, smartboards etc must be understood and practiced prior to practicum. (Mentor, 2012)

The Pre-service Teacher Inquiry Project

As noted previously, the pre-service teacher inquiry project afforded "learning to practise in practice, with expert guidance" (Darling-Hammond, 2010, p. 40). The purpose of the inquiry task was for an interdisciplinary team of pre-service teachers to: develop a sense of the breadth and depth of the relationship between their teaching and student learning; seek and engage with a range of perspectives about a local school issue; and collectively construct teacher practical knowledge.

The process involved: (1) identifying a local school priority related to teaching and learning; (2) exploring and generating ideas and perspectives that could inform possible solutions; (3) identifying and enacting a set of justifiable strategies; and

(4) critically reflecting on the enactment of the strategies including possible further refinement.

The following example demonstrates how pre-service teacher inquiry alters the conventions of practicum. The pre-service teachers worked collegially with academics and teacher-mentors to apply a set of collaboratively generated pedagogical principles, grounded in the school context, to their own practice. Most importantly, this process stimulated conversations about practice that aimed to build coherence and integration between university and school-based learning. These conversations were about how each inquiry project informed individual pre-service teacher knowledge about working in open-plan learning environments and incorporation of personalised learning pedagogy.

The school priority identified at Grevillea College was engaging boys through technology (discussed in chapter 5, case study 2). The pre-service teacher team (discipline mix: mathematics, mathematics/science, humanities, English/IT) met to talk about what they did and did not know about this priority, and to discuss what they wanted to achieve. They agreed to individually search for games-based learning ideas. A lecturer provided them with a set of readings about games-based learning; the expert mentor organised a survey of all students in the learning community about their use of games and why they enjoyed using games to learn. The pre-service teachers communicated via email, texting, and social media to share ideas, links, and resources.

After two weeks the pre-service teachers met with a lecturer at the university café to discuss their thoughts, and to generate a set of teaching ideas they could each apply to their teaching. They agreed on the following games-based learning properties: games are fun; the games context is captivating; games are success oriented; games broaden the learning space beyond the immediate; students invest emotionally in their game play; students control their learning/game space; and games allow for different levels of learning.

After further discussion with the expert mentor, each pre-service teacher then devised a lesson, or a series of lessons, in their discipline area based on the application of these principles. This was not additional work, as they had to plan and enact a series of lessons anyway; the use of teacher inquiry informed their day-to-day practice and framed the planning and review discussions with teacher-mentors.

After they had taught their lessons, the pre-service teachers met again to share what happened and reflectively discuss how this process had changed their practical teaching knowledge. The pre-service teachers also outlined how they would change their approach or strategies if there was a further iteration. These conversations about practice were valuable interactions that modelled a process of professional learning and adaptation. The final step was to present key findings to all staff in the school community about what they had learnt about games-based learning, through a presentation to a staff meeting.

DISCUSSION AND IMPLICATIONS

Integration and Coherence

Integration concerns how the pre-service teacher values, makes sense of, and assembles the knowledge, relationships, and interactions between university and school-based preparatory experiences. Evidence of integration can be identified in changes to pre-service teacher practical knowledge. This is not a precise formulation, as teaching practical knowledge is more correctly imagined as a narrative that is learnt, applied, and reformed based on context and experience. Knowledge as narrative is a useful frame for pre-service teachers, as it affords engagement with diverse perspectives, informs reasoning for practice decisions, and encourages complex interplay between theory and practice ideas and strategies.

Coherence is the degree to which teacher educators and teacher-mentors intentionally frame and make sense of the conceptual intersection between theory and practical knowledge. This is evident in the formal and informal discourse between these key players, and subsequent interactions with pre-service teachers.

Based on the literature and the case study, Table 8.6 identifies a number of strategies for building coherence and integration, specific to preparing pre-service teachers for the affordances of open-plan learning environments. These affordances have been identified by Deed and Lesko (in press). Each affordance is then linked to strategies that would be enacted by teacher educators, teacher-mentors, and pre-service teachers. The process of teacher preparation is about the grounding of conceptual ideas-in-play into personal practice decisions.

Open-plan learning environments, for example, can express and authorise the concept of community (Deed & Lesko, in press). This generates the possibility of teaching in a community-like environment. In a community it is possible to move from a ratio of one teacher and twenty-five students to three teachers and at least seventy-five students. Each teacher potentially becomes responsible for all the students within their community. Pre-service teachers placed into this type of school space want to make personal sense of the possibilities of the different learning environment. They want to know what works, and how this contributes to their teacher practical knowledge. The question for teacher educators is what activities can frame and structure the learning experience.

Table 8.6 suggests that placing pre-service teacher teams in a community where they are expected to plan, work and reflect relationally may improve integration and coherence. Framing this experience by the use of an inquiry project allows pre-service teachers to personalise the experience and the subsequent learning while co-constructing knowledge and practice.

Building Adaptive Expertise

Coherent and integrated teacher preparation provides the basis for building adaptive expertise. A developmental pathway allows pre-service teachers to become more

Table 8.6. Building coherence and integration in teacher education for open learning environments.

Features of open learning environments[1]	Means of building coherence & integration	
	University strategies	*School-based strategies*
School-less space	Identification of teaching and learning questions related to new educational space.	Identification of local school priorities, models, and strategies.
Humanism and democracy	Introduction to theoretical models and pedagogical approaches that support autonomous and active learning.	Seeking and engaging with a range of diverse perspectives and practices during practicum.
Student agency	Introduction to theories and models of agency complementary to autonomous and active learning.	Practicing teaching approaches that support autonomous and active learning.
Community	Support and scaffolding team teaching and collegial collaboration.	Team-based planning, communication, and review processes, including placing pre-service teachers in project or inquiry teams.
Flexibility	Introduction to theoretical models for learning in open-plan and virtual learning environments.	Applying a range of pedagogical approaches appropriate to flexible use of space.

[1] (categories based on Deed & Lesko, in press)

efficient and effective in their application of teaching practical knowledge. This is evident when pre-service teachers move from a restricted and solution-oriented view to taking a more planned, complete and complex view of problems, generating alternative teaching solutions. By applying the expert model (Sternberg & Horvath, 1995) to the case study data it is possible to identify the characteristics of expertise (knowledge, efficiency and insight) required for pre-service teacher adaptation to open learning environments:

— Knowledge of: local school protocols; teaching space layout and organisation; school and lesson structures; and planning models; a variety of pedagogical models; strategies for management of large student groups; team-teaching models; teaching and learning models for open-plan learning environments; and competence in use of ICT.

— Efficiency demonstrated by: a flexible orientation to other perspectives; experience in teaching across a range of disciplines and using a range of pedagogical models; experience in ways to organise and use large open-plan learning environments; team-teaching strategies, including planning, observation and discussion with experienced teachers; and ICT problem-solving skills.
— Insight demonstrated through: flexibility; creativity; initiative; open-mindedness; a sense of how to judge effective and efficient teaching and learning strategies; and a sense of how ICT can be used for learning and teaching.

CONCLUDING COMMENT

What then can be said in response to the question posed at the start of this chapter: how to prepare pre-service teachers for the differences inherent in the nuanced and multi-faceted work of teaching in open-plan learning environments?

Open-plan learning environments, technology and related pedagogies have broadened the conception of teaching and learning. One implication is that teaching is no longer a purely isolated and largely autonomous activity. Teaching now includes activities in a range of physical and virtual, formal and informal, contexts, with a range of student groupings, and in various collaborative configurations. This is evident in the context of community school spaces, and teacher preparation partnerships and related learning activities between universities and schools.

The case study showed that over three years pre-service teachers were provided with preparatory experiences that framed and focused productive participation in the culture, narrative, and community of practice of being a teacher. This was both a collective and a personalised experience, as pre-service teachers constructed personal teacher knowledge, and enacted and validated agency and practical reasoning.

In the case of preparation for open-plan learning environments, we identified that teacher-mentors, teacher educators, and pre-service teachers needed to develop additional knowledge and skills in: teaching and learning in open-plan settings; team teaching; curriculum differentiation and personalised learning; and effective use of ICT. The inter-related nature of the conceptual and practical basis for teaching adaptation to different learning environments was explored in the pre-service teacher inquiry project reported in the case study. In particular the inquiry project required an expansive view of workplace learning, calling on expertise within and beyond both the immediate school and university experience.

Overall, open-plan learning environments require a change to teacher preparation models, one where pre-service teachers project themselves as adaptive experts, simultaneously building expertise teaching knowledge and skills that can be applied across a variety of teaching and learning contexts.

SECTION THREE

LEARNER EFFECTS AND IMPLICATIONS

VALERIE LOVEJOY

9. STUDENT VIEWS OF PERSONALISING LEARNING IN OPEN-PLAN UP-SCALED LEARNING COMMUNITIES

> I like that you get to be with different kids that have different likes and dislikes. They can help you in certain ways, say they might be creative and have really good ideas.

This is one Year 7 student's positive response to learning with peers in flexible open-plan settings. Open-plan settings have created a new potential for student input to improve the quality of relationships, effective teaching, and personalised learning by enabling new notions of participant partnership and agency in learning communities. For this potential to be realised, both teachers and students need to imagine new roles and spheres of influence for students in these settings.

In chapters 9, 10, and 11 we analyse students' perceptions about and practices of learning and wellbeing in the new settings. In chapter 9 we (a) review the rationale for taking account of student views about their learning and wellbeing at school, (b) identify challenges in eliciting student input to improving learning communities, including research methods that monitor these inputs, (c) analyse examples of student viewpoints and teacher responses, and (d) suggest ways of encouraging fruitful dialogue. We note the challenges for teachers in this aspect of community life, as eliciting student views either confirms or contests teachers' notions of good practice, posing challenges for how teachers should respond (Cook-Sather, 2006; Taylor & Robinson, 2009). In chapter 10, we analyse teacher input and student responses to the TA program as a contribution to student learning and wellbeing. In chapter 11, we review the literature on student wellbeing to frame the evolution of practices in the BEP schools. We include teacher and student responses and examine gender differences in student wellbeing.

RATIONALE AND CHALLENGES OF LISTENING TO STUDENT VOICE

In order for learning to meet their needs, learners' voices are vital in making choices and decisions about the nature and method of their learning. We agree with Rudduck and McIntyre (2007) that the commitment of modern educators to schools as learning communities justifies the incorporation of participant views in planning and reflecting on learning spaces and programs, in order to make them function more effectively. Drawing on Cook-Sather (2006), Bragg (2007), Robinson and Taylor (2007), and our research over three years, we characterise student voice as the expressed views of students who are actively contributing to improving the quality of their learning experience. We agree with Cook-Sather (2006) that student voice encompasses not only the opportunity to speak one's mind, but also to be heard and counted by others, with a potential influence on outcomes. Acting on student opinion can potentially improve the practice of teachers, foster better teacher-student relationships, and empower students in matters concerning their learning (Mitra, 2007; Kincheloe, 2007; Rudduck, 2007).

The key questions for leaders and teachers in organising teaching for learning are what, when, where, how, why, with whom, and at what pace students are expected to learn in these settings, yet, in our study, student interest in these questions is mostly limited to how and with whom they learn. This raises complex questions about relationships between participants and structures for learning experiences. We acknowledge that the degree of agency imagined for, or permitted to, students depends on how teachers view these matters and the purposes for which they seek and use student input (Lodge, 2005; Mitra, 2007; Fielding, 2004a). We concur with the rationale of these researchers for eliciting and addressing student voice, including promoting young people's rights (Convention of the Rights of the Child, 1989), developing their role as key stakeholders in their education, and preparing them for active citizenship in a democratic society. We suggest that students of low socio-economic backgrounds are likely to need encouragement and teacher assistance to develop confidence in expressing their views.

We acknowledge that the term 'student voice' often over-simplifies diverse, competing and contradictory viewpoints, expectations, and needs, raising significant challenges for staff (Reay & Arnot, 2002). We also recognise that unequal power relations problematise student consultation. The possibility of misrepresentation in presuming to speak for, or about, others is acknowledged as a potential pitfall for both teachers and students (Fielding, 2004a, Mannay, 2010). We suggest that how student input is gathered is of fundamental importance to avoid this danger. We acknowledge that traditional methods, such as surveys or interviews, where we may influence data collection, and distort outcomes, by the specific questions formulated, by the language in those questions that may be unfamiliar or irrelevant to the students' interests, and by the selection of data to be reported. However, we suggest that these pitfalls can be mitigated by careful trialling of questions, listening to student feedback, and using direct quotation in reporting. We used student surveys, observations of classes, and teacher and student interviews to inform our analyses. We also employed a 'students as researchers' (SAR) project, in which, in consultation with researchers, students led investigations to identify student perspectives on the new open-plan settings, the efficacy of the TA program, perceptions of belongingness, and school culture, thus enabling a greater sense of commitment to, and ownership of, research results. Keeffe and Andrews (in press) describe the agency involved in adolescent-friendly research methodologies. They emphasise a level of active and embodied participation to encourage an intense form of reflection that is able to overcome the barriers to authentic responses inherent in the power structures of school hierarchies. Further, we agree with Mannay (2010) that creating visual representations can enable greater participant control in the data-production process and have incorporated these methods in our SAR research (for detailed reporting on the SAR project see chapter 10).

In this way, we have sought to overcome the twin concerns of a) tokenistic gathering of student opinion with no effect on outcomes, and b) an uncritical privileging of some student views over other participants in school settings (Fielding, 2004a; Alcoff, 1991). We agree with Fielding (2007) that, as voice is only created in relationship with others, in a school setting, a genuine student voice will emerge when students and teachers are engaged in informed and genuinely democratic discussions about teaching and learning. Such discussion is central to the development of student personhood. Self-development is the iterative identity construction that develops through interaction with others (Giddens, 1991). We suggest that 'relational agency' is central to the wellbeing of students and teachers (Edwards, 2007, 2009; Prain et al., 2013; Sugarman & Martin, 2007), and that a genuinely personalised learning environment will emerge only from teachers and students listening to each other and working together. Up-scaled learning communities unsettle traditional student/teacher relationships. As Engeström (2001, p. 137) argues, transformation can occur through reconceptualising the object and motive of the activity (in this case dialogue for the purpose of school improvement), to embrace "a radically wider horizon of possibilities", including new roles for students and teachers and a wider sphere of influence for students. Acknowledging that teachers and students have separate but interconnecting roles and responsibilities in teaching and learning, we nevertheless argue that sharing responsibility for school improvement powerfully enhances the participants' separate contributions (Edwards, 2011; Prain et al., 2013).

ELICITING STUDENT VOICE

In this chapter we explore student views and teacher responses in order to identify what enables and constrains student voice in the new settings. We first report on student perspectives on the extent to which personalised learning strategies in the open-plan settings have added to a sense of wellbeing and improved academic engagement and efficacy. Second, through a series of vignettes, we report on examples of principal and teacher responses to student opinion in these settings. To this end we used a case study approach, incorporating analyses of quantitative and qualitative data (Green, Camilli, and Elmore, 2006; Tashakkori and Teddlie, 2010; Yin, 2008). Quantitative data included the Personalised Learning Experience Questionnaire (PLEQ) (see chapter 2).

In order to capture the developmental aspect of personalised learning, qualitative data included individual student interviews conducted with 28 Year 7 and 33 Year 10 students from the four BEP schools. Students selected by each school represented a range of motivational and achievement levels which the teachers characterised as high, medium, and low. Ten interview questions sought student responses to the enablers and challenges of the open-plan learning environments, perceptions of their personalised learning experiences, their relationships with other students, and their relationships with teachers. The researchers reported thematised student views to staff at the four schools, illustrating the report with a sample of student responses. De-identified interviews were also sent to schools with full student responses. Four subsequent interviews with school principals garnered leadership responses to student opinions and projected actions.

STUDENT PERCEPTIONS OF THEIR READINESS FOR VOICE

Student responses to the PLEQ are relatively consistent over the three years from 2011 to 2013 and, where the highest possible response was 5.00, display a narrow range of responses between 2.93 and 3.98 on the Likert scale (see Figure 9.1 and chapter 2 for full scale details). The highest scales (consistently over 3.50 on the Likert scale) related to three self-directed learning scales (self-management, desire for learning, and self-control), cognitive engagement, assessment congruence with planned learning, and academic efficacy. The lowest scales (below 3.00 on the Likert scale) related to shared control, assessment student consultation, and individualisation.

The highest scoring scales suggest that students have a positive opinion of their own capacity for independence and self-direction while the lowest scoring scales suggest that the weakest area is the limited opportunities for students to have a say (voice) in their learning. The scale related to self-report of disruptive behaviour appears to be the lowest scale but it is a negative scale (see chapter 2). It is possible that the more students believe they are competent to direct their own learning, the higher their expectation of teacher consultation and negotiation. Gender differences suggest further ways of considering the relationship between the highest and lowest scales.

The gender graph (Figure 9.2) reveals that the boys in BEP schools have a slightly lower sense of their ability to self-direct their learning than girls, combined with a slightly higher degree of satisfaction with the degree of control they are able to exercise over their learning. A possible explanation is that the lower the belief in ability to self-regulate, the lower the expectation of teachers in consultation and shared control. However, though they are still at a higher level than the boys, the scales related to girls' perceptions of their ability to self-direct their learning show a slight decline over the three years of the survey together with a slight decline in the scales that relate to the degree of control they are able to exercise over their learning. On the other hand boys' perceptions of their ability to self-direct their learning have risen slightly over the three years, while their perceptions of the degree of control they are allowed to exercise are either stable or slightly rising. This movement suggests that both boys and girls may be affected in their positive perceptions of cognitive engagement, and skills in self-direction, by the degree to which they perceive that

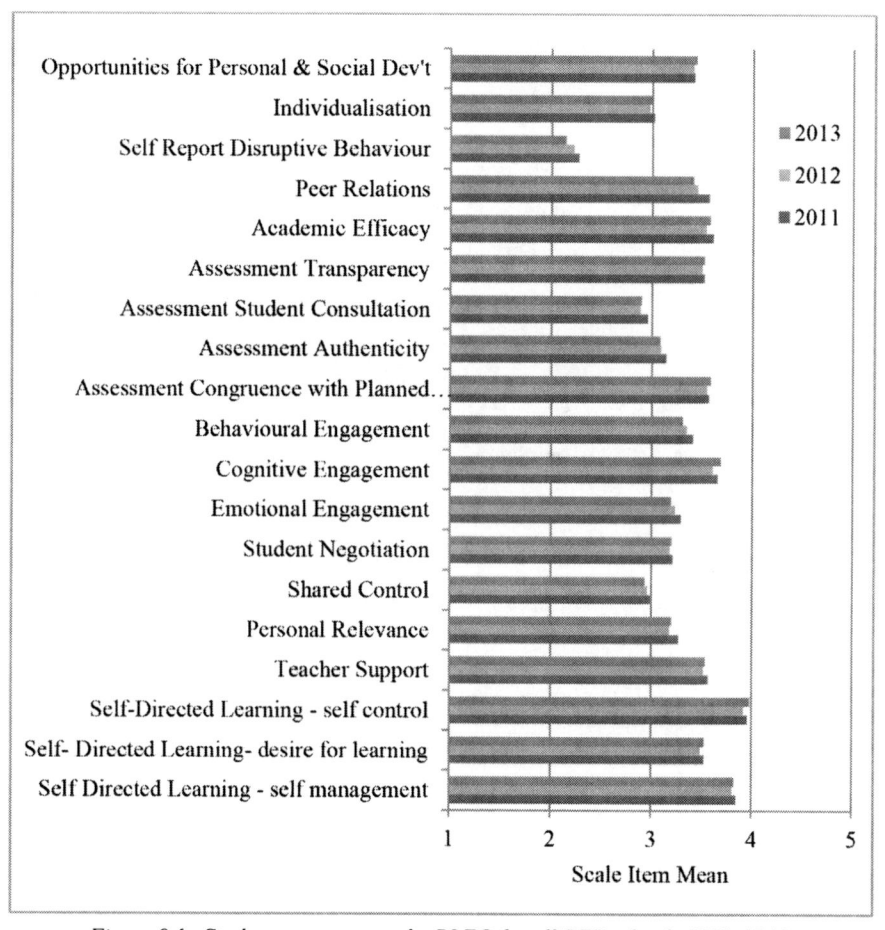

Figure 9.1. Student responses to the PLEQ for all BEP schools 2011–2013.

teachers' negotiate and share control with them. That is, the more teachers negotiate with both girls and boys, and share control with them, the greater the positive effect on their perceptions of their ability to self-direct their learning. This proposition needs further research to establish its validity. What is clear is that the lowest scales concern shared control, negotiation and individualisation, suggesting that teachers face ongoing challenges in allowing students to have more say in their learning.

STUDENT VIEWS OF PERSONALISED LEARNING IN OPEN-PLAN SETTINGS

The interview questions in Table 9.1 were prompts for students we interviewed about their views on the learning environment and relationships with their peers and teachers.

V. LOVEJOY

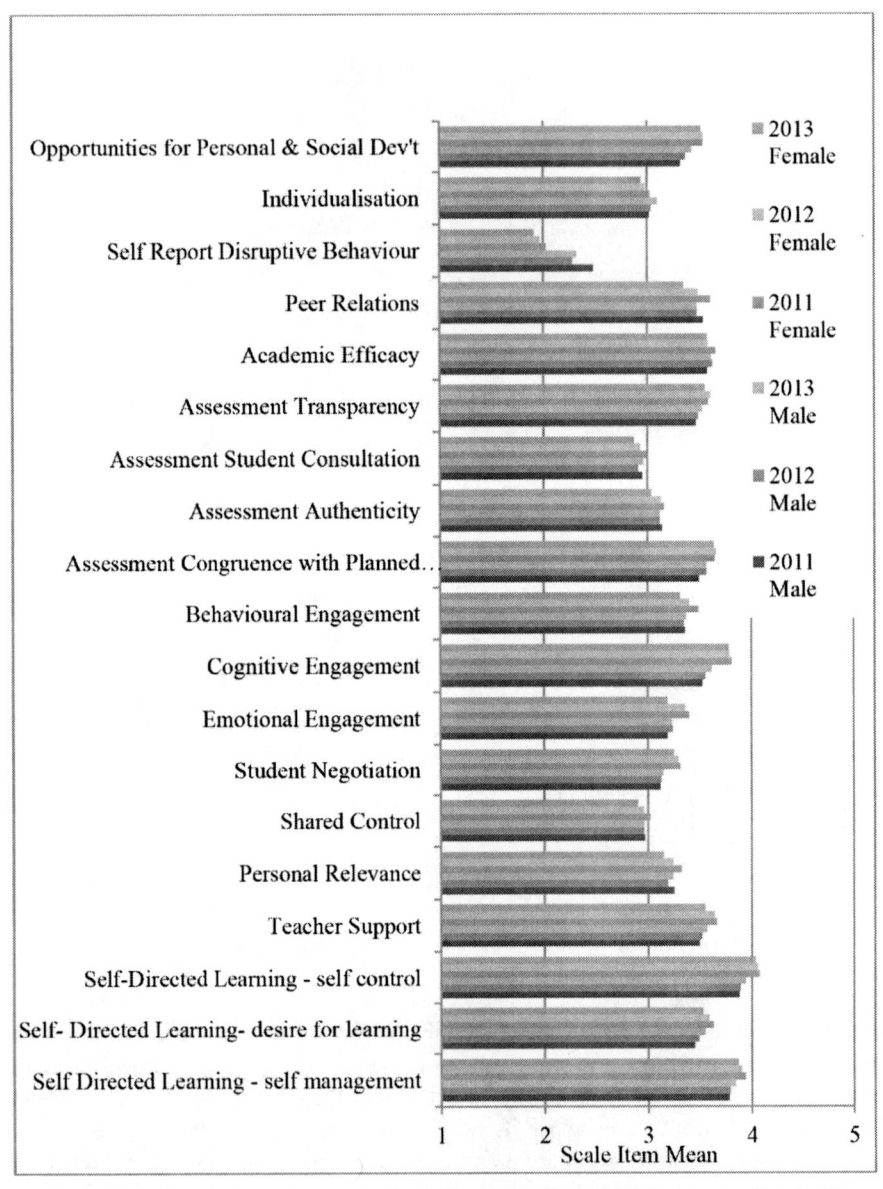

Figure 9.2. Survey responses to the PLEQ by gender for all BEP schools 2011–2013.

Students' interview responses have been thematised into perspectives on the physical learning environment, relationships with peers and teachers, and learning experience in the open-plan settings.

Table 9.1. *Interview questions on personalised learning and relationships in the open learning environment.*

Themes	Questions
Learning environment as a physical place to learn in	What do you like about the new learning environment? Why?
	What don't you like about the learning environment? Why?
	What would make the learning spaces better for you?
	Which space at your school do you really like to be? What do you do there?
Student wellbeing and peer relationships in the learning environment	How do you feel in your learning neighbourhood?
	How well do you know the other students in your learning neighbourhood?
	What advice would you give to a new student coming into your learning neighbourhood?
Teacher-student relationships in the learning environment	Have you noticed any differences in the ways your teachers teach in the new learning environment?
	What advice would you give your teachers about teaching in these settings?
	Think of a teacher who cares about you. Tell me what he/she does. Does this help you learn? Contrast with other teachers.

Student Perspectives on the Physical Learning Environment

> It feels less like a school. I know that sounds weird but when you think of a school you think of one room sitting there quietly for 70 minutes. In the open areas you can talk a bit more. It makes you feel more relaxed. (Year 10)

The students were enthusiastic about the open learning spaces mainly because of the greater sense of freedom of movement they create, but also because of the potential for improved relationships. They appreciated the opportunities the space provides to mix with a larger range of students and learn from a variety of teachers who have different skills and teaching styles:

> You are not with the same people all the time. You meet more students and when you have one teacher they are good at one thing and not at another thing (Year 7).

The main disadvantages of the open-plan settings, according to both Years 7 and 10 students, are noise and distractions. They could not imagine solutions to these problems, perhaps reflecting their historical lack of voice. The Ironbark College students participating in the SAR project added that the increased space brought with it opportunities for drifting to other classes "when something more interesting was going on" or "hiding in the corner and playing games". While the spaces are assumed to create increased visibility, they also allow freedom of movement that can be used responsibly or irresponsibly.

As an antidote to large open-plan settings, favourite spaces at school, linked to informal times of the school day, are generally intimate outside spaces where students socialise in their own 'territory' with a few friends. Cross-community friendships are common by Year 10. The global learning centre, a safe, staffed, and friendly inside space was favoured by both Year 7s and 10s while Year 10s sometimes nominated a specialised learning area, such as drama, technology, or visual arts, as their favourite space.

The junior Ironbark College students (SAR interviews) were adamant that the outside spaces had not been well planned. They wanted playgrounds with "monkey bars, flying foxes and slides". Students' request for a graffiti wall (through the SRC) has been agreed to, but the SAR leaders felt that "inside everyone is fine, but outside, "everything has been made picture perfect, but they have forgotten about the whole-school feel". Comments that there is nothing to do, "we get told off when we kick the footy" were supported by the SAR leaders.

Most students experience positive feelings of wellbeing in the open-plan learning environments. Common adjectives to describe Year 7 feelings included "happy", "relaxed", "good" and "safe", concentrating on the physical environment, while the more complex responses of Year 10: "relaxed", "calm", "belonging", "grateful", "respected", and "challenged", suggest their feelings were closely linked to relationships with peers and teachers. Open-plan spaces do not suit every student's needs though few students (4 of 28 in Year 7, and 4 of 33 in Year 10) expressed negative feelings. Adjectives, such as "nervous", "scared", and "edgy", reflect the new status of Year 7s in the school, while negative Year 10 responses such as "frustrating", "disappointing", and "angry", reflect disappointment in their learning experience.

Student Perspectives on Relationships with Peers and Teachers in the Settings

The visibility of the spaces seems to have lessened overt bullying so that most students feel safe and happy at school, confirmed by interviews with the principals and teachers. The presence of TA groups (see chapter 10) gives students a sense of belonging. TA groups were established to mitigate the possible alienating effects of larger learning communities and open-plan learning environments by the personal connections students could establish in these groups of 25 students.

> I could probably name every single person. I'm always friendly to people and smile, so I guess I know them quite well". (Year 10)

Though friendship groups were much smaller (typically five to ten), all Year 7 and Year 10 students feel they know the students in their TA well, and reflecting their longer time at school, Year 10s had a much broader acquaintance with others in their learning community:

> I know a lot of people but they have their own friends. My friends have grown quite a bit over the years. We wind each other up and have fun. (Year 10)

While both Year 7s and Year 10s emphasised that new students need to work at making friends in order to fit in, Year 10s' stronger sense of identity is reflected in advice to new students to "be yourself".

Positive effects of new learning environments on relationships with teachers are evident in Year 10 advice to students. They warned of the consequences of "dumbing yourself down" on academic grades, showing off as "giving the wrong impression", and "being scared of the teachers", as missing an opportunity for assistance. The strong advice to "ask teachers" suggests a confidence in teacher/student relationships:

> We have a lot of fantastic teachers here who would do anything for students. A lot of people write them off and don't get to know them. Teachers are willing to do a lot for you (Year 10).

The biggest differences students noticed in the new learning environments were the improved teacher/student relationships (Year 7, 12 comments, Year 10, 12 comments):

> If you're having a few social issues, like you've got things going on at home, I've noticed they're nicer to you. They're easier on you and they ask you how you are going all the time. They really do care. (Year 7)

Year 10 students were more aware than Year 7 students of the physical effect of the learning environment on teacher/student relationships:

> I think they can be more free, such as us being more free. They feel they can interact better with the kids. . .you can actually have a chat with them about what they're doing at the weekend. The buildings have changed the people—it's good. (Year 10)

Good relationships with teachers were particularly important for Year 7 students (11 of 33) whose advice to teachers included "to listen", to be "kind and helpful", to "give everyone a fair go", and importantly, to "try and stay happy even if you're not feeling that way so kids don't think it's their fault". Year 10s are more likely to value a teacher who had established a respectful, egalitarian relationship with them: "he talks to me like I'm a friend—like we're equal" and one who is willing to "put in the extra yards" of availability beyond class time. A sense of humour is a highly valued attribute at both year levels and both appreciate an enthusiastic, "joyful" teacher who communicates their passion to the students.

Student Perspectives on their Learning Experience in the Open-Plan Settings

Students who have experienced team teaching and greater collegiality enthused about the positives. Year 7s had positive responses to teacher collaboration because it gave them access to more teachers' expertise, teachers seemed to have better knowledge when working together, and students received help more quickly. One student appreciated the opportunities in team teaching for moderation: "When they are marking work, they talk to each other and basically it's a big team effort. It's better because teachers mark differently". It is somewhat disturbing that over 15 % of the students interviewed (5 of the Year 7s and 5 of the Year 10s) have noticed no change in the way their teachers teach in the open-plan settings (see chapter 7 on teacher adaptation).

Few students had noticed differences in curriculum organisation and content (around 10 % of responses). Year 7 students at Whirrakee College were positive about their experience of ability grouping "you know everyone's on the same page so you can advance when you want to, or go back when you want to" while Year 10 students focused on the increased interest and variety that new technologies (such as smart boards and netbook computers) have brought to their lessons.

STUDENT VOICE: ENABLERS AND CONSTRAINTS

These student perspectives support arguments about the risks of essentialising student voice (Taylor & Robinson, 2009; Fielding, 2004a). Reay and Arnot (2002), quoted in Fielding and Rudduck (2002, p.4), pointed out that "there is no homogeneous pupil voice even in a single working group, but rather a cacophony of competing voices". Listening to, and acting upon, student views is a complex task that involves taking into account multiple perspectives of students of diverse ages, abilities, motivations, and backgrounds. The local context provides a further filter on the lens of student views. Our limited research has provided a small snapshot of a range of student views. Nevertheless, we suggest there is enough common ground about student adaptation to their new learning environment for leaders and teachers to take note of factors that will both reassure and challenge them. The honesty, insight, and practicality of student opinion demonstrates that students, even at Year 7 level, have much to offer in discussions of matters of school improvement and effectiveness. Trusting students to conduct research into specific matters such as the teacher advisor program has elicited fruitful ideas for program improvement (see chapter 10).

The improvements students have experienced in relationships can be partially explained by changes in organisational structures, whereby the four BEP schools are each organised into four learning communities (see chapters 1 and 4). Staffrooms based in each learning community are easily accessible to students, and shared bathroom facilities mean that traditional barriers are broken down. Students and staff encounter each other not simply in class but as community members in a shared space. Positive student comments on the experience of freedom that the flexible, open-plan settings provide, and the quality of the relationships with teachers, suggest that students are, on the whole, appreciative of the opportunities for more relaxed and friendly relationships that the open-plan settings have enabled. As the bedrock for an improved experience of teaching and learning for students, this achievement cannot be underestimated. Teacher advisors, who mentor, and advocate for students in their care, have the closest personal relationships with students, and also teach their students in one or more subjects, creating the opportunity for a more intimate knowledge of each student's needs and preferences (see chapter 10).

The areas where students appear to be least satisfied are those areas that relate to their learning. The desire for more control over their learning (PLEQ survey), the relatively few comments regarding changed teacher practice in the open-plan settings (interviews), the suggestions for more engaging and active learning (SAR project and interviews), and the issues of noise and distraction (interviews), all point to a hesitation among some teachers to change from traditional teaching methods to more inquiry-based problem-solving approaches involving teacher and student teams.

Adaptation to these settings has proved a greater challenge for teachers than students (see chapter 7). Team teaching requires team planning, negotiation and reflection, which takes time from a busy teacher's schedule. Further, some teachers fear that team teaching a larger number of students will lead to a loss of connection with individual students. However, teachers competing for students' attention in separate classrooms within an open-plan setting create the noise and distraction problems observed by students. Additionally, catering for the learning needs of twenty-five students with a wide range of abilities (see chapter 7) is a very difficult task. Students appreciate the increased opportunities for learning that team teaching (where it occurs) provides, by mixing with greater numbers of teachers and students. Working in teams makes the task of differentiating the curriculum easier. The open-plan spaces better enable the organisation of flexible groupings for this purpose. However, working in teams requires the development of a quality, challenging curriculum based on sound pedagogy. This requires time for planning and up-skilling of teachers.

As the schools are in a transitional phase, leaders have reported that increased visibility in open-plan settings and the requirement for changed teaching methods have exposed a poverty of pedagogy. Over the past three years, consultants have been employed to assist schools to create model lessons to ensure improved teaching, and to build a robust curriculum that supports differentiation as a first step to a team-teaching approach (see chapters 1 and 3). A complicating factor has been the transition from a state based to a national curriculum. This is now in place in all schools, but is a generalised template that requires work at the individual school level on specific units of work, resources and activities to adapt it to the needs of local students.

While students want more active participation in decision-making about their learning, as well as the learning itself, teachers traditionally see themselves as predominantly responsible for these matters. Layers of tradition and history engraved within school artefacts, rules, conventions, and roles have the potential to inhibit the new division of labour that occurs in the expansion of student voice (Engeström, 2001; Murphy and Rodriguez-Manzanares, 2008). Consultation with students, incorporation of student ideas into planning, and sharing responsibility with students for their individual progress have been traditionally limited to formal channels such as Students Representative Councils (SRC) and the limited goal-setting activities undertaken by teacher advisors in conjunction with students (see chapter 10). Some teachers find the pressure of raising academic standards for all students, an expectation of the Federal and State governments that accompanied the building of new schools, and which is measured by nationwide testing in English and mathematics at Years 7 and 9 levels (NAPLAN), difficult to balance with allowing students more control over their learning (see chapters 2, 4 and 10).

The silencing of student voice is not a matter of teacher resistance alone. Students appear to self-limit their views to areas they feel justified or competent to comment on. Students of low socio-economic background may be particularly reluctant to encroach upon ground traditionally regarded as the territory of teachers. Thus, students may perceive negative consequences of open-plan settings but be unable to suggest modifications. Students have ideas to offer about how, and with whom, they should learn. However, they have little to say about other vital questions relevant to personalising their learning experience such as what, when, where, and why they learn.

RESPONDING TO STUDENT VOICE IN BEP SCHOOLS

We do not pretend that these are easy issues to address. While the literature on student voice is strident about the need for students to have a say in their learning, it is less concerned with: recognising the pressures on teachers that inhibit genuine consultation; addressing the need for professional learning to develop skills in acting on student input; ways of differentiating the curriculum to better cater for individual student needs; and learning to work relationally with other professionals and students to ensure the best learning outcomes for students.

Student voice is being encouraged and affirmed in various ways at our case study schools as the following examples demonstrate. The principals' response to the annual PLEQ has been to acknowledge that the area needing most work is that of 'shared control'. However, teachers are charged with lifting the academic performance of students and perceive that giving students more control over their learning may threaten their achievement levels.

Grevillea College

The Principal of Grevillea College explained the student lack of satisfaction with shared control as a result of a tightening of control over absenteeism and an increased emphasis on literacy and numeracy. At this school, progression to the next year level depends on satisfactory attendance and academic performance. The Principal suggested that girls, whose satisfaction levels were lower than the boys, were frustrated by increased surveillance and less subject choice. The Principal acknowledged the students' dissatisfaction, but believed that a temporary tightening of control in order to raise academic standards was a greater necessity.

Students at this school exercised their voice by holding a protest meeting, on the school oval in November 2012, over staffing and program reductions (*Bendigo Advertiser*, 9 November 2012). The students claimed they had not been consulted about the changes before they were implemented. The Principal responded by inviting students to her office to discuss the issues, listening to their concerns, and explaining the necessity for the reductions. The Principal considered the matter a misunderstanding and strongly rejected the suggestion that the students were being silenced. On this occasion, some teachers supported the students as they also felt a lack of consultation. At this school, student voice representatives in each TA feed in their ideas for community improvement through their SRC representatives (see chapter 6 for further detail). According to the Principal, their ideas generally reflect traditional matters of concern, such as school socials and end of year programs for senior students, rather than learning issues.

Whirrakee College

The Principal of Whirrakee College responded to the students' perceptions that they had little control over their learning by encouraging independent, resilient learners. Recognising that the journey towards becoming a self-regulated learner is developmental, the Principal, who is also the Year 10 coordinator, incorporated opportunities for leadership by setting up a mentoring program in which Year 10 students worked with Year 7, 8 and 9 buddies and junior TA teachers to provide guidance and support to junior students. He encouraged independence and responsibility through the use of ICT. Students read school bulletins online and scan in their attendance electronically. This school has improved its attendance record through this process to well above the state average (see chapter 2). In addition, a personal student dashboard ensures that students set goals, and allows them, their parents and their teachers to monitor their academic progress (see chapter 5 and Prain et al., in press). Additionally, Year 10 students may use up to three periods a week to "follow their passions", a privilege that encourages students to be self-motivated and involved members of their local community, who are responsible for completing their academic tasks. Students in Year 10 have their own unsupervised common room, in which they can eat, study, and meet with their friends. This has been an appreciated and respected privilege. Younger students observe these privileges and aspire to the increased independence that comes with age at this school. Responding to the results of student interviews, in which students perceived that Years 8 and 9 students were not finding the buddy program useful, the Principal demonstrated his responsiveness to their views by modifying the program so that students were placed with Year 7 students only.

Ironbark College

SAR leaders invited the coordinator of the teacher advisor program at Ironbark College to be present at their reflection session (see chapter 10 for details of this research project). This invitation indicated not only the strength of the respect of student leaders for this teacher, but their conviction that he needed to hear what they had to say. After listening to the session, the coordinator became aware of the varying quality of TA sessions. The importance of teacher commitment to the success of the TA program was confirmed. Despite his work in this area, the students made it clear that the TA program needed further attention. A poor TA leads to an unsatisfactory and poorly delivered program. The coordinator expressed his intention to follow up this avenue of student opinion and was receptive to the idea of student input into the program activities (see chapter 10). However, to this point, traditional understandings of teacher and student roles and division of labour have limited the impact of student ideas regarding the content, methodology and quality of the TA curriculum (Engeström, 2001).

Melaleuca College

Melaleuca College has reorganised the school structure for 2014 into four learning communities comprising Years 7-10 students, in place of year-level learning communities (see chapters 4 and 11). This decision was influenced by observation of the successful use of this structure in two other schools. Significantly, the decision was made after a combined staff and Year 9 student visit to these schools. Discussion with staff and students about their learning community structures elicited such positive responses that both staff and students were convinced that change would benefit Melaleuca College. Year 9 students were selected on the basis of their maturity and because they had potentially the most to lose from a multi-year-level learning community, as the Year 10 community (to which they were about to progress) had more privileges and greater flexibility than the younger year-level communities. After the school visits, Year 9 students spoke to the Year 7 and 8 communities, convincing the younger students of the benefits of change. Though a formal student vote was not taken, this involvement of students in an important school decision is an acknowledgment that all participants' views should be considered in an organisational change that affects teaching and learning.

Reflection on student voice in BEP schools

Traditionally, appointed student leaders (through the SRC) play a role in bringing the concerns of students before the teachers and principal. However, it is understood that areas where students are entitled to speak and be listened to are limited to aspects that do not threaten teachers; those concerning student social activities rather than the central purpose of schooling—teaching and learning.

The increased sense of community and agency in learning communities is responsible for heightened student voice in the BEP schools. Leaders in the BEP schools are committed to listening to students, engaging in dialogic problem-solving (Grevillea and Whirrakee Colleges) and involving students in discussions on structural reorganisation (Melaleuca College). Though this represents an extension of traditional student inputs on social matters, the content of their views has not, thus far, extended to matters of teaching and learning. However, these school principals have demonstrated their determination to begin the process of involving students in systemic change by inviting researchers to seek student opinion on teaching and learning within the schools.

VALUE AND LIMITATIONS OF OUTSIDER RESEARCH

In this instance, eliciting the opinions of students about the quality of their personalised learning in open-plan settings has been the task of a university research group, rather than the teachers themselves. Detailed reports on both surveys and interviews have been presented at staff meetings in which staff members were invited to respond to, question, and discuss the implications of student comments with the researchers. Despite the researchers' efforts to inform staff, students were not communicating their opinions directly to their teachers. Survey and interview questions were designed by the researchers rather than by the students. To verify that survey questions were comprehensible to students, they were trialled with a group of students and modified as a result of their feedback (see chapter 2 for more detail). Nevertheless, researcher-designed tasks filtered student responses. Furthermore, researchers interpreted student responses and selected what to report to principals and teachers. These limitations reflect the concerns about the power dynamics of student voice research raised by Fielding (2004a). To lessen these limitations, the SAR project encouraged student control of question design, student conduct of interviews, and reflection on results of their research (see chapter 10). In individual interviews, we encouraged students, with a range of achievement and motivation levels, to put forward their views in many non-traditional areas, including their experience of personalised learning, the open-plan learning environments, and their views on teacher adaptation to, and practice within, these settings.

FUTURE DIRECTIONS FOR STUDENT VOICE

As in any healthy ecosystem, in order to sustain schools as healthy communities of learning, the everyday and ongoing needs of learning community members need constant monitoring (see Prain et al., in press). With opportunities for informal conversations and discussions among teachers and students, the open-plan settings create the conditions for democratic monitoring processes which call upon the input of all community members. Students, in relating better to their teachers, are also freer to talk to them about their concerns and suggestions. Prain et al., (2103) and Edwards (2011), argue that the "relational agency" of teachers and students should be encouraged to achieve the best outcomes in teaching and learning. Sharing different perspectives and working together will ensure optimal teaching and learning outcomes. Student expression of learning needs and preferences is only the beginning of this process. The role of teachers is to encourage appropriate ways of expression, encourage open communication, and to act on student initiatives. Listening to, and consulting directly with students about the best ways to meet those needs is another step. Students who feel their needs are being addressed will be more motivated and responsible. However, even this will not satisfy the student desire for more control over their learning unless the students are given choices about, and responsibility for, their learning.

Fielding (2004a, 2004b) and Cook-Sather (2006) advocate a dialogic approach to student voice research, in which teacher and student partners listen respectfully to each other, discuss issues, and work together to improve teaching and learning practices. It is easier to ignore, or fail to act upon, student input when not directly engaged in listening to student voices. The dialogic approach involves relinquishing of sole control by teachers and trust in the students' knowledge and right to speak. It represents a change in the traditional teacher/student role.

School leaders, especially principals, with their broad vision for their school as a community of learners where all players contribute to learning success and student development, play a critical role in encouraging teachers to make these changes to democratic dialogue and shared control over learning (Mitra, Serriere, and Stoicovy, 2012).

The formal structure of a teacher advisory is one forum for teacher and student dialogue about matters of teaching and learning. In this daily session, teachers and students can engage in individual and small group discussions, teachers can guide students in the skill development needed to enhance confidence in their voice, demonstrate practical listening skills, and genuinely seek feedback on teaching programs. A limited beginning has been made with goal-setting activities and identification of learning styles at Ironbark and other colleges. However, the direct link of TA with learning needs to be strengthened (see chapter 10). More specific discussion about students' personal learning needs and critiques of the quality of their learning could be gainfully added to the social and emotional learning of the TA program. Inviting and acting on student feedback on the TA curriculum itself is an ideal way to begin. In this way students are "learning to represent themselves to the world" (Benhabib, 1992) by exercising their voice in a safe setting. Teachers and students are practising the skills of listening, understanding, and respecting each other's views and, because teachers are also teaching students in core subjects, finding ways to move closer to creating personalised learning experiences. Edwards (2011) drawing on Benhabib (1992), argues that the capacity to reverse perspectives and seek understanding with the 'other' produces a form of common knowledge based on shared understanding that is a vital prerequisite for relational action.

Implementing structures, time, and space to formalise these discussions and mutual decision-making, would seem to be necessary to counter the traditional role understandings that work against relational communication. Grevillea College has implemented a formal avenue for student voice that attempts to reach the broader student population. Students are encouraged to feed ideas on community improvement through a student representative in their TA group who reports to a student voice committee (see chapter 6 for more detail). Though suggestions rarely concern matters of teaching and learning, when formal structures are created that encourage listening and understanding student views, common knowledge is created that allows a solution orientation.

Creating a forum for thorough review of, and potential change to, teaching and learning practices would seem to be an avenue for collectively thinking about how to organise and vary the learning experience. A student learning committee that meets regularly with teachers and leaders, with representatives from all year levels, but weighted towards the senior students with their greater maturity, would serve the purpose of concentrating attention on the areas of learning which would result in a widening of the students' sphere of influence. In order to understand each other's perspectives, listening skills and the ability to understand other perspectives would be required as teachers, for example, explain their current rationale, and students recount their learning experiences. The trust and commitment built between teachers and students in these new settings is the basis on which such a forum could be founded. As well as an expectation that students have a voice about learning, a student learning committee would encourage growth in independence and responsibility among the student representatives. The matters for discussion in these learning committees could be decided in TA sessions and these sessions also used for reporting to all students. Such encounters may initially threaten the traditional school frameworks that teachers and students are comfortable with. However, such potential unsettling or conflict, as Engeström (2001) argues, creates the very conditions for finding new solutions to difficult challenges, in this case the challenge of addressing the vital task of ensuring that learning is stimulating, rewarding, and personally challenging for all students.

MARY KEEFFE

10. BUILDING RELATIONSHIPS: TEACHER ADVISOR PROGRAMS IN BEP SCHOOLS

INTRODUCTION

In this chapter, we investigate why and how teacher advisor (TA) programs were developed in the BEP schools, including challenges in using these programs to build strong relationships between teachers and students. We claim that an effective TA program will provide learning experiences and changed relationships that improve student autonomy, or the ability for students to make their own informed decisions in living and learning contexts. We aimed to research the following questions:

1. What were the initial purposes and roles of the TA program?
2. How did the TA curriculum evolve in each school?
3. What were student responses to the TA program?

We found that the TA program developed in three broad phases in each school and they included: role clarification, a defined curriculum, and links with learning. The phases describe emergent pathways for the development of the role of the TA group that may be relevant to all attempts to build meaningful relationships in schools. Consistent with Niska's (2010) research, our study found that strategic considerations involved capacity-building for teacher agency, and confidence to collaborate with students, and to develop their social, emotional and learning resilience. The purposeful success of a TA program, however, depended on a deep appreciation of student agency as it was developed through reflective problem-solving in life and learning contexts (Engeström & Sannino, 2010). In this chapter we describe each phase of the TA experience, the contentions that emerged at each iteration of the program, and the structures that evolved over time. We complete the chapter with a detailed review and analysis of students' perspectives on a TA program.

Research Methods

In researching these questions we used qualitative data that included teacher and student interviews, classroom observations, and document analysis related to the goals and development of the TA programs over three years. Interviews with six principals, twelve neighbourhood leaders, three TA program coordinators, six beginning and seventeen experienced teachers, and fifteen students provided perspectives from those involved in the program. We focus mainly on Ironbark College as the site where the TA program was most developed over the three years (see also chapter 6). A students-as-researchers project (SAR) conducted in the final year of the study examined students' perspectives on the value and effects of the TA groups at Ironbark College (see rationale in chapter 9). Rudduck and Fielding (2006) argue that student research projects can remain ineffectual in authorising student voice unless organisational barriers are identified and reduced. In this SAR project, students were involved in each phase of the research: developing the research questions, methods, and data analysis. Data were collected through focus groups with Years 7, 8 and 10 students, and interviews with their teacher advisors. Year 10 student leaders conducted four focus groups with Years 7 and 8 students about their perceptions of the schools' TA program, the learning spaces, and feelings of wellbeing at school (see also chapter 11). Photovoice methods incorporated into the study elicited images and dialogue that represented student responses to the TA program. The SAR leaders then reflected on positive, negative, and interesting aspects or PMI (De Bono, 1987) of the teacher advisor program and made suggestions for improvement. Data from all sources in the study were analysed using a qualitative coding method of recurring themes, cross-referencing, and participant review at various stages of the study.

Background to the TA Programs in the BEP Schools

Historically, TA programs arose from the belief that meaningful relationships between teachers and students could promote engagement with school activities and improve learning outcomes (Butler, Schnellert, & Cartier, 2013). The original plan for the BEP identified the TA group as the main motivator for the changed relationships required to achieve this goal. In 2001, the Canadian government believed that students at high risk of disengagement (poverty, rural isolation and learning difficulties) could develop meaningful relationships with teachers and engage with a school culture that prioritised personal learning. In 2003 a group of BEP teachers were invited to Ontario to preview the progress of Canada's legislated requirement for TA groups in schools. However, the program was disbanded in 2005 because:

> Instead of creating a connection between each student and a teacher who could mentor and guide them, (the TA program) was seen as a burden for which teachers were inadequately prepared and in which students were "wasting their time". (Earl, Freeman, Lasky, Sutherland, & Torrance, 2002, p. 77)

The Ontario experience foreshadowed similar initial concerns raised in the BEP schools about teachers' lack of willingness or expertise to undertake TA work. While a personal development curriculum linked to student learning and belonging is held in high regard in schools (see Engeström, 2011), these effects are difficult to achieve, and evidence of the benefits of TA programs are weak. Three potential phases of TA program development emerged through our study. Phase one involved a clarification of the purpose and role of the TA. During this phase, the schools wanted a shared vision of the role so that students and teachers could have changed relationships through high expectations of meaningful school experiences (Hallinan, 2008). Schools and teachers initially believed they had the capacity to realise those expectations, but the TA time lapsed into administrative or chat sessions. Each school grappled with emergent issues that related to a clear vision for the purpose of the role (Levin 2009), new skills and organisational structures for mentoring and support (Phillippo, 2009), and professional development (Niska, 2013). Phase two entailed developing, enacting and evaluating a formal TA curriculum to guide TA activities and to address the limitations of the scope of the role as it was experienced in most schools. The pervasive need for constructive and supportive decision-making in life and learning for students from challenging backgrounds resulted in the emergence of phase three of the TA, where schools aimed to establish links between the TA curriculum and school engagement. This final phase is ongoing.

THE PURPOSE AND ROLE OF THE TEACHER ADVISOR

Each school in the BEP defined the TA role in different ways. As noted in chapter four, the differing SES profiles of the schools meant that schools adapted their TA programs to their perceived local needs. At all four schools, the role of TA as the student's advocate and mentor was a primary purpose.

At Whirrakee College, the school with the highest SES profile, the TA was expected to:

- improve student outcomes;
- improve student connectedness to peers, to teachers and to school;
- reduce student alienation from school;
- minimise student absenteeism from school;
- ensure effective communication between school and parents;
- ensure high levels of compliance with the college's school uniform policy;
- encourage high levels of compliance with college values and the student code of conduct;
- improve student organisational skills. [Whirrakee, TA role statement]

The role statement implies a strong administrative function. The Principal at Whirrakee College explained that daily personalised reminders in student notebooks obviated the need for students to listen to teachers about meaningless details such as bus travel, excursions and sporting events. He believed that TA time should promote student independence and that students would achieve this with the use of the dashboard (see chapter 5):

> The TA group is not needed any more for the Year 10s. They can access the notices themselves and we have log on technology to track absenteeism - so we have changed the TA group to study time. [Principal, Whirrakee]

At Whirrakee College, the TA plays an important role in Year 7 students' transition to secondary school. The TA is the students' first point of contact and the teacher to whom they are most closely connected. The TAs work with the students on a curriculum based on social and emotional learning. The topics to be covered weekly are outlined in the students' diaries that they bring each day to class. As students progress through the college, they become increasingly independent of the TA teacher.

The content of the TA time at Grevillea College is used for student silent reading with the aims of settling students before they begin their formal classes, encouraging students to read, and allowing time for the TA teacher to individually mentor one or two students in each session. Initially, each teacher was responsible for 12 students, but a reduced staffing profile and budgetary pressures resulted in an increase to 25 students per teacher at Grevillea College.

At Melaleuca College, although a teacher advisor role had been implemented to create connectedness and to develop teacher-student relationships, there was no agreed curriculum for the daily teacher advisor period. Some teachers resisted any attempt to change from their traditional role of checking attendance and passing on administrative information to their students, and this resulted in an ad hoc approach to various activities. One teacher developed a values and skills program based on the Stephen Covey's book "The 7 Habits of Highly Effective People" (1989), while others participated in competitive sports activities in order to provide fun-based team experiences.

In 2014 a new curriculum for the teacher advisor period was introduced at Melaleuca College. All students were provided with a student planner, (and teachers with the accompanying teacher manual), which included diary space and weekly focus topics on life values, learning and self-management skills, and strategies for improving health and wellbeing. Learning community leaders explained that the combined groups of Year 7-10 students made it more difficult to plan a teacher advisory curriculum for the learning community as a whole. The commitment to the curriculum was not consistently uniform as one learning community leader introduced a program where the students in the community were nominated to "make a difference" outside the school. The students then reported to the whole learning community about what they had done.

Ironbark College developed the most advanced curriculum over time, based on advocacy, problem-solving, and learning. The strategic approach to the importance of the role, and the evolution of the program itself, provide an insight into how a TA group can provide a consistent and supportive approach to learning, decision-making, collaboration, and meaningful relationships. From the outset the Principal at Ironbark College considered that teachers needed to change their expectations about limited responsibility for students:

> If it was a semester length unit, you'd hear them in the staff room saying, 'I've only got a few weeks left with that kid and I'll never see them again'. They

just wanted to wash their hands of behaviour issues and things like that. That wasn't changing anything. It was just preserving the culture of reduced care.

To alter these attitudes the Principal made the purposes of the TA program explicit and encouraged teacher 'buy in' through collaboration, reflection, professional development, and role clarification. Teacher professional development, and the establishment of supportive protocols in the neighbourhood structures, raised the awareness of the theoretical basis for the TA program. Teachers were actively involved in the evolution of a prepared curriculum and they learned from each other through modelling the skills involved in student support and home or family communication. The induction process included improving teachers' understanding of the impact of poverty, the reasons for students' difficult behaviours, and developing better communication skills to reduce conflict rather than to escalate it. This professional development contributed to teachers and students reporting a calmer and friendlier environment where the responsibility for all students was shared. Training in restorative practices and explicit teaching of the school values assisted both students and teachers to come to a shared understanding of the expectations for living and learning in these new learning spaces. The TA curriculum was shaped and reshaped as knowledge grew about the needs of the students and the teachers.

The school raised the profile of the TA program by making the curriculum activities compulsory. The roles and expectations were made explicit in the school's policy documents, and every teacher in the school was involved with a group of students. The principal argued that advocating for the needs of students and teaching them problem-solving skills for life and learning were part of a teacher's regular duties and responsibilities. Professional learning, modelling and distributed leadership provided support for teachers to build their capacity to manage their own professional growth and their changed, perhaps more intense, relationships with the students and their complex lives. Teachers began to trust each other in sharing professional responsibilities and gaining skills.

DEVELOPING A TEACHER ADVISOR CURRICULUM

As teachers began to advocate for the needs of students and communicate with families, they realised how pervasive student problems were. Poverty, high risk behavior, poor self-esteem, and low levels of learner resilience challenged student decisions and confronted teacher responsiveness on a regular basis. To address these challenges, the next phase of the development of the TA program involved a structured curriculum that linked students' personal reflections with constructive decision-making and learning.

Teachers were paired to complement each other in gender, experience, outlook on life ("I'm very creative and he is so down-to-earth" – experienced teacher), and areas of expertise. Pairs of teachers, often one male and one female, were allocated to a group of about 25 students who worked together, but each teacher had particular responsibility for half of the group. The TAs stayed with the same group of students for four years so that continuity would build trust within relationships for students, teachers and peers. The students met as a group for 20 minutes with their TA at the beginning of each day. While these 20 minutes were a more informal period within the school day, the TAs followed a curriculum aimed at teaching social and emotional competencies. Some explicit health topics (drug education, mental health, relationship education) were included in the curriculum. The TA also assisted students to plan their learning goals and their future learning pathways. The formal TA curriculum was followed two days per week, with one day for an assembly, and another two days for the TA groups to choose activities that were interesting or relevant for the specific group, such as sport, walking, or discussions.

The TA curriculum was structured along developmental and thematic lines that involved reflecting on social and learning contexts, and discussing implications of the contentious issues raised. The dialogic, problem-solving approach aimed to teach learner resilience in an explicit way, while at the same time develop problem-solving and reflection skills in everyday contexts. Maslow's (1954) hierarchy of needs informed the choice of themes for each year level. For example, topics for discussion for Year 7s related to safety needs: emotions and emotional management; positive participation in TA, class, school and community; working on strengths; and communicating feelings. Contentious topics such as bullying, drug education, and mental health issues were used to provoke discussion within the group. In a similar way, belonging, love needs, and relationships were explored with Year 8 students. Year 9 students investigated esteem needs, stress, and self-discipline, while the Year 10 curriculum extended esteem and self-understanding to include community, communication, and post-school options.

Sugarman and Sokol (2012) recommend critical reflection through problem-solving as an effective means to build personal awareness and agency. In a typical scenario, the students examined information about an issue, discussed a contentious scenario, analysed possible solutions, and evaluated the consequences of these choices. In effect, the students modelled and practised problem-solving with the support and critical awareness of peers and the teacher advisor. They also learned to respect the opinions of others, and understand the level of risk involved in expressing personal opinions, when those opinions had yet to be explored and validated.

LINKS WITH LEARNING

In our appraisal of the TA group so far, we have focused on the caring and advocacy attributes of teachers as they responded to the diverse needs of the students. However, Lowenstein (2009) claims that TA programs can be coherent and manageable if all the activities in the TA group are linked directly to learning. He argues against developmental or counselling approaches to claim that a more learning-centred paradigm will contextualise learning in the students' lives, and suggests that the TA should focus on making the skills for self-guided learning explicit. The TA curriculum at Ironbark has three priorities that include advocacy, problem-solving, and learning. With regard to the TA curriculum, and the explicit links with learning, the teacher advisor is expected to assist students' decision- making on learning goals, curriculum choices, learning pathways, study skills, subject selection, and career aspirations.

At strategic times through the year, students examined their own attitudes and practices in planning, engagement, and achievement in learning. The TA negotiated learning goals with each student in the areas of literacy, numeracy, and one other area as chosen by the student:

> Yes, they (TA) really do help us find our learning goals. They try. Some kids need a lot of help figuring out their goals. At the start of the year we spent two weeks doing learning goals [Jade, Year 9].

Literacy and numeracy goals were related to the student's performance levels and were often checked with the student's subject teacher. The optional learning goal may have been related to the student's interest or performance in another subject (for example, to attain level 6 in Arts or to pass technical design), a personal goal (for example, to complete all my homework, or to participate in the drama club), or a school goal (for example, to play in the girl's netball team and win the final). In the negotiation of learning goals, the TA encouraged each student to consider current performance, possible achievement, strategies for success, support networks, and future learning pathways. Questions such as: What do I want to achieve? How will I do that? and Who can help me? guided the discussions. Other planned learning skills' topics included study skills, planning for assignments and exams, identifying barriers to learning, homework, subject choices, and learning pathways. The dialogic, collaborative basis to the TA discussions helped students to become aware of their own learning progress and more responsible for the choices they made in learning. At the same time, the teachers gained a deep understanding of their students' perspectives on learning, their learning difficulties, and their personal ambitions.

EFFECTS ON TEACHERS AND STUDENTS

Our examination of the role of the TA, as it has been variously interpreted in this study, raises the contentious issue that supporting students in their social and emotional growth must be part of the defined responsibilities of the teacher. It seems unrealistic for schools to have responsibility for academic attainment alone. A focus on pedagogy related to a discipline area will not necessarily make extenuating demands on relationships between students and teachers. The advocacy, nurturing, reflective, and caring role to support students in their social and emotional growth while they progress through school does, however, demand a high level of relational agency. This study found that the teachers were able to assimilate the complex issues related to helping students to become more confident in their decision-making. The teachers needed a lot of strategic encouragement from the school, professional growth, and consistent networks of support from within the school community to develop that level of professional confidence.

Phillippo (2011) argues the organisational climate of the school can provide support for teachers to realise their own agency as they assist students to grow in self-awareness and confidence. We found that students developed a strong sense of safety and belonging at school, which they attributed to the relationships they had established through the TA program. Teachers at Ironbark also found it rewarding to be more aware of, and responsive to, student needs:

> It's a teacher/student relationship. It's not over familiar but you get to know them well. You talk to the parents on the phone, you talk to the kids a lot, you know what's going on in their lives. If there is something concerning them it comes out quickly and easily and gets dealt with too. It's a lot more caring and there's a lot more family feel to it. [Hilary, Experienced Teacher]

Students developed a mature sense of diversity and collegiality. The TA groups remained together for four years and TA teachers were timetabled to teach their students as often as possible. This resulted in peers acknowledging and appreciating their differences and a sense of mutual respect developed within the groups:

> Our class, I'll be honest, is one of the worst classes that's full of a few interesting characters. She (TA) kind of understands them which is a really good thing and we generally get along pretty well together. There are a couple of kids in the class who might muck about a bit but they are generally very well meaning and get along well with each other. (Student, Year 9).

Most students perceived the TA as a trustworthy person who could be relied upon, who knew them well, and who cared for them and helped them with their problems:

> The teacher [TA] we have is our go-to teacher so if we have any problems in the school yard or any classmate problems we can go and talk to them without going to our neighbourhood leaders or people we are not sure of. We know and we've known them for the whole time we've been here (Female student, Year 8).

> I personally have a pretty good relationship with her. I think she's a pretty good teacher. She interacts well with all the students and understands where they're coming from in most situations. (Male student, Year 8)

STUDENT PERSPECTIVES ON THE TEACHER ADVISOR PROGRAM

Overcoming status dimensions of power and control to establish meaningful relationships in schools is very difficult (Mitra, 2010; Keeffe and Andrews 2011). Traditional interpretations of the students' role depicts them as passive and powerless, with an inability to have opinions about the conduct of their learning or shared decision-making (Fielding, 2007). While these themes were explored in chapter 9, our intention here is to examine students' perspectives of the TA as they overcome the resistance of strategic, historic, illusory, personal, communication, or cultural barriers to develop meaningful relationships.

The purpose of the final stage of the Students as Researchers (SAR) program was to gather student opinion about the TA program, guide the students through an analysis of the data that they had gathered, and include their considered perspectives in our understanding of the roles and functions of the TA groups. Keeffe and Andrews (2009) argue that students prefer active involvement with research methods, as a means to overcome the barriers to participation in research in a school environment. Shohel (2012) concurs and claims the elicitation of photos can provoke an emotional response that leads to deep interpretations of the symbolic image and context. As the students had been instrumental in devising research questions, conducting focus groups, and analysing data, they were ready for the next challenge of the photo voice research method.

Students were asked to take photographic representations of the TA group: as they experienced it (purposes and outcomes), and as it could be experienced (possibilities and changes). The photos in this study were developed and then used as a thoughtful and active provocation for data analysis. Students explored the themes that emerged from the data by grouping the photos and adding their choice of other symbolic statements. They used the photo elicitation to discuss supportive and contentious aspects of the TA program, and provide insightful comments about their experiences within the TA environment.

To the SAR students the TA represents: safety (fire extinguisher), harmony (chairs in a circle), friendship, (goldfish swimming together in a bowl, Figure 10 b), growth (eagle soaring high, Figure 10a), creativity (art work), teamwork (tug of war), cooperation and sharing (glue stick, Figure 10c), positive change and improvement (shapes in a circle) and importantly, their voices being heard (loud speaker, Figure 10d). It does not mean crowding (topographic view of a city), constriction (barbed wire fence), threats to safety (holes in the fence), or a waste of time (rubbish bin).

Reiterating these perspectives, the SAR interviewees felt the relationships they had established with their teacher advisors, and other students in their teacher advisor group, contributed strongly to their feelings of wellbeing and safety at school. They liked having a teacher with whom they had a close personal relationship and felt that this teacher understood them so well that they knew how they were feeling. They enjoyed those aspects of the TA curriculum that seemed to be directly relevant to their lives, such as bullying (see Figure 10.2).

On the other hand, some structures and activities in the TA program were unpopular with the SARs (Figure 10.2). Some did not like "circle time", a time when students gather in a circle for discussion, as it made them feel "intimidated", while others disliked writing on worksheets and found the activities "boring". Some students wanted to be able to mix more with students from other learning communities and other year levels. Some younger students felt they did not know the older students in their own learning communities. Further, as they did not mix with students from

M. KEEFFE

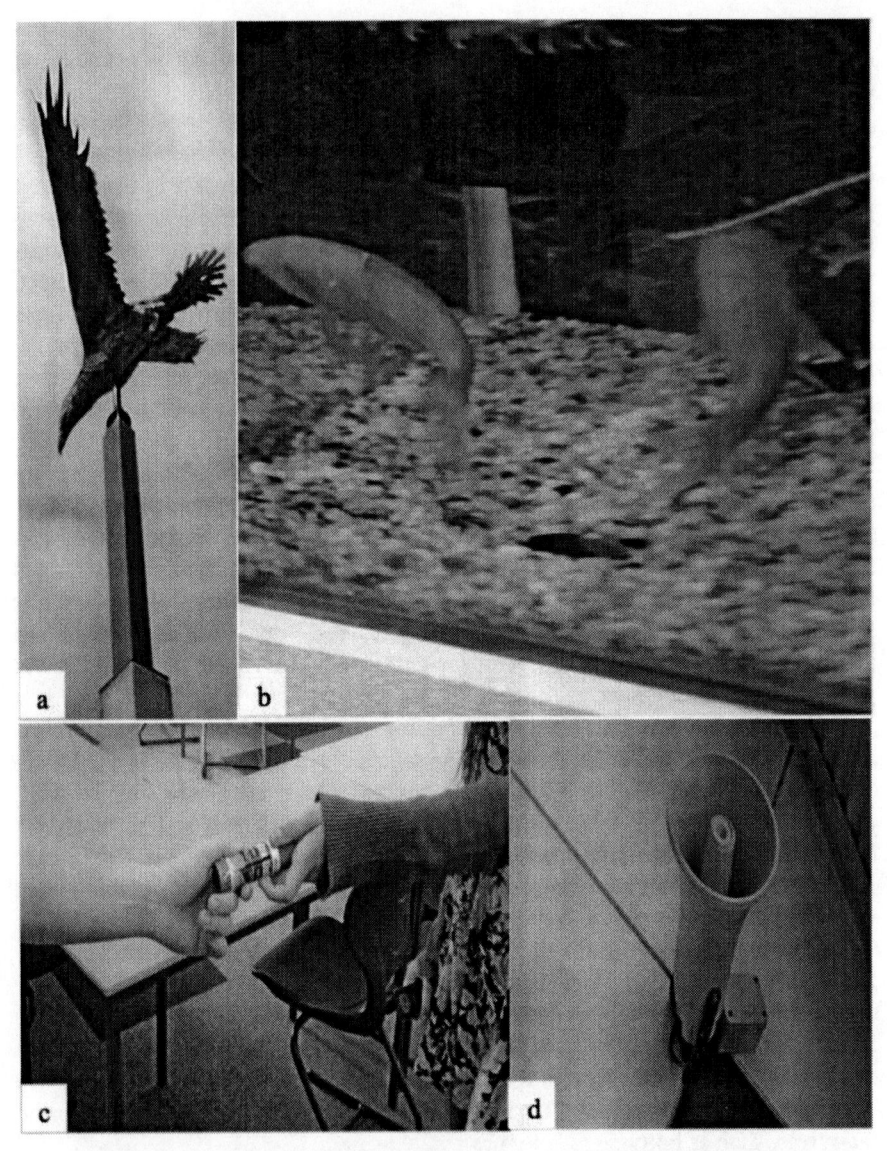

Figure 10.1 Student explanations of SAR photographs representing TA

(a) *"TA makes you grow and soar as a person, like the eagle soaring high."*
(b) *"The fish are friends like us in TA—they are happy swimming together."*
(c) *"The glue stick represents sharing and compromise. In TA we cooperate and problem-solve."*
(d) *"In TA we can speak out, our voice is heard, everyone gets their time to speak and be heard. We have time to share our views. It builds confidence which extends beyond school. TA teachers are our friends."*

Figure 10.2 Student whiteboard summary of TA positives and negatives

other learning communities they dreaded Year 9 when, due to increased subject choices, they would be mixing with different students.

Reflecting on these responses, and their own experiences, the SAR group suggested that TA activities should more closely match the interests of the students. A way to ensure this would be to ask the students to evaluate the TA curriculum and make topic suggestions. Further, in TA sessions, students should be engaged in more active learning to address the dislike of written worksheets. This would assist in distinguishing TA from regular subjects. Outdoor activities are very popular and students thought that they could be utilised more. It was felt that school camps were an excellent way of mixing students from different communities and should be encouraged, while joining of senior and junior TA groups would allow better community contact between seniors and juniors within learning communities, and encourage peer mentoring.

DISCUSSION

The TA program at Ironbark College progressed from the teachers' recognition that their student cohort faced many challenges, to the need for an explicit curriculum based on strong relationships between participants. Daily life difficulties were sometimes overwhelming for students to the extent that they would impinge on their motivation, resilience, and academic success. Teachers acknowledged the range of difficulties students experienced, but at first they were confident that they already possessed the appropriate skills to address changed relationships and to explicitly teach personalised learning skills. This study shows that such a level of confidence, based on former experience, was not justified. A traditional response to student needs was inadequate, and a recurring barrier to changed relationships and the development of the students' ability to make autonomous decisions about their life and learning contexts. A whole-school approach was required to change the culture of school responsiveness. This study shows that the TA program can be instrumental in developing a person-centred approach to students and their learning (Woods & Gronn, 2009). Inherent in the changes required for school responsiveness and cohesion from the TA group was building teacher capacity. A detailed program of TA learning activities within the curriculum helped build teacher confidence in addressing contentious issues, quickly leading to new ways of assisting students to improve their understanding of themselves and their learning.

Edwards, Lunt, and Stamou (2010), argue that collegial support, as a network of shared understandings and strategic actions, will facilitate professional growth. The paired teacher structure implemented at Ironbark provided an opportunity for peer mentoring and a shared responsibility for the wellbeing of students in their TA group. Together, the teachers were able to discuss the difficulties their students experienced and propose strategies to manage support. Broad examples of complementarity included: shared roles and responsibilities where one teacher would be parent contact while another provoked lively discussion in the groups; different personalities, so each could relate to students in different ways; and different gender, age and experience. However, the consistent feature of all TA groups was the commitment to build trust in an environment where all students could feel safe.

The teachers were able to build the quality of their professional, relational agency over time. The boundaries of experience identified by Edwards (2011) were extended by the demands of the TA program, but the structures provided by the school defined a level of professional growth that was expected and supported. The advocacy role of the TA also strategically aligned teachers with a level of care for a particular group of students. By advocating for the needs of their students, teachers were provided with a platform to know and understand the particular needs of each student, to collaborate with their colleagues to raise the awareness of particular students' needs, to propose different approaches to student learning, or to provide advice on contentious issues in students' lives. The efficacy of the collaborative effort improved as colleagues became partners in making informed decisions about student support.

Consistent with the Ontario experience, the teachers at Ironbark initially regarded the prescribed curriculum as a burden. They were concerned about discussing contentious topics with their students and they perceived that they lacked professional expertise in guiding social/emotional learning. Phillipo (2009) argues that the teacher advisor role is very complex and teachers are more likely to be successful in the role if the role statement and strategic supports within the school align. According to the students, teachers, and the school administration at Ironbark, a successful teacher advisor was one who made the students feel confident and resilient.

In time, the positive attributes of the teacher advisors included:

- confidence in their relationships with the students in their group;
- communication in constructive ways with parents or carers;
- an ability to share resources and ideas with their colleagues;
- advocacy for the needs of the students;
- a positive connection with youth culture and problem-solving;
- a sense of pride in encouraging students to excel in their interests and strengths;
- confidence in the provision of positive support for students to maintain a level of resilience when issues were challenging.

However, some teachers were unable to cope with the more intense experience of relational agency required from the program. While most teachers grew to meet the challenge of critical reflection in the TA role, one person in the study tried to maintain the traditional powers of authority and control. In this situation, mentoring from colleagues, modelling from the neighbourhood leaders and professional development from the administration were not helpful. His colleagues described his assertive mistakes:

> I think he runs it like a class. It's based on fear I think, he is abrupt or... always has to have that loud teacher voice. And you feel like saying just chill out. They're not going to eat you or be nasty to you. But it's really hard to talk to people about stuff like that. [TA, beginning teacher.]

Sugarman and Martin (2011) claim that personal agency is emergent, developmental, and reflective. To this extent, the design of the TA program created the opportunity for students to become critically aware of their abilities to make decisions about their own futures. The problem-solving nature of the learning activities in the TA program allowed for the discussion of diverse opinions and life views, where possibilities and options could also be proposed. The developmental nature of the design of the program was consistent with the increasing complexity of students' lives as they matured. The feedback from the SAR project indicated that some activities were irrelevant. This was an alert to staff that students wanted some say in the choice of activities. Since then, according to the coordinator of the teacher advisor program, students have been collating and co-presenting a selection of learning activities based on popular music, computer games and role play. These co-presentations have increased the level of enjoyment and active involvement for students and discussions are often more relevant, grounded and spontaneous.

IMPLICATIONS OF THE TEACHER ADVISOR PROGRAM
FOR PERSONALISED LEARNING

The skills of personalised learning need to be taught in an explicit and structured way. This process must begin with students understanding themselves better as learners. When students are informed of their own learner strengths, interests and abilities, and they are able to critically evaluate their own learning styles and habits, it is more likely that students will make informed decisions about their own learning choices and pathways. Problem-solving and critical reflection are skills that are valuable in learning and in life. By linking the two in a structured program schools are developing relational agency to promote student and staff wellbeing.

Students need a meaningful relationship with at least one person in the school setting. In this case, the TA should know the student well and be able to advocate for their learning and social needs. The TA is also the first contact with the school for the parents, thus forming a reliable network of support for students when they experience difficulties.

Students learn from their peers particularly when social and emotional contexts are in some way contentious. A TA program is able to provide structure and support to make this problem-solving process explicit and reflective.

A structure of support is required to build teacher capacity for the range of problem-solving contexts that are addressed in students' lives. Paired teacher advisors, a structured program and mentoring provide a collegial network of support for all teachers.

We have argued that relational agency can be theorised as both sociocultural (Edwards, 2011) and psycho-social (Sugarman and Martin, 2009), providing explanatory frameworks to understand the goals and means through which professional and social/emotional learning is fostered for participants in the TA program. In this way the TA groups at Ironbark provide a developmental and social context in which teacher and student participants practise their ability to interact, listen, empathise, express opinions, collectively problem-solve and become more confident in decision-making. This exploration of the TA programs shows that a whole-school approach is required to personalise learning, in order to raise the level of students' autonomy and self-awareness through critical reflection and decision-making in life and learning contexts.

CATHLEEN FARRELLY

11. STUDENT WELLBEING IN OPEN-PLAN UP-SCALED LEARNING COMMUNITIES INCLUDING GENDERED EFFECTS

WELLBEING AND SCHOOLING

In Australia, like most developed countries, educators are concerned about increasing adolescent mental health problems, self-harm, suicide, obesity, violence, poor levels of academic achievement, and associated low levels of social capital and community cohesion (Putnam, 1993). This is the case particularly among lower socio-economic status (SES) groups. Schools are perceived as ideal sites to implement wellbeing strategies as an educational aim (see O'Brien, 2008), as research has identified a significant link between positive student wellbeing and improved learning (Seligman, Ernst, Gilham, Reichvich, & Linkins, 2009; Fredrickson, 1998; Bolt, Goschke, & Kuhl, 2003; Fredrickson & Branigan, 2005; Rowe, Hirsch, Anderson, & Smith, 2007, Isen, Rosenzweig, & Young, 1991; Kuhl, 1983, 2000). This focus on schooling, while not denying the intractability of structural inequality (see Berliner, 2006), recognises the powerful role schools can play in creating safe, supportive relationships and learning spaces for young people.

In this chapter, we report on (a) the wellbeing issues that formed the context for renewal and reform in the Bendigo Education Plan (BEP) schools, (b) the recommendations of the BEP Steering Committee (2005) to improve student wellbeing, (c) some school-based attempts made over the past three years to address issues of wellbeing, and (d) the gendered outcomes arising from these changes. We also report on new insights into the factors that impact on students' wellbeing in open-plan settings. Quantitative data drawn from our multi-dimensional model of learning and wellbeing in open-plan settings and qualitative data from student and teacher interviews are used to explore attempts to improve wellbeing.

Characterising Student Wellbeing

Although 'wellbeing' is a commonly used term, there is little consensus about its meaning, with philosophical, economic, psychological, sociological, and medical perspectives adopted. Definitions of wellbeing variously include elements of happiness, life satisfaction, flourishing, a balanced or meaningful life, reaching one's true potential, freedom and choice, resilience, emotional literacy, engagement, a positive sense of self, and the active pursuit of physical, mental, emotional, and spiritual health (see Australian Catholic University (ACU) and Erebus International, 2008; Coleman, 2009). Wellbeing is culturally specific and impacted by individual capacity. It is therefore important to remember that measures of wellbeing may not be accurate across various populations, time, and contexts, and that aggregated measures of wellbeing can only be indicative of average or 'typical' cases.

Most wellbeing models focus on holistic adult or life span wellbeing rather than the wellbeing of young people within the context of secondary schooling (Huebner, 1997; McLaughlin, 2008; Palombi,, 1992). This study explores self-reported levels of wellbeing and investigates the relationship between other school environment factors and wellbeing within the open-plan settings of the BEP schools. Wellbeing is understood as being underpinned by social, emotional, and cognitive capacities, and there is a strong argument that improved wellbeing can improve academic success. Adolescent wellbeing is also impacted by gender (Bolognini, Plancherel, Bettschart, & Halfon, 1996; Bergman & Scott, 2001; Almquist, Östberg, Rostila Edling, & Rydgren, 2013; Løhre, Moksnes, & Lillefjell, 2013). This is an important issue given the increasing gender gap in academic outcomes. Females are outcompeting males in all subjects except mathematics. They are also graduating tertiary education at higher rates than their males in developed countries (Buchmann & DiPrete, 2006; OECD, 2009; Quenzel & Hurrelmann, 2013).

Drawing on Allardt's theory of welfare (1976, 1981, 1989), Konu and Rimpelä, (2002) take a sociological perspective of wellbeing, and position health and wellbeing as an entity within schooling. Allardt conceptualises wellbeing as a state in which it is possible for someone to satisfy his or her needs including material and non-material needs. Allardt divides these needs into three categories: 'having', 'being' and 'loving', identifying indicators for each of these categories. 'Having' refers to material and interpersonal needs, indicated by objective measures of the level of living and environmental conditions, and subjective feelings of satisfaction or dissatisfaction with living conditions. 'Being' denotes personal growth needs indicated by objective measures of people's relation to society and nature and subjective feelings of alienation or personal growth. 'Loving' refers to the need to relate to others and develop social identities, indicated by objective measures of relationships to other people and subjective feelings about social relations, happiness, or unhappiness.

Konu and Rimpelä's (2002) conceptual model is useful to our investigation of wellbeing in open-plan settings. It stimulates thinking about the complexity of the school environment, and the relationship between key factors of that environment and wellbeing. We are similarly interested in identifying the relationships among factors that indicate learning conditions in open-plan settings including: levels of perceived personalisation of learning and assessment, support from teachers, self-directed learning, personal relevance, shared control, and factors that indicate wellbeing within open-plan settings. We include in our model the following indicators of student wellbeing: peer relationships (loving), self-report of disruptive behaviour (being), individualisation in terms of the tailoring of learning tasks to individual students interests and abilities (having), and opportunities for personal and social development (having) (see chapter 2 for details of our model). Some of the factors explored in our model overlap with those in Konu and Rimpelä's model; however, there is considerable difference between the two, including the context in which our model was tested.

Student Wellbeing in Bendigo Education Plan Schools

As stated in chapter 4, three of the four BEP secondary colleges are identified as below the Victorian state average according to the Index of Community Socio-Educational Advantage[1] (ICSEA). While the ICSEA is developed using data on students' parental income, education, and employment levels, the impact of disadvantage can be identified in the education, health, and wellbeing statistics of Bendigo's adolescents themselves. In 2006, a year after the establishment of the BEP, 19.4% of school leavers were disengaged (that is not involved in either further education or employment) compared to the state average of 15.4%, the school retention rate for Years 7-12 was 73.4%, compared to the state average for all government schools of 78.8%, but significantly above the average of 68.5% for rural schools (Bendigo Loddon Primary Care Partnership (BLPCP) 2012, p. 104; DEECD 2011, p. 23).

The BLPCP Community Health and Wellbeing Profile reported that, in 2009, 50.6% of Bendigo students aged 10-17 reported having recently experienced bullying compared to state average of 44.6%, self-harm leading to hospitalisation at a rate of 0.9 per 1000 (an increase from 0.5 in 2005), compared to the state average of 0.6, and were more likely to be victims of crime (22 per 1000) than the state average for their age group (17 per 1000) (BLPCP, 2012, p. 14). Students in Years 7, 9, and 11 reported higher rates of psychological distress at 15.1% than the state average of 13%, while 56.1% reported having positive psychological wellbeing compared to the state average of 61% (DEECD, 2011). The rate of teenage births in the Bendigo region is higher than the state average at 19.7 per 1000 females aged between 15-19 years compared to the state average of 10.3 in 2005 (BLPCP, 2012, p. 99).

These statistics reveal significant and entrenched health and wellbeing problems within a context of poverty and disadvantage. However, that is only one side to the story. These young people are also often highly resilient, independent, intelligent, and creative, and have strong connections and networks within their communities. They are supported by creative, passionate, and caring parents, teachers and other community members, who work hard to meet the needs of these young people, challenging them to achieve at the highest levels and increasing their life chances (BEP Steering Committee, 2005). Their family's often vigorous desire for education parallels those who are better off (see Angus, 1993; BEP Steering Committee, 2005) contradicting simplistic homogenous discourses that mark the poor as deficient, while ignoring existing structural inequalities both within schools and in the wider community. The knowledge and skills of many teachers working in these settings is focused on respecting and accommodating student needs and differences, and refusing to underestimate their knowledge, experiences and capabilities. They do this within a complex context of standardising imperatives, accountability frameworks, and an expectation of doing more with less. Our survey data revealed students in the BEP schools have high levels of self-efficacy and self-control suggesting that students have a positive sense of their own ability to cope with school tasks. Self-efficacy and social competence were identified by Rutter (1990, p. 311) as "robust predictors of resilience".

In providing insight into Bendigo secondary students' perceptions of their connectedness and satisfaction with schools and teachers prior to the establishment of the BEP, a survey of 421 Year 10 students revealed that 25% of these students leave school without good memories (BEP Steering Committee, 2005). The results of this survey were consistent with data from the Attitudes to School Survey conducted in 2004 and 2005[2]. It was also found that the lower the achievement, the lower the level of satisfaction with school, and the more frequently students represented their school negatively. The majority of students in Year 10 reported positive relationships with their teachers, rating them highly for helpfulness and responsiveness, although this was dependent on how well the student was faring at their school. These students frequently reported criticism of their teachers' classroom management, discipline, lack of fairness and willingness to help with personal problems, and reported their pedagogy as unengaging. Successful academic students claimed higher levels of motivation than those with lower academic skills, but some data reported a perceived lack of challenge, and a lack of subject choice particularly for high achieving students at Year 10 level (BEP Steering Committee, 2005). They wanted breadth, choice, and good teaching in an 'adult environment'.

Our research aimed to understand student perceptions of these new open-plan settings and their impact on wellbeing. To this end, we surveyed approximately 2300 students across all year levels (7–10) in the four BEP schools each year from 2011 to 2013 using our Personalised Learning Experience Questionnaire (PLEQ) (see chapter 2 for details). The schools' annual Attitudes to School Survey data was also examined for the years 2009 to 2012, including two years prior to the students relocating to the new open-plan settings. We aimed to gain insight into the factors influencing wellbeing in these open-plan settings, and to understand how students and teachers perceive wellbeing in these settings. Our research also explored perceptions of student wellbeing through student and teacher interviews undertaken in all of the BEP schools.

TEACHERS' UNDERSTANDING OF STUDENT WELLBEING

Research has revealed teachers to be powerful agents in the lives of young people because they are often identified as the most frequently encountered non-family member who takes a personal interest in them. They are confidants and provide positive role models for personal identification (Howard, Dryden, & Johnson, 1999). Further, Howard et al. found that achievement in school is linked to environments where teachers teach for mastery, curricula is relevant to the needs of students, and assessment is authentic. Students contribute to the governance of their classrooms, where "rational, human and consistent" behaviour management approaches are used, where teachers are "warm, approachable, fair and supportive," and where a range of ways of being successful are offered to students (Howard et al., 1999, p. 318).

When nine teachers, including two principals, from all four BEP schools were asked how they defined student wellbeing, their answers revealed considerable insight into the complexity of the concept, and a strong sense of responsibility towards students' wellbeing. They were all aware that these students often had factors impacting negatively on them that neither they, nor their students, could control. Nevertheless, they had considerable confidence in the belief that school can contribute to students' wellbeing. Each one of these teachers conceptualised wellbeing in a holistic way including physical, social, emotional, and intellectual aspects. They saw the need for strong relationships between teachers and students, and between students, in a safe and supportive learning environment, as essential to wellbeing and improved learning outcomes. An assistant principal noted that:

> If a student is not tracking well personally, it has a huge impact on their learning, their concentration, their ability to feel confident in the class. ... Usually we will see that in behaviour as well.

These staff believed that relationships had to be fostered and nurtured by the staff to allow students to develop trust. This was sometimes difficult for students who were not well supported by their own parents, or who in some cases had experienced abuse.

RESULTS OF STUDENT SURVEYS

The data from the BEP schools' Attitudes to School Survey provide indicators for student wellbeing and student relationships on an annual basis. The indicators of student relationships in Tables 11.1 and 11.2 reflect students' perceptions of their connectedness to peers, classroom behaviour, and safety, while student wellbeing was rated on their own morale and distress at school. Table 11.1 includes students who began Year 7 in 2009 and completed Year 10 in 2012. Table 11.2 includes the results for students who began Year 7 in 2010 and completed Year 10 in 2013. Most of these students had experienced at least three of their four years in the new open-plan settings. Grevillea and Whirrakee were the last to complete their building program and, as a result, include a small cohort that did not relocate to the open-plan settings until mid-2011.

The values in these tables are the difference between the average cohort score and the state average. The arrows indicate where the differences were above (↑), below (↓) or within 0.1 (→) of the expected values based on state-wide data.

Table 11.1. Student relationships and wellbeing for student cohort commenced Year 7 in 2009 and completed Year 10 in 2012 in all BEP schools.

School	Year 7 in 2009 Student relationships	Wellbeing	Year 10 in 2012 Student relationships	Wellbeing
Whirrakee	0.06	−0.22	0.22↑	0.39↑
Ironbark	−0.29	−0.11	−0.15↑	−0.02→
Melaleuca	−0.20	0.02	−0.22→	−0.27↓
Grevillea	−0.24	−0.06	−0.31→	−0.34↓

Table 11.2. Student relationships and wellbeing for cohort who commenced Year 7 in 2010 and completed Year 10 in 2013 in all BEP schools.

School	Year 7 in 2010 Student relationships	Wellbeing	Year 10 in 2013 Student relationships	Wellbeing
Whirrakee	0.01	−0.29	0.15↑	0.40↑
Ironbark	−0.18	−0.29	−0.16→	−0.05↑
Melaleuca	−0.30	−0.36	−0.26→	−0.27→
Grevillea	−0.23	−0.24	−0.49↓	−0.74↓

Tables 11.1 and 11.2 indicate that for both cohorts, in each of the BEP schools, students' perceptions of student relationships all improved when compared to the state average, some noticeably. The only exception to this was Grevillea College for both cohorts. Students' ratings of their own wellbeing at school reveal improvement at two of the schools (Ironbark and Whirrakee) for both cohorts. In addition, the Year 7, 2010 cohort at Melaleuca maintained its ratings in relation to the state average. These results suggest that up-scaled open-plan learning communities do not contribute to decreased school wellbeing and connectedness, safety and positive behaviour. Ironbark College, a low SES school, specifically focused on ensuring student connectedness and wellbeing, providing significant opportunities for the development of relationships between students and between students and teachers (see chapter 10).

The results of our own Personalised Learning Experience Questionnaire (PLEQ) (2011-2103) suggest that there is a complex interplay of factors influencing school wellbeing and that changing only one or two factors will not necessarily provide a direct effect on wellbeing. Our multidimensional model detailed in chapter 2 revealed that learning environment (including teacher support) and self-efficacy were positively associated with wellbeing. There was no significant change in student

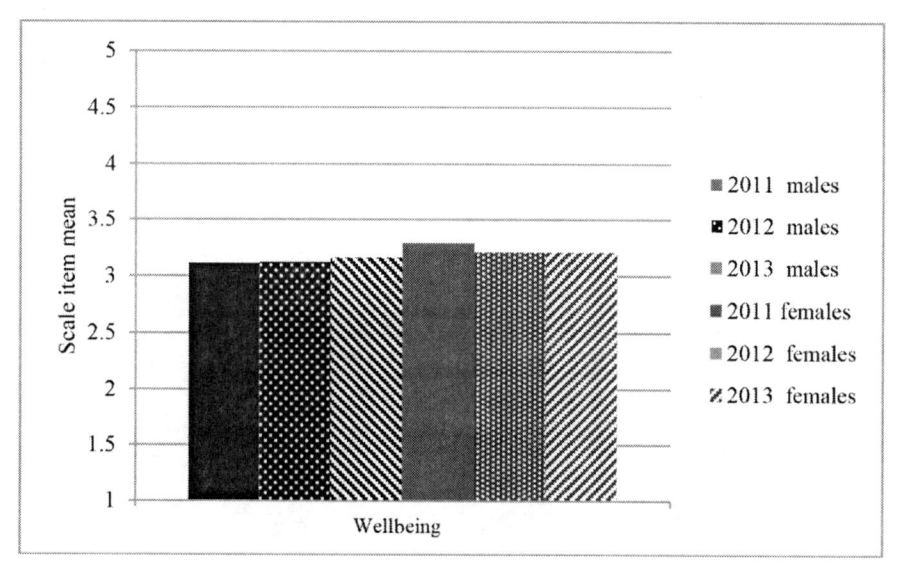

Figure 11.1. Aggregated wellbeing scales by gender and calendar year.

wellbeing in the BEP schools over the survey period, which is contrary to the results of the Attitudes to School Survey. This may be due to the different instruments used. The Attitudes to School Survey included a greater number of indicators of wellbeing and student relationships than the PLEQ. However, the results of the PLEQ survey revealed significant gender differences. Age-based differences were also found, with a decline in wellbeing from Year 7 to Year 8 followed by a gradual increase to approximate Year 7 scores by Year 10.

Scores (Figure 11.1) from aggregating the four wellbeing scales (i.e. peer relations, self-report of disruptive behaviour, individualisation, and opportunities for personal and social development) in the PLEQ revealed a slight improvement in wellbeing for male students and a slight decrease in wellbeing for female students from 2011 to 2013. However, the wellbeing scores were slightly higher across all the survey years for female students than those for the males.

When each of the wellbeing scales is examined (Figure 11.2), female students were found to have significantly ($p<0.01$) lower self-reporting of disruptive behaviour and higher levels of perceived opportunities for personal and social opportunities than males, while males reported significantly more positive levels of peer relations.

These results support the socialisation thesis of Quenzel and Hurrelmann (2013) regarding growing educational success of females and the decline of success in males. Quenzel and Hurrelmann argue that while peer relations are important for both adolescent males and females, males tend to have more friends and spend more of their free time with them than females spend with their friends. According to Quenzel and Hurrelmann, male peers "provide a compensatory function for social

C. FARRELLY

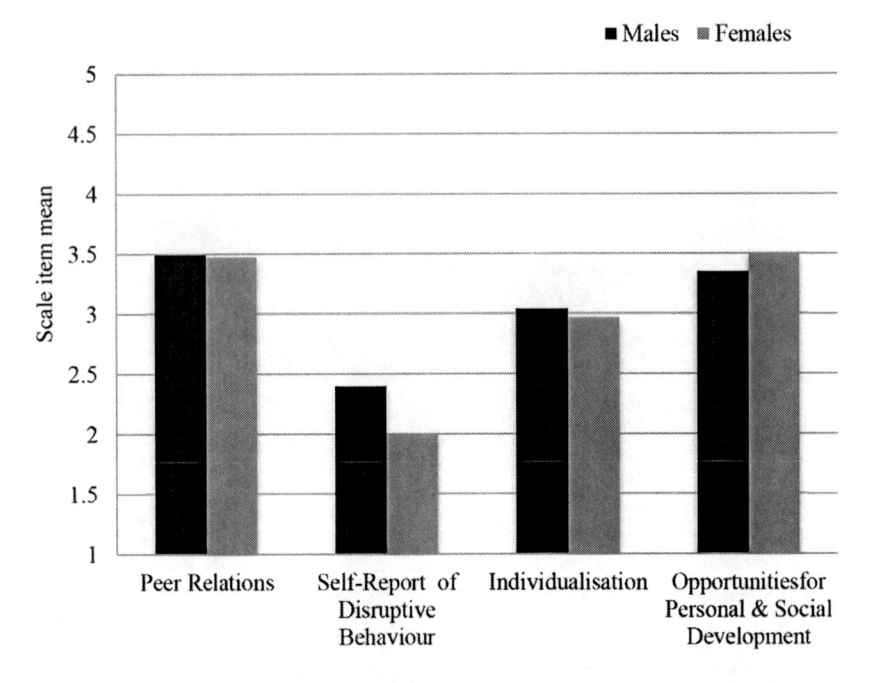

Figure 11.2. All wellbeing scales by gender for all schools, 2011–2013.

requirements and school performance expectations" which in turn leads to reduced academic motivation. In our interview data, one of the most common reasons given by both male and female students for their preference for open-plan learning spaces, was that they liked being able to easily interact and see their friends. This might have greater impact for males as it may allow them to interact more with their peers during class time and consequently contribute to reduced on-task behaviour. The significantly ($p<0.01$) higher self-reporting of disruptive behaviour, and lower levels of self-management and cognitive engagement by males, in this study of up-scaled, open-plan settings, resonates with Quenzel and Hurrelmann's explanatory theory that males are socialised away from academic success. Conversely, they argue that young women have significantly stronger values and skills that contribute to successful school performance (p. 78).

A recent study by Løhre, Moksnes, and Lillefjell (2014, p. 94), found that although there were no gender differences in self-rated school wellbeing, factors associated with student wellbeing revealed significant gender differences. Males who received academic support from teachers were two to three times more likely to report good school wellbeing whereas females' wellbeing was not impacted by levels of teacher support. For females, perceived loneliness at school was negatively associated with school wellbeing. The impact of these factors was apparent two years after they were first measured for both males and females (p. 94).

STUDENT WELLBEING

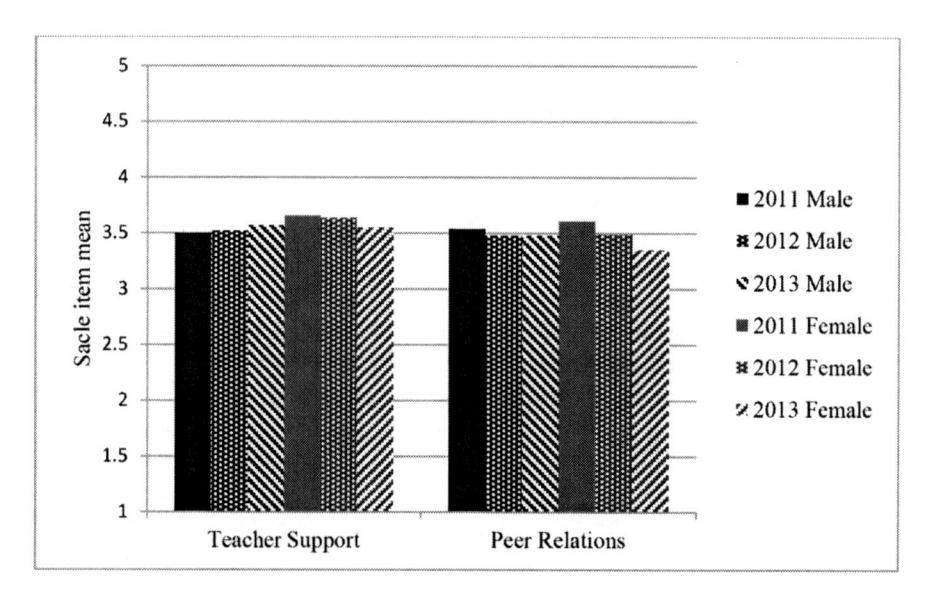

Figure 11.3. Teacher support and peer relations by gender and calendar year for all schools.

Although not significant, male students in our PLEQ study showed some improvement in their perceptions of levels of teacher support (one of the learning environment scales), whereas female students showed a slight decline in peer relations over the survey period (2011–2013) (see Figure 11.3). However, when examining the year by year scores, females had slightly higher scores for teacher support and peer relations in 2011 and 2012 but lower scores than males in both scales in 2013. These results suggest that the open-plan settings might be a factor impacting more on males' perceptions of some factors associated with wellbeing. Further research in these settings is needed to assess the veracity of this trend and its impact on wellbeing over time.

Legewie and DiPrete (2012) found that resistance to school by males was not only a function of their class background or their masculinity, but also the "local cultural environment of the school and classroom", and that males were more sensitive to human and cultural capital resources in schools (pp. 32–33). The results of our research indicate that the learning environments provided by open-plan settings can impact on factors relating to wellbeing, but further research is needed to examine their impact on academic outcomes.

We can only surmise the reasons for the trending decline in peer relations for female students; however, our interviews with teachers indicated that girls were more likely to be both subjects, and perpetrators, of cyber-bullying. The teachers indicated that the use of social media, and subsequent cyber-bullying, had increased during the research period as the use of personal devices increased. Teachers explained that they were devoting growing amounts of time to assisting students to deal with this issue. Some teachers thought that because social media enabled more school colleagues (friends or otherwise) to see bullying online, the victims of bullying may feel more "on display" in the open-plan learning spaces, subjecting them to even more humiliation. It was evident from the teacher interviews that male students had considerably less involvement with, and spent less time on, social media and cyber-bullying.

Another teacher was concerned that while the school had increased the options for more vocationally oriented subjects for students at Years 9 and 10, most were traditionally male oriented subjects including the trade subjects. She felt that fewer options were available for girls and suggested that this may have had an impact on students' perceptions of self-directed learning and the learning environment.

It is important to recognise that there is considerable variation in academic and wellbeing needs within the male and female cohorts. Our quantitative data discussed above suggests that improving student wellbeing is complex, and requires a multi-dimensional approach.

WHOLE-SCHOOL APPROACHES TO IMPROVE STUDENT WELLBEING

As a result of BEP recommendations to improve student wellbeing, a variety of school-based programs and interventions have been implemented across the schools. These include the structuring of student groups and learning spaces, the provision of specialised support services, curriculum development and new teaching approaches, and strategies to improve relationships. The case studies that follow describe examples of these measures.

The first case study outlines the development of a Student Support Centre at Whirrakee College that assisted primary school students to transition into a new open-plan secondary school. The aim was to ensure students felt comfortable and safe as they transitioned to secondary school. The second case study explores structural changes at Melaleuca College that aimed to improve student relationships, social and emotional skills, and learning success. The final case study provides an overview of a whole-school multi-dimensional approach to improving wellbeing undertaken at Ironbark College.

CASE STUDY 1: WHIRRAKEE COLLEGE

The Student Support Centre (SSC) at Whirrakee College was established as an "umbrella" to provide whole-school programs to develop personal skills, and to provide support to all students in the school. The SSC staff consists of two social workers (equivalent to a half-time position for each learning community of 300 students), a part-time school nurse, a school chaplain and a part-time disability worker. The SSC is situated in a dedicated area within the confines of one of the school's learning communities. The SSC focuses on all students and provides prevention and intervention programs. The centre provides particular support for students with learning difficulties, students transitioning into the school, particularly those from smaller primary schools, students with mental health problems, and students who are disengaged from school or 'school refusers'. In order for the centre to become a positive space for all students, and to reduce the stigma often associated with 'student welfare', staff within the centre are strongly linked into the learning communities. For example, the social workers undertake a range of roles not typically associated with student welfare, including participation in Year 10 camps and organising student work experience. The school nurse and other centre staff run wellbeing programs that focus on issues raised by the students themselves. The school attendance officer is also located in the same space. By the time the students have spent four years at the school they will have all attended the centre for a variety of reasons. The team leader noted that students now just pop in saying "I just want to chat about my friend", whereas initially they may have worried that other students might see them entering the centre.

In conjunction with the teacher advisor program (see chapter 10 for details), which assists students to develop relationships with teachers and peers, an extensive transition program was developed to assist students in their progression from smaller primary schools into the college. Transition to secondary school is a big step for most Year 6 students, and most students moving to Whirrakee College come from smaller schools that have limited or no experience of open-plan learning settings. Often both students and parents are anxious about how they or their child, will cope, and a significant number of these students already have patterns of school refusal and low levels of self-efficacy. An online 'dashboard' (see chapter 4 for details) can be accessed by parents and teachers at any time. The dashboard, which provides all student work requirements, results, class attendance, and behaviour monitoring, is central to school processes and can be overwhelming for both students and their parents. A 10–15 day transition program begins in the May of the year before transition. The SSC team ensures background information is gained from the students' previous schools to identify their specific social, emotional and educational needs. The transition program enables students to become familiar with the physical environment of the school, begin to build relationships with their future learning-team mentors, and to make new friends.

Students identified, through educational and psychometric testing, as having specific learning needs, are provided with individual support and educational plans. These plans are included on the dashboard. Students with Autism Spectrum Disorder (ASD) are often stressed by noise or visual stimulation which can be problematic in an open-plan learning community. Teachers are given instructions on how to identify and reduce such stressors through information shared on students' individual learning plans. Strategies might include allowing students to use headphones to work independently, to move to a breakout room, away from larger groups of students, or to take a short walk when their levels of anxiety rise.

The SSC staff acknowledged that a number of their students suffered from abuse, family separation, trauma, mental health problems, and parental mental health problems, and that the wellbeing of these students is a priority. The student wellbeing coordinator explained that she says the following to students, especially to students suffering a mental illness:

> Our first priority is not to get you into the classroom and make sure all those learning assessments are being ticked off. We need you here healthy, happy and feeling safe. When that happens, the learning will come from it.

There is a tension here between the school's academic expectations for students indicated by the dashboard, and the need to individualise the measures of success for students. One staff member noted that schools are increasingly data-driven and sometimes overlook the reasons for students' successes or otherwise. She said that while the dashboard reported on what students had done, or had not done, and student absenteeism, it did not recognise the significant achievements made by many students.

> They might be a carer for someone at home or they've had an illness themselves, so there's many things they can look at on their dashboard that don't show that they're having success. For a student [who is a carer] turning up five days a week should be praised for that and [that should be] congratulated as a success. And their parents should be as well for getting them here. I think it is important for us and for teachers to understand that the students that they're working with, data aside, are going to experience success in different ways. (Female teacher)

A significant advantage of the dashboard, however, is that it enables staff to meet individual student needs, where a large student population would normally limit staff capacity to do this. The access to specific student information allows all staff, including casual relief teachers, to respond to students in ways that most suited their needs.

CASE STUDY 2: MELALEUCA COLLEGE

This case study focuses on the structural changes at Melaleuca College over four years as it attempted to create learning communities that were more conducive to improved wellbeing for teachers and students. All BEP colleges structured their learning spaces differently (see chapter 4). Some learning spaces included a range of year levels, while others had only one or two year levels.

Melaleuca College began with a combined Years 7 and 8 in two learning communities, and Years 9 and 10 each in a separate learning community. After two years of this arrangement, and in response to timetabling, and other problems, the Years 7 and 8 were also separated. Along with these separate spaces, areas of the school playground were allocated to younger students, and others to the Year 9 and 10 students. Teachers reported that this not only segregated the students from one another but also the teachers. Teachers in the Year 7 and 8 learning communities expressed considerable concern about behavioural issues and learning engagement.

At the end of 2013 the learning communities were restructured to include all year levels from 7 to 10 in each of the neighbourhoods within each learning community. This resulted in reduced student movement between buildings for core subjects. A buddy system was developed whereby a Year 10 student was linked with a new Year 7 student. This was identified as significantly improving the transition of these students into the Melaleuca College. In addition, one learning community leader opened the learning community from 8am because students often wanted to talk to her when there were fewer students around.

At the time of writing, teachers reported dramatic improvement in the atmosphere of these learning communities after only one term (10 weeks). One Year 8 teacher reported significantly reduced levels of misbehaviour and an improved learning environment assisted by reduced student numbers. The playground segregation was removed and teachers believe that the level of conflict in the playground has declined. The segregation in the school playground was also removed which, according to one teacher, seems to have reduced the bullying problems.

CASE STUDY 3: IRONBARK COLLEGE

The final case study is examined through the lens of the World Health Organisation (WHO) Health Promoting Schools Framework (HPS) (WHO, 1996). The HPS framework is based on worldwide research that suggests that successful promotion of health and wellbeing can be achieved through three interrelated areas in schools: (1) organisation, ethos, and environment; (2) curriculum, teaching, and learning; and (3) partnerships and services.

School Organisation, Ethos, and Environment

Students generally welcomed the newly built open-plan learning spaces. Most students we interviewed felt happy and safe within the spaces and enjoyed the design and sense of freedom, although they noted noise levels were sometimes problematic (see also chapter 9). This sense of safety was also apparent in data from the Attitudes to School Survey. Students commented that the teachers spoke more quietly and tended to raise their voices far less than they had in the traditional classrooms, something that the students agreed created a much better social environment.

As noted in chapter 4, the organisation of the school into Years 7-10 learning communities had a positive effect on student wellbeing. This sense of belonging and connectedness to a community afforded students more consistency in their relationships because they stayed in the same learning community with the same teachers for four years. Both staff and students acknowledged this.

> I think it's really good because you can connect and bond with the same people throughout your whole school life. It's good that we have the same teacher so you get more confident to talk to them about anything that's happening in school and with other classmates as well. (Year 8 girl)

> I think the greatest change has been how the spaces have provided that opportunity for those relationships to really grow and expand. Everything is transparent. The kids see teachers teaching, other than just their own teacher. They get to know teachers outside of their own class. (Assistant principal)

Some students also identified the value of having older students and even siblings in the same learning community.

> Its good having older kids in there as well to try and help you out, its good having older kids and younger kids, its good having a bit of a range…my brother was in the same community as me [when I came in Year 7] so he was in the class next door which was completely open so he could help me. It was good. (Year 10 girl)

A wellbeing team, consisting of social workers, a chaplain, a psychologist, a nurse, an indigenous worker, an attendance officer, and an intellectual disabilities coordinator, provides support for staff and students. The referral system was reviewed and redeveloped to ensure that all students who wanted to access the wellbeing team were able to do so, and that when necessary, the wellbeing team was able to refer students to the best external services available. Both the TA and students can approach members of the wellbeing team for support. Where possible, the wellbeing team works with the families of students and this assists in developing a closer relationship with the school. In answer to a question regarding where the line is drawn between the responsibilities of the school and others, the school chaplain stated that there was:

> No line [between school and home]. We deal with or work [with] the families. Myself, and I know other wellbeing team members, make a lot of home visits. Usually, or if not always, we speak to the parents in relation to what's happening at school with the students. If their behaviour is really questionable then usually the TAs have rung them, and often it will be a referral to the chaplain or wellbeing team to follow up, and then we keep in touch with parents.

Policies and procedures were redeveloped to support the new structures and a positive school culture. A staged response to poor student behaviour was introduced whereby classroom teachers take initial responsibility for dealing with the problems and the assistant principal or principal is the last step, usually in extreme situations. This provides for greater shared responsibility for students. School uniform policies were couched in ways that considered what might be going on for the child who is failing to wear the correct uniform. Such policies support the ethos of the school, which is focused on positive and respectful relationships, and contribute to the promotion student and staff wellbeing.

Procedures for student management are perceived to be extremely important in developing a school culture of consistency and security. Explicit teaching about core values related to community, opportunities, relationships, expectations, and achievements, and constant reference to them when talking with students, enhanced the shared culture. One teacher suggested that, although the learning communities tended to function like four mini-schools due to variation in how teachers were implementing the procedures, there was enough consistency to ensure that all students and staff were aware of the expectations for learning and behaviour. Staff members knew what to expect from week to week and this allayed past fears about managing student behaviours. This sense of consistency is important for students' sense of security and fairness.

Clearly the development of this positive social environment within the learning communities required new ways of being a teacher. Much of the change, one teacher claimed, required "learning how to communicate with the kids" (Male teacher). These skills were taught to teachers who rehearsed and practised them in a context of growing relational agency. While teachers recognised the need for co-responsibility for the wellbeing and learning of all students, they also recognised their own strengths and weaknesses in relation to this. Discussion around the importance of the school values for teachers and students allowed teachers to reflect on their development needs and to draw on their colleagues' knowledge and skills. Community leaders and teacher advisors would often model communication strategies, or the implementation of TA learning activities, for their colleagues and then discuss these experiences.

Student referrals to the wellbeing team were discussed at executive level and included the child psychologist, assistant principal, wellbeing coordinator, and attendance officer. They identified the best course of action, agency or service for the referred student. The learning-team members learnt from each other and this led to new ways to understanding and responding to student needs. One staff member who had been involved in student wellbeing for many years noted that referrals to the wellbeing team had decreased over the past few years. He put this down to improved relationships, communication, and shared responsibility for students.

Physical Environment

While the class structures within the open-plan settings were designed to improve relationships and the overall culture of the school, the physical environment, including the design of the open-plan learning spaces, also contributed to students' wellbeing. The changes to the school's built environment were, and continue to be, welcomed by the students. A lack of graffiti and damage to the learning spaces is further testament to student appreciation. All the teachers interviewed commented on the significant decline in student misbehaviour in these new spaces.

The protocols for the use of inside spaces are perceived as contributing to a sense in students that their school cares about them. Initially, as per tradition in most schools, the students were not allowed inside the learning communities at all during their lunch period. One learning community leader suggested that given that the school communities include both students and staff, students should be allowed inside these spaces during lunchtimes, and on particularly cold days during recess periods. While this teacher's learning community agreed to this change, there was some opposition to the idea from staff in other learning communities. Further work with staff, a trial, and finally an agreement, led to the protocol that students can be inside for three days a week, unless it is inclement weather. In interviews, students often referred to inside spaces as their favourites, including the library and the couches in the Einstein areas (see chapter 9). Staff reported that another significant outcome of this arrangement was a decrease in problems in the school grounds during lunch and recess.

The physical environment outside the learning communities is considerable in size. Areas between the buildings are landscaped as passive recreation areas and spaces further from the buildings provide opportunities for major games such as netball, basketball, cricket, and football. Students from both Year 7 and Year 10 highlighted the lack of playing equipment (see also chapter 9). Playground equipment has been identified as inducing physical activity thereby contributing to the physical and social health of students (Ramstetter, Murray, & Garner, 2010; Parrish, Okely, Stanley, & Ridgers 2013). Acknowledging this, one assistant principal said:

> It might have been the end of last year, we painted a whole lot of down-ball squares [on the ground] and the kids we had playing down ball…it's very popular. It begs the question why do kids come out of primary school and suddenly they go from having all this play equipment to nothing?

A male leading teacher recalled being on edge when he was on yard duty in this first year of teaching at the school:

> Maybe it was because I was a first-year teacher, but I was always looking for trouble, … looking for smokers or kids doing the wrong thing, whereas now, my yard duty consists of playing down-ball with the kids or wandering around and having chats with little groups of kids who are basically sitting around having their lunch and talking. So it's a really good feeling.

The Ironbark College case study highlights one school's attempt to improve wellbeing through a whole-school approach. In response to these changes, our survey analyses revealed a significant increase in perceptions of teacher support and peer relations for males in the new open-plan settings. However, there was a slight decrease in perceptions of teacher support and peer relations for females. These outcomes suggest that males are perhaps more responsive to changed school environments than females and that it cannot be assumed that all changes will affect all students in the same way.

Curriculum, Learning, and Teaching

The TA program (detailed further in chapter 10) in this school was focused on social and emotional learning and the development of close, positive and supportive relationships between teachers and students, and between students. Students in this school reported high levels of satisfaction with their TAs and almost always identified them as a key support person to whom they took their problems and concerns. These positive and caring relationships set the tone for the culture of care across the whole school.

Ironbark College provides Physical, Health and Sport Education (PHASE) as a compulsory subject for Year 7 and 8 students and elective health and physical education subjects for Years 9 and 10. Students at all levels are required to participate in sports with the opportunity for students to experience a variety of sports. Students are also encouraged to participate in community sporting clubs. The teachers perceived sport and physical education as contributing to social, teamwork and leadership skills, as well as physical health. PHASE also includes the range of topics found in most health education programs including anatomy, fitness, body image, mental health, drugs and alcohol, and sexuality education. The interview data indicated that there was considerable overlap between the TA and the PHASE curriculum, although this did not seem to be orchestrated. There may be opportunities to strengthen the links between these two areas in order to provide improve sequencing and time allocation to discrete topics.

Partnerships with Parents and Other Services

Ironbark College employs a student engagement worker, who is a teacher skilled in counselling 'at risk' students, to reconnect these students with the school. This role resulted from a teacher identifying students who were spending their days on the local streets. The student engagement worker's role was to work one-on-one with these students to provide the motivation and skills to return to school and to work in partnership with parents where possible. This often involved phone conversations before school, or actually going to a student's home to coax him/her out of bed. This was enabled only after the engagement worker developed a trusting relationship with the parents, and often resulted in parents gaining the confidence to assert themselves with their adolescent. It also meant preparing students for their first step back into the school ground, practising scripts on what to say to groups of students, and even to teachers who demanded to know where they had been.

The role also involved working with teachers to ensure that they were willing to take students back and were prepared for their return. Welcoming these difficult students, whom the teachers had been relieved to see drop out of school, wasn't always easy. Perhaps the biggest challenge for the student engagement worker were to create a teacher culture that valued students' rights to return to school, that valued these students' right to be respected in the same way as more motivated students, and that understood the difficulties that these students were experiencing beyond school.

A number of disengaged students were in Out-of-Home-Care, which meant they lived away from their parents, usually with foster parents or in residential care homes. Some had been involved with the justice system. The wellbeing team at Ironbark maintained strong relationships with relevant service agencies in order to ensure suitable and relevant education plans were put in place for these students. The sphere of influence of school staff in this context clearly extends beyond their traditional roles and beyond the school boundaries.

Development of relational agency (Edwards 2005, 2007, 2011; Prain et al., 2013) among teachers, principals, the student engagement worker, and those from outside services is necessary if student wellbeing is to be maximised. There are significant cultural differences between professionals in support services beyond the school, and teachers within the school. According to the student engagement worker, it took a number of years to develop relationships to the point where the teachers and social service professionals were using the same language.

The commitment of the school leadership team to this program was exemplified by their willingness to create the student engagement role without any extra funding. According to the student engagement worker, the development of policy and procedures for student management mentioned above included a focus on ensuring that "no one [was] getting lost or forgotten".

CONCLUSION

The story of the BEP schools' approaches to improving wellbeing over a three-year period reveals the need for a commitment by the school leadership team and all staff members to a whole-school approach. This means prioritising wellbeing and its costs in school planning, ensuring staff members develop a broadened understanding of their teaching role, and up-skilling teachers in communication and relationship building skills. Relational agency is developed through shared responsibility for student wellbeing, which requires teachers to take risks, share and reflect on their experiences while learning from one another, including non-teaching colleagues. An expanded sphere of influence for school staff through the development of stronger relationships with students, parents, and community support services beyond the school boundaries, is also an outcome of a focus on student wellbeing.

Open-plan settings in up-scaled learning communities can stimulate a rethink of the physical and social organisation and overall ethos of schools. While open-plan settings offer increased flexibility for team teaching and personalised curriculum, they also require high levels of structuring and organisation to ensure students remain connected, and have a sense of belonging, to the school.

The curriculum, learning, and teaching in any school can support or detract from student wellbeing. The content of health and physical education and teacher advisory curricular must ensure the explicit teaching of physical, social, emotional, problem-solving skills, and general health and wellbeing knowledge. The explicit teaching and reinforcement of shared values through these programs, along with a culture of high academic expectations, can contribute to a positive school climate and improved educational outcomes for students.

The case studies above illustrate examples of programs and interventions that can contribute to a whole-school approach to the promotion of wellbeing. These include: the provision of dedicated wellbeing services and the development of stronger partnerships between parents, teachers, and community services such as Whirrakee's SSC, Ironbark's wellbeing team and student engagement worker; the creation of a positive and caring ethos as implemented at Ironbark though the explicit teaching of school values; the development of school policies sensitive to the students' wellbeing needs, and a TA curriculum focussing on social and emotional skills; and the physical design and organisation of learning spaces, exemplified by Melaleuca's experiments with learning community groupings, which allow students freedom to utilise spaces most conducive to their learning needs, as apparent in all BEP schools.

Our study provides new knowledge in relation to student wellbeing in open-plan settings. We have found that males perceive significantly higher levels of peer relations and teacher support than do females, albeit with significantly higher levels of self-reported disruptive behaviour. These results suggest that while males may be more sensitive to changed learning environments, these spaces may also offer greater potential for improving male student wellbeing. However, the results of our surveys also revealed evidence of a slight decline in perceived levels of teacher support and peer relations for females. These findings suggest that changed learning environments may affect male and female students in different ways. Further research is required to establish the levels of consistency in the changes across learning communities, and to identify the impact of various learning environment factors on male and female perceptions of their school wellbeing.

Our research reinforces the complexity and multi-dimensional nature of student wellbeing. It is therefore difficult to isolate and recommend changes that will guarantee improved student wellbeing, and it is likely that only whole-school approaches will be successful. A whole-school approach requires continual review of the school organisation, ethos, physical and social environments, the curriculum, and learning and teaching strategies, and partnerships with parents and other relevant services. Our research indicates that schools can have an impact on teacher-student and student-student relationships, as well as student perceived comfort and safety in open-plan settings through curriculum and organisational interventions where there is a collective responsibility for student outcomes.

SECTION FOUR

CONCLUSION AND IMPLICATIONS FOR LEARNING IN LIKE SETTINGS

VAUGHAN PRAIN, PETER COX, CRAIG DEED, DEBRA EDWARDS,
CATHLEEN FARRELLY, MARY KEEFFE, VALERIE LOVEJOY, LUCY
MOW, PETER SELLINGS, BRUCE WALDRIP & ZALI YAGER

12. NEW PRACTICES, NEW KNOWLEDGE AND FUTURE IMPLICATIONS FOR LEARNING IN OPEN-PLAN SETTINGS FOR LOW SES STUDENTS

In this book we have identified many BEP implementation effects, some expected and others less predictable. We also recognise that many effects and outcomes have arisen from altered conditions since the development of the BEP's original goals nine years ago. In summarising these findings we are particularly interested in focusing again on new knowledge about the relationship between up-scaled learning communities and learning and wellbeing for predominantly low SES students. In this chapter we review our major findings, addressing each of the research questions posed in chapter 1.

1. What are the individual and combined effects of the proposed strategies on students' academic efficacy, performance, and wellbeing?
2. What are the effects of these strategies on teachers' and students' practices and beliefs about effective learning?
3. What do teachers and students perceive as enablers and challenges in this educational initiative?
4. What are the theoretical and practical implications of this study for a systemic approach to addressing effective schooling for similarly disadvantaged students?

STUDENT ACADEMIC EFFICACY, PERFORMANCE AND WELLBEING

As noted in chapter 1, the major strategies of the BEP focused on: rebuilding four schools using contemporary design principles; curricular reform leading to a more explicit; differentiated curriculum that replaced a traditional age-based curriculum with a stage-based one founded on the state-mandated curriculum; and the development of teacher professional knowledge to enable effective teaching, learning and student wellbeing in these new settings. These strategies were intended to achieve: substantial improvement in student attendance and retention from Years 7–12; significant increase in the range of subjects available to students in Years 9–10; greater challenge for all students, particularly high-achieving students; improved student engagement and interest in subjects, particularly for average and

V. Prain et al. (Eds.), Adapting to Teaching and Learning in Open-Plan Schools, 195–204.
© 2014 Sense Publishers. All rights reserved.

low achieving students, and those from lower socio-economic backgrounds; and improved teaching methods, classroom management, and wellbeing of students.

Our study indicates that the proposed strategies were not all equally pursued for a range of reasons, thus affecting possible findings. For example, the capacity of BEP schools to provide a wide range of student subject and course pathways for Years 9 and 10 students was compromised by restricted staffing profiles in each school. There was also considerable staff turnover in the first years of occupancy of the new buildings, affecting continuity of teacher professional learning and collective expertise.

However, as noted in chapter 2, quantitative data in national testing of reading and numeracy in similar schools (2011-2013) indicate positive trends for student academic performance in these four low SES Bendigo schools. While these schools are not reaching the average expected national performance in these subjects, the results are a positive indicator of significant gains against comparable low SES schools nationwide, and indicate positive outcomes for the approaches to curriculum renewal in these schools. Our survey's emergent model for assessing wellbeing over the three years of the study (See chapters 2 and 11), while not showing significant gains across these years, highlights that no single factor dominates student perceptions of this aspect of schooling, and points to the multi-dimensional complexity in influencing students' perceptions in this area. Our study found that the new settings affected male and female student perceptions of wellbeing differently. A pattern of slight gain in male wellbeing over the three years of the PLEQ was linked to perceived levels of peer relations and teacher support. By contrast, females' perceptions of wellbeing declined marginally over the same time, but remained higher than the males' perceptions (see chapter 11). This suggests the need for further research on factors influencing this pattern as a basis for reviewing and changing practices to enhance the wellbeing of both genders.

As noted in chapter 2, the instrument for measuring the complexity of influences on wellbeing represents methodological comprehensiveness not evident in any past models of constituent components of school-based perceptions of student wellbeing. Analyses of students' perceptions enabled researchers and teachers to track student perceptions of major contributing elements to personalised, quality learning, and to target, track and evaluate possible pedagogical interventions to one or more scales to alter these perceptions. Discussion with participant teachers and students also enabled a shared language to be developed about how to interpret these findings and enhance learning processes for both groups.

EFFECTS ON TEACHERS' AND STUDENTS' BELIEFS AND PRACTICES

The story of the effects on teachers' and students' beliefs and practices from extended experience in the BEP schools is also multi-dimensional. As noted in chapters 3 to 8, the effects on principals' and teachers' beliefs and practices were transformational in that these settings necessitated change to curricular enactment. This is evident in the practical reasoning of principals and school leaders around decisions and revisions to curriculum organisation in and across learning communities (chapter 4), the evolution of teaching teams to optimise differentiated learning possibilities (chapters 3 and 7), the willingness of teachers to give students more autonomy about learning processes and outcomes (chapters 5, 6 and 9), and the range of local initiatives around curriculum renewal (chapter 7). Not all teachers welcomed these changes, and some left these schools, but many embraced the opportunities for collegial in situ support in building and enacting a robust stage-based curriculum. Some have taken up opportunities to offer students more say in what, and how, they learn (see chapters 5, 6 and 9). Our study indicates the necessity of teachers developing a new set of skills to be effective contributors to these learning communities (see Alterator & Deed, 2013). Over and above generic expectations of teachers having current disciplinary knowledge about appropriate content and effective pedagogical skills for catering for all learners, teachers in these settings have to be genuine team players who can collaborate at micro and macro levels of curricular enactment. They need to understand and enact the collective goals of their learning community and school, and are expected to have significant influence on the academic progress and wellbeing of their students.

Our study points to both the scale of the challenge and what may count as signs of success. These signs include teacher willingness to be active, adaptive learning community members who contribute to ongoing innovations in how learning and wellbeing are understood, enacted, assessed, communicated, and celebrated. We noted that in adapting to these new open-plan settings the principals and teachers experimented with different temporal and spatial structures. However, a common theme of this experimentation was the recognised need for structured activity and clear protocols to provide a predictable framework for guided learning, especially in the initial phase of adapting to these new settings. It is clear that more flexible organisation (orchestrated spontaneity) is only possible when staff members and students understand complementary roles and responsibilities in these learning communities (see chapter 5).

Our study also shows that these up-scaled learning communities require a new set of skills from pre-service teachers. These teachers needed preparatory experiences that framed and focused how they could participate in the culture, narrative, and community of practice of these settings. This was both a collective and a personalised experience, as pre-service teachers constructed personal teacher knowledge, and enacted and validated agency and practical reasoning. More broadly, teacher-mentors, teacher educators, and pre-service teachers needed to develop new knowledge and skills in: teaching and learning in open-plan learning environments; team teaching; curriculum differentiation; personalised learning; and effective use of ICT. In their inquiry project, the pre-service teachers needed to expand their understanding of workplace learning, calling on expertise within and beyond both school and university experiences. They needed to project themselves as adaptive experts, simultaneously building expertise in teaching knowledge and skills that can be applied across a variety of teaching and learning contexts, as did their mentors (see chapter 8).

Our research on student beliefs about (and practices in) these settings offers a broadly complementary account of positive adaptation to these new settings (see chapters 9 to 11). As noted in student responses to our PLEQ and in interview comments, students reported positive accounts of their own capacities as learners, and enjoyed access to a wider range of teachers and students in these settings than those usually available in traditional classes (see chapters 9 and 10). The persistent less favourable student responses to the scale in the PLEQ about opportunities for shared control with teachers highlight agency challenges for both students and teachers. As noted in chapter 3, creating the conditions for shared control, particularly with low SES students, entails considerable staff confidence and competence in enacting a robust, stage-based curriculum that can support this negotiation of goals and approaches. We have reported on some successes in this area (see chapters 3, 5, 7 and 9), but recognise that this aspect of a quality learning environment requires significant professional learning for teachers, and a developmental trajectory for students, in understanding and enacting their role and responsibilities in their own learning. Our study reports on initial adaptation to the new settings, but there is evidence of teacher uptake of opportunities to negotiate curricular requirements to meet student needs and interests. Quantitative and qualitative data also highlight students' positive perceptions of the new settings and provide evidence of encouraging academic gains.

ENABLERS AND CHALLENGES IN OPEN-PLAN SETTINGS

Teachers' and students' perceptions of enablers and challenges in this educational initiative partly confirm a longstanding literature on conditions that support or block long term whole-school change to new conditions or practices (see Fullan, 2007). However, these new open-plan, up-scaled learning communities also highlight new enablers and blockers to adaptation. As noted by Fullan (2007) and many others, whole-school change traditionally depends on effective leadership, whole staff buy-in to a new vision of practice, and sustained support to design, enact and review new practices. These conditions played out in each school and learning community, affecting the degree and duration of teacher uptake of expectations and enactment of new practices. At the same time, the vistaed visibility (or multiple framed visual perspectives) of the new open-plan settings, the shared space, the scope for aggregating groups of students and organising teaching team, acted as enablers for teachers to consider new ways to imagine and enact curricula (see chapters 3 and 7). Challenges around large groups sharing spaces, including increased noise and student distraction, were addressed through a range of strategies, including: development of protocols around student behaviour in these settings; negotiation between teachers about structures and organisation of lessons in the shared space; and recognition of the need for a developmental curriculum for students to participate as positive learning community members (see chapter 9). Students' perceptions of enablers and challenges in the open-plan, up-scaled learning communities matched teachers' concerns about adequate structures and capacity to concentrate in these contexts. At the same time, students often reported on the value of sharing a space with teachers that felt more informal, personal, and safe (see chapters 9 and 10). This ambience represents a significant positive change from the milieu of low SES schools with traditional teaching spaces, and indicates potential for further learning and wellbeing gains.

THEORETICAL AND PRACTICAL IMPLICATIONS

The question of the theoretical and practical implications of this study for systematically addressing effective schooling for similarly disadvantaged students has led to a range of new insights. As noted in most chapters, there is no shortage of prescriptions in the literature on what will enable quality learning and wellbeing for this cohort. Recurrent terms in these prescriptions include claims about the need for more "student agency", more "student voice" "distributed leadership", more "personalisation of learning", and the judicious exercise of "collective expertise". However, this long-standing advocacy of particular constructs/approaches often fails to provide precise evidential accounts of effective practices or gains, or their theoretical underpinnings. Also, as often noted, these constructs often remain ill-defined place-holders in a reform rhetoric about how schooling should be more democratised, in order to meet the needs, and harness the expertise, of students. Our study contributes to this literature by providing an evidence-based account of how these constructs can be defined more sharply and operationalised in this and other contexts.

Probably the most over-worked term in this literature is the construct of 'agency', variously conceptualised psychologically as enacted motivation or intent, and sociologically as successful participation in social practices and use of appropriate artefacts and structures (see Arnold & Clarke, 2013). Drawing on an activity system perspective (see Engeström, 1999), we understood participants in these new contexts as necessarily acting out new roles, rules, goals, outcomes, and new divisions of labour, drawing on new and old material and symbolic tools to shape the scope and nature of activities. Our study points to the necessity of highly resolved structures and shared understandings to support learning, wellbeing, and teacher and student agency in these settings. These include: (a) a comprehensive stage-based curriculum in compulsory subjects to enable effective targeted differentiation of learning tasks, as well as scope for student design and negotiation of learning goals and tasks; (b) symbolic resources that enable teachers and students to design, enact, and review learning goals and outcomes precisely and meaningfully (see chapter 5); (c) processes and routines that enable teachers and students to participate in personal and community development, including celebrations of success (see chapters 9 and 10); (d) understood shared processes for decision-making about learning community rules and protocols; and (e) capacity for all community members to contribute to meaningful review processes around the extent to which rules and practices achieve the learning and wellbeing goals of these schools.

In this way, the new learning communities prompt and reinforce altered and expanded teacher and student spheres of influence as part of the exercise of personal and collective agency. Teachers and students, in theory and practice, can influence what, when, where, how, why, with whom, and at what pace teachers and students learn. This is evident in many formal and informal processes in each learning community (see especially chapters 7 and 10). Spheres of influence in the new settings are more malleable than in traditional classrooms, varying from on-the-fly individual actions and interactions to sustained explicit teamwork among teachers, among students, and among both groups. However, a repeated theme of attempted changes to curricular processes and organisation point to the need for shared understandings of the purposes for any structural arrangements or changes.

In theorising teamwork in these settings, we consider that Edwards' account of "relational agency", understood as negotiated mutual responsibility between expert participants, has explanatory power to characterise the ontogenesis and maintenance of collaborative processes between teachers (2011, p. 34). However, this raises sharply the question of the extent to which students' "expertise", including their rights and experiential knowledge of their own learning and personal needs should, or could, influence school practices and the development of teacher expertise. For Edwards (2011), relational agency refers to effective co-ordination/integration of diverse professional expertise for the benefit of the child/student, and clearly this applies to teacher teamwork in these settings; however, in this context students can also support peer and teacher learning, depending on the object of the activity and the division of roles (see chapters 5, 6, 9 and 10 for examples). This implies that agency is always shaped by, and has the potential to reshape, the cultural practices in which it is embedded. In the context of these up-scaled learning communities, our study suggests that disadvantaged low SES students have considerable capacity to enact high levels of relational agency, depending on what imperatives, goals, decision-making processes, structures, and divisions of labour evolve in these schools. Our study further suggests that agency for teachers and students in these settings is emergent rather than fixed, depending on these influences.

We were also interested in how these new emergent expressions of agency relate more broadly to change processes. We agree with Engeström (2001) that major changes to activity systems can arise from attempts by agents to address perceived internal contradictions and conflicts (see chapters 6, 9 and 10). However, our three-year research identified multiple catalysts leading to both large and incremental changes. These included: individual or group dissatisfaction with the practicability of an approach or organisational feature (see chapters 5 and 10); experiential prompts from working in these new open-plan settings, leading to collaborative experimentation (see chapters 5 and 7); extensions of prior teacher teamwork (see chapter 7); external pressures on performance in high stakes subjects (see chapters

7 and 10); staff employment changes leading to advocacy by new staff of imported 'proven' new methods (see chapter 11, and Prain et al., in press); and student inputs to curricular matters (see chapter 10). However, as noted in many chapters, the new settings acted as catalysts for less formal interactions among students, and between teachers and students, thus improving the professional and personal relationships of learning community members. In these new contexts of increased civility and heightened self-reliance by students, especially in the upper year levels, there was scope for more cooperative planning by staff and students around choices about how learning is scoped, monitored and enacted.

On the issue of distributed leadership, we found that traditional boundaries of leadership between teachers and students could become blurred by pedagogical principles that were determined by the co-construction of knowledge, the differentiated curriculum, and increasing student autonomy (see chapters 5, 6 and 7). A form of distributed leadership was required that supported teachers to attempt and sustain shared leadership and decision-making. The transition from top-down, hierarchical leadership to more democratic and distributed leadership involved a range of new structures such as the TA curriculum, altered expectations, and changed roles and responsibilities for staff and students in each school. The open-plan spaces continued to have an informing influence on the transparency of the processes required. Initial teacher leadership possibilities emerged from the learning community and neighbourhood structures where colleagues mentored and supported each other with direct responsibility for the wellbeing and learning of the students in their care. Community leaders worked collaboratively with teacher advisors and relationships improved between teachers, students, and parents. Consistent with the changing patterns of leadership in the schools, themes related to student leadership are now emerging. Leadership structures emerged that encouraged a sense of belonging and roles based on personal agency, to create an environment for students where their perspectives are valued as agents, and decision-makers, in their own educational experience (see chapters 6 and 9).

Do the new open-plan spaces really matter in these change processes to teachers' and students' roles, symbolic tools, dispositions and practices, and in what ways? We recognise that the new buildings did not automatically alter pedagogy and behaviour, but they functioned as a catalyst for change, and prompted strong positive and negative assessments. Following Foucault (1977), some researchers have been quick to condemn any signs of increased surveillance of student behaviour (whether virtual or actual) as evidence of unnecessary intrusion on student rights and privacy (see Hope, 2005) as well as unwelcome monitorial panoptic control over teacher behaviour in more open settings (Markus,1993). We recognise potential dangers in this regard, and that some teachers in the BEP schools disliked the new public dimension to shared teaching when contrasted to the hidden sanctum of the traditional classroom. For some, the visibility inhibited their usual personas with students or was distracting because of the intensification of diverse activities within shared spaces. However, for many teachers these new conditions for collegial support, orchestrated spontaneity, informal learning, and team-play were embraced as significant gains in their professional and personal lives (see Prain et al., in press). On the parallel critique of another form of intensification in schooling, an increase in trivial learning, or what Biesta (2009, p. 3) decries as the "learnification of education", we acknowledge that there are risks around trivial busy lock-step learning (and teaching for the test). However, we would claim that these distortions are best addressed through a deeply robust curriculum that invites students' most imaginative problem-seeking and solving as they engage with disciplinary and transdisciplinary methods of inquiry and new forms of knowledge (see Prain et al., in press). We argue that the new settings could be used to support Biesta's (2009) richer sense of ultimate purposes for schooling. The open-plan settings exposed the fragmentation of past teacher goals and practices, and prompted new curricular consolidation (see Figure 12.1).

We have claimed often in this book that the new spaces have been a catalyst for change and gains, and consider that affordance theory is useful to explain some of the character of the new interactions between participants and the physical/cultural resources and tools that influence adaptive new practices in these settings. Drawing on Gibson (1979), Greeno (1994), Norman (1999), and others, we define affordances as recognition of the reciprocities between features in the environment and prompts/sustenance of an agent's or team's goals. Primary affordances such as increased visibility and larger open-plan spaces enable secondary affordances such as reconfigured group sizes, greater freedom of assembly for subgroups, and in some instances, a more embodied, active engagement with the curriculum beyond the scale of a classroom (see Prain et al., in press). New physical features of layout, such as the placement of highly accessible staff areas adjacent to classrooms, has the effect of intensifying the perception and reality of shared daily space between teachers and students, increasing informal conversation and incidental learning opportunities. Similarly, the properties of culturally-designed objects (such as the dashboard in chapter 5) affords opportunities to teachers to customise/constrain/expand circulation of feedback by controlling recipient access of online messages to particular students, their parents, and relevant teaching staff. This design feature also supports targeted feedback and opportunities for students to track and interpret their progress in both academic subjects and participation in co-curricular participation, thus increasing students' responsibility for monitoring and addressing their own learning.

THRESHOLD OF CHANGE

We have learnt much from this study about the new challenges teachers and students face in adapting to these new spaces. We recognise the ongoing tension between (a) the need for structures, certainty, and reward from participating in predictable workable practices around mainstream curricular imperatives, and (b) the need to acknowledge new forms of agency offered by both new virtual resources and the changing expectations, capacities, goals, representational resources, and the new horizons of learning community members in the open-plan spaces. This is especially the case in conceptualising and enacting personalising of learning. As we have shown in detail (see chapters 3, 5 and 7), these settings can provide ongoing refinement of strategies over time to personalise learning for both teachers and students. This process is partly about all the well-recognised strategies for differentiating curriculum in traditional classroom settings through varying goals, tasks, and assessment methods for different learners and learner groups. However, there is also scope for teachers and students to take up new opportunities in what we characterise as a "threshold of change" (see Figure 12.1).

We recognise the dangers of simplification and undue abstraction in any representation, but our threshold area in Figure 2.1 is intended to show the complex unpredictable sources and opportunities of change processes and outcomes. These shifts in practice can be prompted by many different participant perceptions of affordances. These can be temporal (micro/macro from moments to years), spatial (enabled by closed, open, and indeterminate spaces and their interplay), symbolic (as in templates, curricular prescriptions, learning community rules), improvised, expedient, or principled. The changes will then appear variously inevitable, unpredictable, in some cases a false step, improvised, and/or necessary, depending on the mindset of individuals and groups, and their degree of familiarity with the settings.

We began this book by noting many current concerns about the future of secondary education. These include the unpredictability of future knowledge-generating sources and practices for teachers and students in this century, as well as the uncertainty of what will count as worthwhile learning content and processes. Our study provides

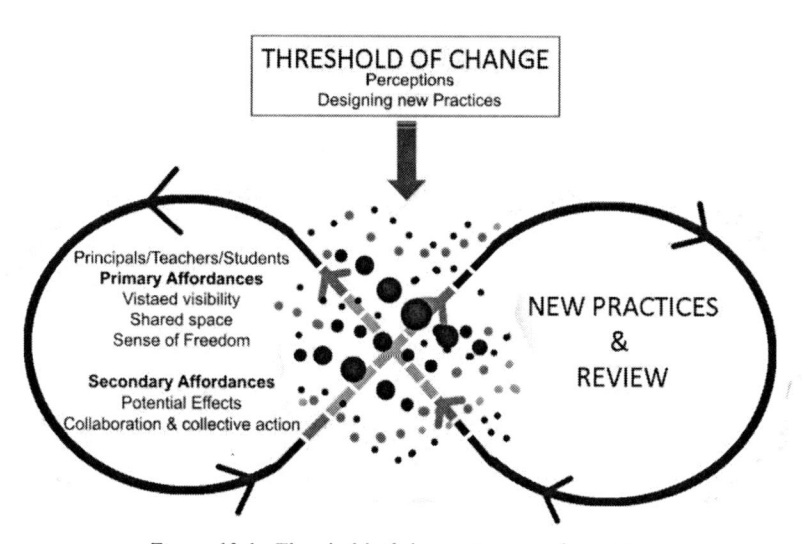

Figure 12.1. Threshold of change in open-plan settings.

positive leads for how this threshold of change in up-scaled learning communities can be understood and welcomed in the context of advancing the education and wellbeing of low SES students. Given the entrenched history of academic and wellbeing failure for this cohort in traditional classrooms, our findings provide some positive leads about addressing these problems, while also acknowledging the major challenges in altering participant expectations, roles, and expertise.

We consider that there are larger lessons for other secondary educational settings about collective effort. The traditional classroom has a mythic history of positive and negative associations about how to organise and optimise student learning. On the negative side, it has been denounced as a dated, constraining space, where a single teacher has to cope with addressing the abilities of students ranging across up to eight year levels, and some students merely serve institutional time. On the positive side, it has been viewed as a space where teachers can productively constrain student focus, so that privacy, security, and order restrict student attention in generative ways. Our study points to ways in which up-scaled learning communities can both preserve some of the benefits of the traditional classroom, such as focused connectedness between teachers and students, but also introduce new benefits, and more diverse networks for participants involved in this threshold of change. These include scope for richer personalised/collaborative learning and community building through team-teaching, where new virtual and actual spaces can be customised in situ to address personal and shared student and teacher interests and needs. This augmentation of collective effort and expertise makes sense for many teachers in our study, and could be adapted to other like contexts.

ANNE EDWARDS

13. EPILOGUE

The Epilogue's role is to connect the strands of a narrative and perhaps hint at future developments, and this is exactly what the research team has asked me to do. The book is, in many ways, an account of two parallel journeys. First is the change voyage for Education in Bendigo, which is given direction by the Bendigo Education Plan (BEP). Second is the intellectual journey taken by the research team, as they brought to bear their different research lenses on the evolution of the BEP, in their research programme. There are therefore at least two interlinked processes to bring together, and a strong sense that what we have read in this book might only be the beginning.

The story of the BEP is a fascinating account of a radical approach to systemic educational change in one city. It was recognised from the outset that the Bendigo Education Plan would be premised on a disruption to the existing schooling system, new schools would be built, learning communities established and there would be a focus on individual learners. The accounts offered in this book are therefore not merely of an intervention with a simple focus on pre- and post-testing. In addition, they chart the implementation and implications of intertwined change at every level: pedagogic spaces; school leadership; teacher education from pre-service to in-service; curriculum; assessment; and above all how children and young people are seen as learners.

The research programme was therefore both exciting and hugely demanding. It needed to capture systemic shifts and also the individual and interactional adjustments and initiatives that advanced the change. I was therefore delighted to see how the team dealt with the challenge. Their attention to systemic change drew with delicacy on the work of Yrjö Engeström and his collaborators in Helsinki; while their analyses of learning and the sites of learning involved elaborations of my own work on relational agency and relational expertise (Edwards, 2010, 2012). Interestingly, the relational concepts arose in part from my attempt to understand the interactional changes which can produce systemic change (Edwards, 2009). Both approaches therefore draw on the cultural historical legacies of Vygotsky and Leont'ev and are entirely compatible, each augmenting the other.

A primary contribution from Engeström's research programme is an analytic understanding of what is gained by taking a dynamic system as a unit of analysis (Engeström, 1999). His much borrowed triangular representation of an activity system is therefore never more than a snapshot of a system in which the internal relationships are open to constant change. By recognising the dynamic nature of systems in flux, the researchers have used Engeström's working of activity theory as a powerful tool with which they can begin to make sense of the complex shifts they observed.

Engeström is a sophisticated thinker whose own empirical work has led to his recognition of the complexity of change across distributed systems, in ways which are relevant to the study. The BEP involved a set of activity systems, such as schools, teacher training programmes and so on, each with their own histories and motives. As a result of the BEP, each experienced shifts in the division of labour, the rules of practice and the purposes of work; yet, at the same time, the Plan required these shifts to be aligned so that different activity systems were aiming at compatible long term outcomes. Engeström is well aware of these kinds of challenge. Writing of how spacio-temporally distributed collaborations are "fragile, open and literally under construction" (Engeström, 2005, p.324), he emphasised the need for organisations to develop what he called "collective intentionality capital" and "object-oriented inter-agency". Both of these concepts were offered as resources for collaborations, which were not embedded within existing institutional structures with strong histories.

Reflecting on the future of activity theory, in ways which again reflect the fluid realities of the BEP, Engeström later suggested:

> In social production or peer production, the boundaries and structures of activity …systems seem to fade away. Processes become simultaneous, multidirectional and often reciprocal. The density and crisscrossing of processes make the distinction between process and structure somewhat obsolete. The movements of information create textures that are constantly changing but not arbitrary or momentary…..So the constantly moving texture is also multilayered and historically durable. (Engeström, 2009, p. 309).

The ambitious research programme reported in this book is recording such a history, capturing the erosions of boundaries, the different layers that are produced and their interweaving. The authors are therefore offering much more than an evaluation. They are also revealing some of the nonlinear creativity, negotiations and compromises that are the back-stage work of institutional change; and which might be described as building the "collective intentionality capital" and "object-oriented inter-agency" that make for successful and fluid collaboration.

My own work on relational expertise and relational agency, now includes attention to the "common knowledge" built when collaboration across practice boundaries is achieved (Edwards, 2010, 2011, 2012; Edwards & Thompson, 2013). Here common knowledge consists of "what matters" for each participant and can be used as a resource to mediate inter-professional collaborations, enabling the alignment of motives while working on complex tasks. One interesting area to explore in the case of the BEP, given its ambition, scale and social relevance, would have been just how the different elements in the education system exercised relational expertise.

In particular, how they constructed, sustained and deployed common knowledge and mutual respect for each other's motives as a resource, when taking forward the different elements of the Plan and weaving the rich texture of the new school system.

So, despite the delicacy with which they used activity theory, the research team might have gone a little further with their systemic analyses; but the same cannot be said of their focus on children and young people as learners. The agency of learners as they engage with meaning is central to the Plan and threads its way through the analyses in the book. The team, however, wear their scholarship lightly when explaining how learning involves connecting personal agentic sense-making with public meaning. I shall therefore use the prerogative of the Epilogue and indulge in a little elaboration.

Equity concerns underpin both the BEP and the research programme. It therefore comes as no surprise that the accounts of the different sub-projects are suffused with Vygotsky-informed ideas; or with concepts, such as distributed leadership, which are entirely compatible with Vygotskian emphases on creating enabling environments.

Vygotsky's psychology was developed during a period of social turmoil in the post-revolutionary Russia of the 1920s and early 30s. His view was that society might be improved by ensuring that the most robust conceptual tools were available to all; once people could grasp these tools they could use them to work on and improve the conditions of their existence. It was a psychology with considerable potential for informing pedagogy. It is a psychology which also aligns well with the equity intentions of the BEP; and with its recognition of the importance of the agency of the learner in connecting with meaning. Let us therefore unpack some of the ideas that underpin the pedagogy supported by the research programme.

In his writings Vygotsky distinguished between sense and meaning, while seeing them as dynamically inter-related. He argued that individuals are involved in personal sense-making when they engage with the meanings that are publicly valued. He explained, somewhat enigmatically, as follows: "...[s]ense is what enters into meaning" and "...[t]he formation of sense is the product of meaning" (Vygotsky, 1997, pp. 136-7). In brief, he was pointing to dialectic process where public meanings are there for us to work with and on, meaning is made, and our sense-making is part of the process of meaning-making. This is a form of constructivism, but a version that emphasises public meaning alongside individual sense-making and involves effort. It requires the exercise of human agency as well as a particular role for the teacher (Edwards, in press).

Vygotsky did not write of agency, but the concept is strongly implicit in one of his central ideas about human learning: the social situation of development. Rather than denoting a social environment, the term explained the developing child's changing relationship with her immediate environment over time. At the core is the idea that the learner creates her own social situation of development by propelling herself forward and tackling new demands. Vygotsky explained that changes within the social situation of development, i.e. learning, are marked by new structures of 'consciousness' (Vygotsky, 1998, p. 199) which in turn alter the child's relationships with experienced reality. Therefore as fresh structures of consciousness emerge, defunct relationships fade away and new ones are formed so that children are repositioned as agents within the practices in which they are participating. Vygotsky's learner is therefore intentional, self-regulating, creating networks of relationships with the world and finding as a consequence that "... [n]ew connections appear between experiences when they acquire a certain sense." (Vygotsky, 1998, p. 291).

Because social situations of development are created by sense-making agentic learners and not by teachers, the role of the teacher is not the deliverer of a curriculum. Instead, the purpose of teaching is to create the environments in which learners are able to move themselves forward creating their own social situations of development. At the same time, teachers need to make demands on learners which ensure that in their sense-making they engage with publicly valued meanings. Vygotsky, in Educational Psychology, the book based on his lectures for beginning teachers between 1921 and 1923, outlined what he saw as the limitations of teaching as curriculum delivery.

> The teacher ... has to become the director of the social environment which, moreover, is the only educational factor. When he acts like a simple pump, filling up the students with knowledge, there he can be replaced with no trouble at all by a textbook, by a dictionary, by a map, by a nature walk......When he is simply setting forth ready-prepared bits and pieces of knowledge, there he has ceased being a teacher (Vygotsky, 1997b, p. 339).

The alternative way of working, whether designated as personalisation or enabling the creation of a social situation of development, is of course extremely demanding for teachers. Unsurprisingly a number of teachers resigned during the implementation of the Plan, and the team wisely examined the implications of the BEP for initial teacher education and school leadership. The Plan required a systemic change, and a shift in one element, if it is to be of significance, will have implications throughout the wider more diffuse system.

The work of the research team has therefore been crucial in providing conceptual tools, which have allowed participants in the changing Bendigo education environment to find ways of stabilising and taking control over what they were doing. Introducing the idea of personalisation, for example, appears to have created the opportunity for discussions about its purposes and implications which have, in turn, made visible what matters for all the participants, allowing each group to use the concept of personalisation to shape its next moves.

Another concept they have used, as I have already indicated, is relational agency, derived from my own work. As the team has explained, I have used the term mainly to discuss how professionals from different practices align their interpretations of complex problems and then their responses to them (Edwards, 2005, 2010, 2012). The concept has nonetheless travelled and has been put to use by other researchers in other contexts. In doing so it has sometimes been fashioned to tackle different problems, a process which as a Vygotskian I find fascinating and legitimate.

In the present research programme relational agency is being used for a fresh purpose, and in a way that I am sure would have met with Vygotsky's approval. In chapter 3, after an overview of how personalised learning has been evaluated and critiqued, relational agency is introduced as a way, of understanding how teachers and students may work alongside each other. In doing so they can develop the co-regulation that can lead to the self-regulation that the agentic learner needs; and help the learner's personal sense-making connect with the public meanings that are carried in the curriculum.

In the concluding chapter of Educational Psychology (Vygotsky, 1997b), Vygotsky outlined what he saw as successful teaching. In summary, it is not a matter of the teacher facing the student and telling what needs to be known. Instead, teacher and student should work alongside each other on culturally relevant problems which require the student to engage with public meaning. The role of the teacher is to help the student continuously expand their interpretations of the problem and to conversationally enhance the repertoire of concepts that they bring to bear on each new interpretation. I have gone some way beyond Vygotsky's actual text in this summary, but this is the pedagogical model that can be gleaned from a reading of that chapter.

How the research team has taken the concept of relational agency and embedded it into their own pedagogic model is an exciting and highly appropriate development. As I have already indicated, relational agency is just one of three linked concepts, the others being relational expertise and common knowledge (Edwards, 2010, 2012). All of these concepts have considerable pedagogic potential in explaining, for example, the planning and enactment of cross-curricular collaborations; seeing others as a resource in group work and being a resource oneself; making one's own knowledge explicit so it can be recognised and accessed by others; the list could go on.

So is my role as Epilogue now done? I hope I have brought attention to how the research programme was not merely an efficient evaluation of an intervention, but was intertwined with, and supportive of, the BEP. The programme has not only provided and refined conceptual tools to be used during the implementation of the Plan, it has also provided an account of the creation of the richly textured system that has been produced in Bendigo.

I also hope I have pointed towards the future. One area for further development might be how the different sets of practices, or activity systems if you prefer, were so successfully aligned in taking forward the Plan. Another, and perhaps easier to tackle, would be to work even more overtly with notions of relational expertise and common knowledge, alongside relational agency, as pedagogic resources within the learning communities that have been established. The concepts could also be used to augment understandings of distributed leadership (Edwards and Thompson, 2013); and might also have implications for how schools and initial teacher education work together (Fancourt, Edwards, & Menter, in progress). But let us not forget what has already been achieved. By following the BEP in such a scholarly manner, the research programme has opened and pursued a myriad of lines of enquiry. The current revels may now have ended, but I suspect that, unlike Prospero, the team will find many more themes with which to entrance us.

Anne Edwards
Departmen of Education
University of Oxford

REFERENCES

Adler, J., Ball, D., Krainer, K., Lin, F. L., & Novotna, J. (2005). Reflections on an emerging field: Researching mathematics teacher education. *Educational Studies in Mathematics, 60*, 359–381. doi: 10.1007/s10649-005-5072-6.

Aelterman, A. N., Engels, J. P., Verhaeghe, K., Panagiotou, H. S., & Van Petegem, K. (2002). *Het welbevinden van de leerkracht*. Ghent: OBPWO project.

Akinsanmi, B. (2011). The optimal learning environment: Learning theories. *Design Share Newsletter*. Retrieved from http://www.designshare.com/index.php/articles/the-optimal-learning-environment-learning-theories/.

Alcoff, L. (1991). The problem of speaking for others. *Cultural Critique, 20*(Winter), 5–32. doi: 10.2307/1354221.

Allardt, E. (1976). Dimensions of welfare in a comparative Scandinavian study. *Acta Sociologica, 19*, 227–240. doi: 10.1177/000169937601900302.

Allardt, E. (1981). Experiences from the comparative Scandinavian welfare study, with the bibliography of the project. *European Journal of Political Research, 9*, 101–111. doi: 10.1111/j.1475-6765.1981.tb00591.x.

Allardt, E. (1989). *An updated indicator system: Having, loving, being*. Working papers 48. Finland: University of Helsinki. Department of Sociology.

Allen, J. M. (2009). Valuing practice over theory: How beginning teachers re-orient their practice in the transition from the university to the workplace. *Teaching and Teacher Education, 25*, 647–654. doi: 10.1016/j.tate.2008.11.011.

Almquist, Y. B., Östberg, V., Rostila, M., Edling, C., & Rydgren, J. (2014). Friendship network characteristics and psychological wellbeing in late adolescence: Exploring differences by gender and gender composition. *Scandinavian Journal of Public Health, 42*(2), 146–154. doi: 10.1177/1403494813510793.

Alterator, S., & Deed, C. (2013). Teacher adaptation to open learning spaces. *Issues in Educational Research, 23*(3), 315–330. Retrieved from http://www.iier.org.au/iier23/alterator.html.

Alvermann, D., Peyton Young, J., Weaver, D., Hinchman, K., Moore, D., Phelps, S., Thrash, E., & Zalewski, P. (1996). Middle and high school students' perceptions of how they experience text-based discussions: A multicase study. *Reading Research Quarterly, 31*(3), 244–267. doi: 10.1598/RRQ.31.3.2.

Anderson, M., & Jefferson, M. (2009). *Teaching the screen: Film education for generation next*. Crows Nest: Allen & Unwin.

Andrews, D., Crowther, F., Abawi, L., Dawson, M., Lewis, M., Morgan, A., & Petersen, S. (2011). *Capacity building for sustainable school improvement*. Saarbrüken, Germany: Verlag Dr. Müller.

Angus, L. (1993). The sociology of school effectiveness. *British Journal of Sociology of Education, 14*(3), 333–345. doi: 10.1080/0142569930140309.

Angus, L. (2006). Educational leadership and the imperative of including student voices, student interests and students lives in the mainstream. *International Journal of Leadership in Education, 9*(4), 369–379. doi: 10.1080/13603120600895544.

Apple, M. (2006). Rhetoric and reality in critical educational studies in the United States. *British Journal of Sociology of Education, 27*(5), 679–687. doi: 10.1080/01425690600958923.

Arbuckle, J. L. (2009). *Amos 18 user's guide*. Crawfordville, FL: Amos Development Corporation.

Arnold, J., & Clarke, D. (2014). What is 'Agency'? Perspectives in science education research. *International Journal of Science Education, 36*(5), 735–754. doi: 10.1080/09500693.2013.825066.

Arnot, M., & Reay, D. (2007). A sociology of pedagogic voice: Power, inequality and pupil consultation. *Discourse: Studies in the Cultural Politics of Education, 28*(3), 311–325.

REFERENCES

Australian Catholic University & Erebus International. (2008). *Scoping study into approaches to student wellbeing: Final report*. Sydney: Aust. Catholic University & Erebus International. Retrieved from http://www.sueroffey.com/wp-content/uploads/import/34scoping_study_into_approaches_to_student_wellbeing_final_report.pdf.

Australian Curriculum Assessment and Reporting Authority (ACARA). (2013). *Guide to understanding 2013 Index of Community Socio-educational Advantage (ICSEA) Values*. Retrieved from http://www.acara.edu.au/verve/_resources/Guide_to_understanding_2013_ICSEA_values.pdf.

Australian Curriculum Assessment and Reporting Authority (ACARA). (2014). *NAPLAN 2014: Information for parents*. Retrieved from http://www.nap.edu.au/verve/_resources/naplan_2014_information_for_parents_brochure_web.pdf.

Barmby, P., Kind, P., & Jones, K. (2008). Examining changing attitudes in secondary school science. *International Journal of Science Education*, *30*(8), 1075–1093. doi: 10.1080/09500690701344966.

Barnes, D., & Todd, F. (1977). *Communication and learning in small groups*. London: Routledge & Kegan Paul.

Barrett, P., & Zhang, Y. (2009). *Optimal learning spaces: Design implications for primary schools*. Salford, UK: Salford Centre for Research and Innovation in the Built and Human Environment.

Barton, A. C., & Tan, E. (2010). We be burnin'! Agency, identity, and science learning. *Journal of the Learning Sciences*, *19*(2), 187–229. doi: 10.1080/10508400903530044.

Battisch, V., Solomon, D., Watson, M., & Schaps, E. (1997). Caring school communities. *Educational Psychologist*, *32*(3), 137–151.

Beach, D., & Dovemark, M. (2009). Making right choices? An ethnographic account of creativity, performativity and personalised learning policy, concepts and practices. *Oxford Review of Education*, *35*(6), 689–704. doi: 10.1080/03054980903122267.

Beaty, L. (2013).Confronting school's contradictions with video:Youth's need of agency for ontological development. *Outlines. Critical Practice Studies*, *14*(1), 4–25.

Bendigo Education Plan Steering Committee (BEP). (2005). *Bendigo education plan*. Bendigo: Loddon Mallee Region, DEECD. Retrieved from http://www.weeroona.vic.edu.au/site-content/strategic-plans/BEP.pdf

Bendigo Loddon Primary Care Partnership (BLPCP). (2012). *Community health and wellbeing profile*. Bendigo, Victoria: Bendigo Loddon Primary Care Partnership. Retrieved from http://www.blpcp.com.au/BLPCP%20Community%20Profile%2022%20November_2012.pdf

Benhabib, S. (1992). *Situating the self: Gender, community and postmodernism in contemporary ethics*. New York: Routledge.

Bergman, M. A., & Scott, J. (2001). Young adolescents' wellbeing and health-risk behaviours: Gender and socio-economic differences. *Journal of Adolescence*, *24*(2), 183–197. doi: 10.1006/jado.2001.0378.

Berliner, D. C. (2006). Our improvershed view of educational research. *Teachers College Record*, *108*(6), 949–995. doi: 10.1111/j.1467-9620.2006.00682.x.

Bernstein, B. (1996). *Pedagogy, symbolic control and identity. Theory, research, critique*. London: Taylor & Francis.

Biesta, G. (2009). Good education in an age of measurement: On the need to reconnect with the question of purpose in education. *Educational Assessment, Evaluation and Accountability*, *21*(1), 33–46. doi: 10.1007/s11092-008-9064-9.

Billett, S. (2009). Realising the educational worth of integrating work experiences in higher education. *Studies in Higher Education*, *34*(7), 827–843. doi: 10.1080/03075070802706561.

Billett, S. (2006). Relational interdependence between social and individual agency in work and working life. *Mind, Culture and Activity*, *13*(1), 53–69. doi: 10.1207/s15327884mca1301_5.

Blanchard, J. (2009). *Teaching, learning and assessment*. Milton Keynes: Open University Press.

Boekaerts, M., & Corno, L. (2005). Self-regulation in the classroom: A perspective on assessment and intervention. *Applied Psychology: An International Review*, *54*(2), 199–231. doi: 10.1111/j.1464-0597.2005.00205.x.

Bolognini, M., Plancherel, B., Bettschart, W., & Halfon, O. (1996). Self-esteem and mental health in early adolescence: Development and gender differences. *Journal of Adolescence*, *19*(3), 233–245. doi: 10.1006/jado.1996.0022.

REFERENCES

Bolte, A., Goschke, T., & Kuhl, J. (2003). Emotion and intuition: Effects of positive and negative mood on implicit judgements of semantic coherence. *Psychological Science, 14*(5), 416–421. doi: 10.1111/1467-9280.01456.

Boud, D., Keogh, R., & Walker, D. (1985). *Reflection: Turning experience into learning.* London: Kogan Page.

Boy, A. V., & Pine, G. (1988). *Fostering psychosocial development in the classroom.* Springfield, IL: Charles C. Thomas Pub. Ltd.

Bradley, D., Noonan, P., Nugent H., & Scales, B. (2008). *Review of Australian higher education: Final report* (Bradley Review). Canberra, ACT: DEEWR. Retrieved from http://www.innovation.gov.au/HigherEducation/Documents/Review/PDF/Higher%20Education%20Review_Title%20page%20to%20chapter%202.pdf.

Bragg, S. (2007). *Consulting young people: A review of the literature.* London: Creative Partnerships.

Bransford, J., Brown, A., & Cocking, R. (Eds.). (2000). *How people learn.* Washington, D.C.: National Academy Press.

Brandt, R. (1998). *Powerful learning.* Alexandria, VA: Association for Supervision and Curriculum Development.

Britzman, D. P. (1991). *Practice makes perfect: A critical study of learning to teach.* Albany, N.Y: Suny Press.

Buchmann, C., & DiPrete, T. A. (2006). The growing female advantage in college completion: The role of family background and academic achievement. *American Sociological Review, 71*(4), 515–541. doi: 10.1177/000312240607100401.

Bush, T., & Gamage, D. (2001). Models of self-governance in schools: Australia and the United Kingdom. *The International Journal of Educational Management, 15*(1), 39–44. doi: 10.1108/09513540110380604.

Butler, D., & Winne, P. H. (1995). Feedback and self-regulated learning: A theoretical synthesis. *Review of Educational Research, 65*(3), 245–281. doi: 10.3102/00346543065003245.

Butler, D., Schnellert, L., & Cartier, S. (2013). Layers of self and co-regulation: Teachers working collaboratively to support adolescents' self-regulated learning through reading. *Education Research International,* doi: 10.1155/2013/845694.

Cabitza, F., & Simone, C. (2012). Affording mechanisms: An integrated view of co-ordination and knowledge management. *Computer Supported Cooperative Work, 21*(2–3), 227–260. doi: 10.1007/s10606-011-9153-z.

Calderhead, J., & Shorrock, S. (1997). *Understanding teacher education: Case studies in the professional development of beginning teachers.* London: Falmer Press.

Campbell, R., Robinson, W., Neelands, J., Hewston, R., & Mazzoli, L. (2007). Personalised learning: Ambiguities in theory and practice. *British Journal of Educational Studies, 55*(2), 135–154. doi: 10.1111/j.1467-8527.2007.00370.x.

Carr, S. (2008). *Personalisation: A rough guide.* London: Social Care Institute for Excellence.

Cherry, N. L. (2005). Preparing for practice in the age of complexity. *Higher Education Research & Development, 24*(4), 309–320. doi: 10.1080/07294360500284649.

Cheung, G. W., & Rensvold, R. B. (2002). Evaluating goodness-of-fit indexes for testing measurement invariance. *Structural Equation Modeling: A Multi-disciplinary Journal, 9*(2), 233–255. doi: 10.1207/S15328007SEM0902_5.

Clandinin, D. J. (1985). Personal practical knowledge: A study of teachers' classroom images. *Curriculum Inquiry, 15*(4), 361–385. doi: 10.2307/1179683.

Clark, C. M. (1988). Asking the right questions about teacher preparation: Contributions of research on teacher thinking. *Educational Researcher, 17*(5), 5–12. doi: 10.3102/0013189X017002005.

Cochran-Smith, M., & Lytle, S. L. (1999). Relationships of knowledge and practice: Teacher learning in communities. *Review of Research in Education, 24,* 249–305. doi: 10.2307/1167272.

Cohen, E. (1986). *Designing group work-strategies for the heterogeneous classroom.* New York: Teachers College Press.

Cohen, J. (1988). *Statistical power analysis for the behavioural sciences.* (2nd ed.). Hillsdale, NJ: Erlbaum.

Coleman, J. (2009). Wellbeing in schools: Empirical measure, or politician's dream? *Oxford Review of Education, 35*(3), 281–292. doi: 10.1080/03054980902934548.

REFERENCES

Collinson, V. (1999). Redefining teacher excellence. *Theory into Practice, 38*(1), 4–11. doi: 10.1080/00405849909543824.

Connelly, F. M., & Clandinin, D. J. (1988). *Teachers as curriculum planners: Narratives of experience.* New York: Teachers' College Press.

Cook-Sather, A. (2006). Sound, presence and power: "Student voice" in educational research and reform. *Curriculum Inquiry, 36*(4), 359–390. doi: 10.1111/j.1467-873X.2006.00363.x.

Covey, S. (1989). *The 7 habits of highly effective people.* New York: Simon and Schuster.

Creemers, B., & Kyriakides, L. (2008). *The dynamics of educational effectiveness: A contribution to policy, practice, and theory in contemporary schools.* London: Routledge.

Cutler, T., Waine, B., & Brehony, K. (2007). A new epoch of individualization? Problems with the personalization of public sector services. *Public Administration, 85*(3), 847–855. doi: 10.1111/j.1467-9299.2007.00672.x.

Danielson, C. (1996). *Enhancing professional practice: A framework for teaching.* Alexandria, VA: Association for Supervision and Curriculum Development.

Darling-Hammond, L. (2006). Assessing teacher education: The usefulness of multiple measures for assessing program outcomes. *Journal of Teacher Education, 57*(2), 120–138. doi: 10.1177/0022487105283796.

Darling-Hammond, L. (2010). Teacher education and the American future. *Journal of Teacher Education, 61*(1–2), 35–47. doi: 10.1177/0022487109348024.

De Bono, E. (1987). The direct teaching of thinking as a skill. In M. Heiman & J. Slomianko (Eds.), *Thinking skills instruction: Concepts and Technique.* (pp. 218–229). West Haven: NEA Professional Library. Retrieved from http://files.eric.ed.gov/fulltext/ed306559.pdf.

Dede, C. (2009). *Determining, developing and assessing the capabilities of 'future-ready' students.* Retrieved from http://www.fi.ncsu.edu/assets/research_papers/brown-bag/determining-developing-and-assessing-the-capabilities-of-future-ready-students.pdf.

Deed, C., Cox, P., & Prain, V. (2011). Enablers and constraints in achieving integration in a teacher preparation program. *Australian Journal of Teacher Education, 36*(8), 72–92. doi: 10.14221/ajte.2011v36n8.3.

Deed, C., & Lesko, T. (in press). 'Unwalling' the classroom: Teacher reaction and adaptation. *Learning Environments Research.*

Deed, C., Lesko, T., & Lovejoy, V. (2014). Teacher adaptation to personalized learning spaces. *Teacher Development. 18*(3), 369–383. doi: 10.1080/13664530.2014.919345.

Department for Children, Schools & Families, United Kingdom (DCSF) (2008). *Personalised learning: A practical guide.* Nottingham: DCSF Publications. Retrieved from http://www.essex.gov.uk/Business-Partners/Partners/Schools/One-to-one-tuition/Documents/Personalised%20Learning%20a%20practical%20guide.pdf.

Department for Education & Early Childhoood Development, Victoria, Australia, (DEECD). (2011). *Adolescent community profile (version 2): City of Greater Bendigo 2010.* Melbourne: Victorian Department of Education and Early Childhood Development. Retrieved from http://www.education.vic.gov.au/Documents/about/research/acpgreaterbendigo.pdf.

DEECD. (February 2012). Summary statistics Victorian schools. Retrieved from http://www.education.vic.gov.au/Documents/about/department/2012summarystats.pdf.

DEECD. (2014). *Attitudes to school survey.* Retrieved from http://www.education.vic.gov.au/school/principals/management/Pages/performsurveyat.aspx.

Department for Education & Skills, United Kingdom (DfES). (2004). *A national conversation about personalised learning.* Nottingham: DfES. Retrieved from https://www.education.gov.uk/publications/eOrderingDownload/DfES%200919%20200MIG186.pdf.

Department for Education & Skills (DfES). (2006). *2020 Vision: Report of the teaching and learning in 2020 Review Group.* Retrieved from http://publications.education.gov.uk/default.aspx?PageFunction=productdetails&PageMode=publications&ProductId=DFES-04255-2006&.

Dewey, J. (1985). *Democracy and education, 1916.* J. A. Boydston, & P. Baysinger (Eds.). Carbondale: Southern Illinois University Press.

REFERENCES

Dewey, J. (1996). Essays. In L. Hickman (Ed.), *Collected works of John Dewey, 1882–1953: The electronic edition*. Charlottesville, VA: Intelex Corporation.

Doll, B., Spies, R. A., Le Clair, C. M., Kurien, S. A., & Foley, B. P. (2010). Student perceptions of classroom learning environments: Development of the class maps survey. *School Psychology Review, 39*(2), 203–218.

Domina, T., & Saldana, J. (2011). Does raising the bar level the playing field? Mathematics curricular intensification and inequality in American high schools, 1982–2004. *American Educational Research Journal. 49*(4), 685–708.

Drexler, W. (2010). The networked student model for construction of personal learning environments: Balancing teacher control and student autonomy. *Australasian Journal of Educational Technology, 26*(3), 369–385.

Duckworth, K., Akerman, R., MacGregor, A., Salter, E., & Vorhaus, J. (2009). *Self regulated learning: A literature review*. London: Centre for Research on the Wider Benefits of Learning.

Dunbar, R. (1993). Coevolution of neocortical size, group size and language in humans. *Behavioural and Brain Sciences, 16*(4), 681–694. doi: 10.1017/S0140525X00032325.

Dweck, C. S. (2000). *Self-theories: Their role in motivation, personality, and development*. Philadelphia: Psychology Press.

Eames, C., & Coll, R. (2010). Cooperative education: Integrating classroom and workplace learning. In S. Billett (Ed.), *Learning through practice* (pp. 180–196). Dordrecht: Springer. doi: 10.1007/978-90-481-3939-2_10.

Earl, L., Freeman, S., Lasky, S., Sutherland, S., & Torrance, N. (2002). *Policy, pedagogy and people: Early perceptions and challenges of large-scale reform in Ontario Secondary Schools*. Ontario: The Ontario Institute for Studies in Education of the University of Toronto.

Edwards, A. (2005). Relational agency: Learning to be a resourceful practitioner. *International Journal of Educational Research, 43*(3), 168–182. doi: 10.1016/j.ijer.2006.06.010.

Edwards, A. (2007). Relational agency in professional practice: A CHAT analysis. *Actio: An International Journal of Human Activity Theory, 1*, 1–17. Retrieved from http://www.chat.kansai-u.ac.jp/english/publications/actio/pdf/1_Edwards.pdf.

Edwards, A. (2009). Agency and activity theory: From the systemic to the relational. In A. Sannino, H. Daniels & K. Gutierrez (Eds.), *Learning and expanding with activity theory* (pp. 197–211). Cambridge: Cambridge University Press.

Edwards, A. (2010). *Being an expert professional practicioner: The relational turn in expertise*. Dordrecht: Springer.

Edwards, A. (2011). Building common knowledge at the boundaries between professional practices: Relational agency and relational expertise in systems of distributed expertise. *International Journal of Educational Research, 50*(1), 33–39. doi: 10.1016/j.ijer.2011.04.007.

Edwards, A. (2012). The role of common knowledge in achieving collaboration across practices. *Learning, Culture and Social Interaction, 1*(1), 22–32. doi: 10.1016/j.lcsi.2012.03.003.

Edwards, A. (in press). Cultural historical theory and pedagogy: The influence of Vygotsky on the field. In M. Myhill & R. Maclean (Eds.). *Handbook on life in schools and classrooms: Past, present and future visions*. Dordrecht: Springer.

Edwards, A., & D'Arcy, C. (2004). Relational agency and disposition in sociocultural accounts of learning to teach. *Educational Review, 56*(2), 147–155. doi: 10.1080/0031910410001693236.

Edwards, A., Lunt, I., & Stamou, E. (2010). Inter-professional work and expertise: New roles at the boundaries of schools. *British Educational Research Journal, 36*(1), 27–45. doi: 10.1080/01411920902834134.

Edwards, A., & Thompson, M. (2013). Resourceful leadership: Revealing the creativity of organizational leaders. In A. Sannino & V. Ellis (Eds.), *Perspectives on activity theory.* (pp. 19–38). Cambridge: Cambridge University Press.

Elbaz, F. (1981). The teacher's "practical knowledge": Report of a case study. *Curriculum Inquiry, 11*(1), 43–71. doi: 10.2307/1179510.

Ellstrom, P. (2001). Integrating learning and work: Problems and prospects. *Human Resource Development Quarterly, 12*(4), 421–435. doi: 10.1002/hrdq.1006.

REFERENCES

Elmore, R. (1996). Getting to scale with good educational practice. *Harvard Educational Review*, *66*(1), 1–27. Retrieved from http://www.project2061.org/publications/designs/online/pdfs/reprints/5_elmor1.pdf.
Engels, N., Aelterman, A., Deconinck, E., Schepens, A., & Van Petegem, K. (2000). *Het welbevinden in de schoolsituatie bij leerlingen secundair onderwijs*. Ghent: OBPWO project.
Engels, N., Aelterman, A., Van Petegem, K., & Schepens, A. (2004). Factors which influence the wellbeing of pupils in Flemish secondary schools. *Educational Studies*, *30*(2), 127–143. doi: 10.1080/0305569032000159787.
Engeström, Y. (1999). Activity theory and individual and social transformation. In Y. Engeström, R. Miettinen & R. L. Punamaki (Eds.), *Perspectives on Activity Theory* (pp. 19–38). Cambridge, UK: Cambridge University Press.
Engeström, Y. (2001). Expansive learning at work: Toward an activity theoretical reconceptualization. *Journal of Education and Work*, *14*(1), 133–156. doi: 10.1080/13639080020028747.
Engeström, Y. (2005). Knotworking to create collaborative intentionality capital in fluid organisational fields. In M. Bayerlein, S. Bayerlein & F. Kennedy (Eds.), (pp. 307–336). *Collaborative capital: Creating intangible value*. Amsterdam: Elsevier.
Engeström, Y. (2007a). Enriching the theory of expansive learning. *Mind, Culture and Activity*, *14*(1–2), 23–39. doi: 10.1080/10749030701307689.
Engeström, Y. (2007b). Putting activity theory to work. In H. Daniels, M. Cole, & J. V. Wertsch (Eds.), *The Cambridge companion to Vygotsky* (pp. 363–382). Cambridge: Cambridge University Press.
Engeström, Y. (2009). The future of activity theory. In A. Sannino, H. Daniels, & K. Gutierrez (Eds.), *Learning and expanding with activity theory* (pp. 197–211). Cambridge: Cambridge University Press.
Engeström, Y., Brown, K., Christopher, L. K., & Gregory, J. (1997). Co-ordination, cooperation and communication in the courts: Expansive transitions in legal work. In M. Cole, Y. Engeström & T. Vasquez (Eds.), *Mind, culture and activity: Seminal papers from the laboratory of comparative human cognition* (pp. 369–385). Cambridge: Cambridge University Press.
Engeström, Y., & Sannino, A. (2010). Studies of expansive learning: Foundations, findings and future challenges. *Educational Research Review*, *5*(1), 1–24. doi: 10.1016/j.edurev.2009.12.002.
Epstein, R. (1996). *Cognition, creativity and behaviour: Selected essays*. Westport, CT: Praeger.
Fancourt, N., Edwards, A. & Menter, I. (in progress). Taking a systemic approach to teacher education: The Oxford education deanery.
Farrelly, C., O'Brien, M., & Prain, V. (2007). The discourses of sexuality in curriculum documents on sexuality education: An Australian case study. *Sex education: Sexuality, society and learning*, *7*(1), 63–80. doi: 10.1080/14681810601134801.
Ferrari, J. (2012, October 22). Make it harder for student teachers. *The Australian*. Retrieved from http://www.theaustralian.com.au/national-affairs/education/make-it-harder-for-student-teachers/story-fn59nlz9-1226500290806.
Fielding, M. (2004a). Transformative approaches to student voice: Theoretical underpinnings, recalcitrant realities. *British Educational Research Journal*, *30*(2), 295–311. doi: 10.1080/0141192042000195236.
Fielding, M. (2004b). 'New wave' student voice and the renewal of civic society. *London Review of Education*, *2*(3), 197–217. doi: 10.1080/1474846042000302834.
Fielding, M. (2006). Leadership, personalization and high performance schooling: Naming the new totalitarianism. *School Leadership and Management*, *26*(4), 347–369. doi: 10.1080/13632430600886889.
Fielding, M. (2007). Beyond voice: New roles, relations and contexts in researching with young people. *Discourse: Studies in the Cultural Politics of Education*, *28*(3), 301–310. doi: 10.1080/01596300701458780.
Fielding, M. (2008, June). Beyond student voice to democratic community. Paper presented at the conference New developments in student voice: Shaping schools for the future. Birkbeck College, University of London.
Fielding, M., & Moss, P. (2010). *Radical education and the common school: A democratic alternative*. London: Routledge.
Fielding, M., & Rudduck, J. (2002). The transformative potential of student voice: Confronting the power issues. Paper presented at the annual BERA conference, September 2002.

REFERENCES

Fisher, D., & Khine, M. (Eds.). (2006). *Contemporary Approaches to Research on Learning Environments Worldviews*. Singapore: World Scientific Publishing.

Foucault, M. (1977). *Discipline and Punishment: The birth of the prison*. (A. Sheridan Trans.). London: Allen Lane, Penguin.

Fraser, B. J. (1986). *Classroom environment*. London: Croom Helm.

Fraser, B. J. (1990). *Individualised classroom environment questionnaire*. Melbourne: Australian Council for Educational Research.

Fraser, B. J. (1998). Classroom environment instruments: Development, validity, and applications. *Learning Environments Research, 1*(1), 7–34. doi: 10.1023/A:1009932514731.

Fraser, B. J. (2007). Classroom learning environments. In S. Abell, S. & N. Lederman (Eds.), *Handbook of Research on Science Education* (pp. 103–124). Mahwah, NJ: Lawrence Erlbaum Associates.

Fraser, B. J. (2012). Classroom learning environments: Retrospect, context and prospect. In B. Fraser, K. Tobin, & C. McRobbie (Eds.), *Second international handbook of science education* (pp. 1191–1239). Dordrecht, NL: Springer.

Fraser, B. J., Anderson, G. J., & Walberg, H. J. (1991). *Assessment of learning environments: Manual for learning environment inventory (LEI) and my class inventory (MCI)*. Perth, WA: Curtin University of Technology, Science and Mathematics Education Center.

Fredrickson, B. L. (1998). What good are positive emotions? *Review of General Psychology, 56*(3), 300–319. doi: 10.1037/1089-2680.2.3.300.

Fredrickson, B. L., & Branigan, C. (2005). Positive emotions broaden the scope of attention and thought-action repertoires. *Cognition & Emotion, 19*(3), 313–332. doi: 10.1080/02699930441000238.

French, B. F., & Finch, W. H. (2006). Confirmatory factor analytic procedures for the determination of measurement equivalence. *Structural Equation Modeling, 13*(3), 378–402. doi: 10.1207/s15328007sem1303_3.

Fullan, M. (2007). *The new meaning of educational change*. (4th ed.). New York: Teachers College Press.

Gallimore, R., Ermeling, B., Saunders, W., & Goldenberg, C. (2009). Moving the learning of teaching closer to practice: Teacher education implications of school-based inquiry teams. *The Elementary School Journal, 109*(5), 537–553. doi: 10.1086/597001.

Gibson, J. (1986). *The ecological approach to visual perception*. Hillsdale, NJ: Erlbaum.

Giddens, A. (1984). *The constitution of society: Outline of the theory of structuration*. Cambridge: Polity Press.

Giddens, A. (1991). *Modernity and self-identity: Self and society in the late modern age*. Cambridge, UK: Blackwell.

Gifford, R. (2007). *Environmental psychology: Principles and practice*. (4th ed.). Colville: Optimal Books.

Gilbert. C., August, K., Brooks, D., Hargreaves, D., Pearce, N., Roberts, J., Rose, J., & Wise, D. (2006). *2020 vision. Report of the teaching and learning by 2020 review group*. Nottingham, UK: DfES Publications.

Gillies, R., & Haynes, M. (2011). Increasing explanatory behaviour, problem-solving, and reasoning within classes using cooperative group work. *Instructional Science, 39*(3), 349–366. doi: 10.1007/s11251-010-9130-9.

Gislason, N. (2009). Mapping school design: A qualitative study of the relations among facilities design, curriculum delivery, and school climate. *Journal of Environmental Education, 40*(4), 17–34. doi: 10.3200/JOEE.40.4.17-34.

Glanville, J. L., & Wildhagen, T. (2007). The measurement of school engagement: Assessing dimensionality and measurement invariance across race and ethnicity. *Educational and Psychological Measurement, 67*(6), 1019–1041. doi: 10.1177/0013164406299126.

Gonida, E. N., Kiosseoglou, G., & Voulala, K. A. (2007). Perceptions of parent goals and their contribution to student achievement goal orientation and engagement in the classroom: Grade-level differences across adolescence. *European Journal of Psychology of Education, 22*(1), 23–39. doi: 10.1007/BF03173687.

Good, T. L., & Brophy, J. E. (2008). *Looking In Classrooms*. (10th ed.). Boston: Pearson/Allyn and Bacon Publishers.

REFERENCES

Goulart, M., & Roth, W-M. (2010). Engaging young children in collective curriculum design. *Cultural Studies of Science Education*, *5*(3), 533–562. doi: 10.1007/s11422-009-9196-3.

Grangeat, M., & Gray, P. (2008). Teaching as collective work: Analysis, current research and implications for teacher education. *Journal of Education for Teaching*, *34*(3), 177–189. doi: 10.1080/02607470802212306.

Green, B., & Beavis, C. (2013). Literacy education in the age of new media. In K. Hall, T. Cremin, B. Comber, & L. Moll (Eds.), *International handbook of research on children's literacy, learning and culture* (pp. 42–53). Oxford: John Wiley & Sons.

Green, J. L., Camilli, G., & Elmore, P. R. (2006). *Handbook of complementary methods in education research*. Mahwah, NJ: Lawrence Erlbaum Associates.

Green, R. L., & Etheridge, C. P. (2001). Collaborating to establish standards and accountability: Lessons learned about systemic change. *Education*, *121*(4), 821–829.

Greeno, J. G. (1994). Gibson's affordances. *Psychological Review*, *101*(2), 336–342. doi: 10.1037/0033-295X.101.2.336.

Greeno, J. G. (2006). Authoritative, accountable positioning and connected general knowing: Progressive themes in understanding transfer. *The Journal of Learning Sciences*, *15*(4), 537–547. doi: 10.1207/s15327809jls1504_4.

Gronn, P.(1999). Substituting for leadership: The neglected role of the leadership couple. *The Leadership Quarterly*, *10*(1), 41–62. doi: 10.1016/S1048-9843(99)80008-3.

Gronn, P. (2002). Distributed leadership as a unit of analysis. *The Leadership Quarterly*, *13*(4), 423–451. doi: 10.1016/S1048-9843(02)00120-0.

Gronn, P. (2009). Leadership configurations. *Leadership*, *5*(3), 381–394. doi: 10.1177/1742715009337770.

Grossman, P., & McDonald, M. (2008). Back to the future: Directions for research in teaching and teacher education. *American Educational Research Journal*, *45*(1), 184–205. doi: 10.3102/0002831207312906.

Haack, S. (2004). Pragmatism old and new. *Contemporary Pragmatism*, *1*(1), 3–42.

Habermas, J. (1987). *The theory of communicative action*. Vol. 2: *Lifeworld and System – A Critique of Functionalist Reason*. (T. McCarthy, Trans.). London: Polity Press.

Halliday, M. & Martin, J. (1994). *Writing science: Literacy and discursive power*. London: Falmer Press.

Hallinger, P. (2011). Leadership for learning: Lessons from 40 years of empirical research. *Journal of Educational Administration*, *49*(2), 125–142. doi: 10.1108/09578231111116699.

Hallinan, M. (2008). Teacher influences on student's attachment to school. *Sociology of Education*, *81*(July), 271–283. doi: 10.1177/003804070808100303.

Halpin, D. (1998). Democracy, inclusive schooling and the politics of education. Paper presented at the British Educational Research Association Annual Conference, Queen's University, Belfast.

Hammer, D., & Schifter, D. (2001). Practices of inquiry in teaching and research. *Cognition and Instruction*, *19*(4), 441–478. doi: 10.1207/S1532690XCI1904_2.

Hammerness, K. (2006). From coherence in theory to coherence in practice. *Teachers College Record*, *108*(7), 1241–1265. doi: 10.1111/j.1467-9620.2006.00692.x.

Hargreaves, A. (2003). *Teaching in the knowledge society: Education in the age of insecurity*. Maidenhead: Open University Press.

Hargreaves, D. (2005). *Personalising learning 4: Curriculum advice and guidance*. London: Specialist Schools Trust.

Harlen, W., Holroyd, C., & Byrne, M. (1995). *Confidence and understanding in teaching science and technology in primary schools*. SCRE Research Report: The Scottish Council for Research in Education.

Harpaz, Y. (2005). Teaching and learning in a community of thinking. *Journal of Curriculum and Supervision*, *20*(2), 136–157. Retrieved from http://yoramharpaz.com/publications-en/thinking/teaching-and-learning-in-community-of-thinking/.

Hart, R. (1997*). Children's participation: The theory and practice of involving young citizens in community development and environmental care*. London: Earthscan Publications, UNICEF.

Hartley, D. (2009). Personalisation: The nostalgic revival of child-centred education. *Journal of Education Policy*, *24*(4), 423–434. doi: 10.1080/02680930802669318.

REFERENCES

Hase, H. D., & Goldberg, L. G. (1967). Comparative validity of different strategies of constructing personality inventory scales. *Psychological Bulletin, 67*(4), 231–248. doi: 10.1037/h0024421.

Hattie, J. A. C. (2009). *Visible learning: A synthesis of over 800 meta-analyses relating to achievement.* London, UK: Routledge.

Hoekstra, A., & Korthagen, F. A. (2011). Teacher learning in a context of educational change: Informal learning versus systematically supported learning. *Journal of Teacher Education, 62*(1), 76–92. doi: 10.1177/0022487110382917.

Holmes, J., & Gutierrezz de Pineres, S. (2006). Democratic development: A comprehensive concept of comparative assessment. *International Journal of Social Economics, 33*(1), 54–76. doi: 10.1108/03068290610636433.

Hope, A. (2005). Panopticism, play and the resistance of surveillance: Case studies of the observation of student internet use in UK schools. *British Journal of Sociology of Education, 26*(3), 359–373. doi: 10.1080/01425690500128890.

Hopkins, D., Munro, J., & Craig, W. (2011). *Powerful Learning: A strategy for systemic educational improvement.* Melbourne, Australia: ACER Publishers.

Howard, S., Dryden, J., & Johnson, B. (1999). Childhood resilience: Review and critique of literature. *Oxford Review of Education, 25*(3), 307–323. doi: 10.1080/030549899104008.

Huebner, E. S. (1997). Life satisfaction and happiness. In G. Bear, K. Minke & A. Thomas (Eds.), *Children's needs II* (pp. 271–278). Washington DC: National Association of School Psychologists.

Huppert, F. A., Marks, N., Clark, A., Siegert, J., Tutzer, A., Vitterso, J., & Wahrendorf, M. (2009). Measuring wellbeing across Europe: Description of the ESS wellbeing module and preliminary findings. *Social Indicators Research, 91*, 301–315. doi: 10.1007/s11205-008-9346-0.

Illich, I. (1971). *Deschooling society.* New York: Tony Hall.

Isen, A. M., Rosenzweig, A. S., & Young, M. J. (1991). The influence of positive affect on clinical problem solving. *Medical Decision Making, 11*(3), 221–227. doi: 10.1177/0272989X9101100313.

Jackson A., & Davis, G. (2000). *Turning Points 2000: Educating adolescents in the 21st century.* New York: Teachers College Press.

Johnson, D., & Johnson, T. (1987). *Learning together and alone: Cooperative, competitive, and individualistic learning.* Englewood Cliffs, NJ: Prentice-Hall.

Johnson, D., & Johnson, T. (1989). Towards a cooperative effort: A response to Slavin. *Educational Leadership, 46*(7), 80–81.

Johnson, K., & O'Brien, M. L. (2002). "School is for me": Student engagement and the Fair Go project: A focus on engaging pedagogies in primary classrooms in low socio-economic status communities in south-western Sydney. Paper presented at the Australian Association of Research in Education Conference, Brisbane. Retrieved from http://www.aare.edu.au/data/publications/2004/joh04182.pdf.

Johnston, P., Woodside-Jiron, H., & Day, J. (2000). *Teaching and Learning Literate Epistemologies.* Albany, N.Y: The National Research Center on English Learning & Achievement. Retrieved from http://www.albany.edu/cela/reports/johnstonteachingepist13009.pdf.

Jung, M. L., & Tonso, K. L. (2006). Elementary pre-service teachers learning to teach science in science museums and nature centers: A novel program's impact on science knowledge, science pedagogy, and confidence teaching. *Journal of Elementary Science Education, 18*(1), 15–31. doi: 10.1007/BF03170651.

Kaplan, A. & Maehr, M. (1999). Achievement goals and student wellbeing. *Contemporary Educational Psychology, 24*(4), 330–358. doi: 10.1006/ceps.1999.0993.

Katzenmeyer, M., & Moller, G. (1996). *Awakening the sleeping giant: Leadership development for teachers.* Thousand Oaks, California: Corwin.

Keeffe, M., & Andrews, D. (2011). Students' perspectives on leadership: Interpretation of symbolic. social and cultural capital. *Leading and Managing, 17*(2), 21–35.

Keeffe, M., & Andrews, D. (in press). Towards an adolescent friendly methodology: Accessing the authentic. *International Journal of Research and Method in Education.*

Keeffe, M., Lovejoy, V., Spencer-Jones, D., & Prain, V. (2013). A case study in personalising learning: Relational agency in a visual arts studio. *Australian Art Education, 35*(1–2), 108–125.

Kelly, P. (2006). What is teacher learning? A socio-cultural perspective. *Oxford Review of Education, 32*(4), 505–519. doi: 10.1080/03054980600884227.

REFERENCES

Khine, M. S., & Fisher, D. L. (Eds.). (2003). *Technology-rich learning environments: A future perspective.* Singapore: World Scientific.

Koc, E. M. (2011). Development of mentor teacher role inventory. *European Journal of Teacher Education, 34*(2), 193–208.

Konu, A., & Rimpelä, M. (2002). Wellbeing in schools: A conceptual model. *Health Promotion International, 17*(1), 79–87. doi: 10.1093/heapro/17.1.79.

Korthagen, F. A., & Kessels, J. P. (1999). Linking theory and practice: Changing the pedagogy of teacher education. *Educational Researcher, 28*(4), 4–17. doi: 10.3102/0013189X028004004.

Korthagen, F. A., Loughran, J., & Russell, T. (2006). Developing fundamental principles for teacher education programs and practices. *Teaching and Teacher Education, 22*(8), 1020–1041. doi: 10.1016/j.tate.2006.04.022.

Kress, G., & van Leeuwen, T. (2001). *Multi-modal discourse: The modes and media of contemporary communication.* London: Oxford University Press.

Kubow, P. K., & Kinney, M. B. (2000). Fostering democracy in middle school classrooms: Insights from a democratic institute in Hungary. *The Social Studies, 91*(6), 265–271. doi: 10.1080/00377990009602476.

Kuhl, J. (1983). Emotion, cognition, and motivation: II. The functional signficance of emotions in perception, memory, problem-solving, and overt action. *Sprache & Kognition, 2*, 228–253.

Kuhl, J. (2000). A functional-design approach to motivation and self-regulation: The dynamics of personality systems interactions. In M. Moekaerts, P. R. Pintrich & M. Zeidner (Eds.), *Handbook of self-regulation* (pp. 111–169). San Diego: Academic Press.

Leadbeater, C. (2003). *Personalisation through participation.* London: Demos.

Leadbeater, C. (2005). *The shape of things to come: Personalised learning through collaboration.* London: DfES Publications.

Ledward, B. C., & Hirata, D. (2011). *An overview of 21st century skills.* Honolulu: Kamechamcha Schools-Research & Evaluation.

Lee, M. R., & Lan, Y. (2007). From Web 2.0 to conversational knowledge management: Towards collaborative intelligence. *Journal of Entrepreneurship Research, 2*(2), 47–62. Retrieved from http://citeseerx.ist.psu.edu/viewdoc/download?doi=10.1.1.106.5090&rep=rep1&type=pdf.

Lee, V., & Smith, J. (1997). High school size: Which works best and for whom? *Educational Evaluation and Policy Analysis, 19*(3), 205–227. doi: 10.3102/01623737019003205.

Legewie, J., & DiPrete, T. A. (2012). School context and the gender gap in educational achievement. *American Sociological Review, 77*(3), 463–485. doi: 10.1177/0003122412440802.

Leiringer, R., & Cardellino, P. (2011). Schools for the twenty-first century: School design and educational transformation. *British Educational Research Journal, 37*(6), 915–934. doi: 10.1080/01411926.2010.508512.

Leitch, R., & Day, C. (2000). Action research and reflective practice: Towards a holistic view. *Educational Action Research, 8*(1), 179–193. doi: 10.1080/09650790000200108.

Leithwood, K., Mascall, B., & Strauss, T. (Eds.). (2009). *Distributed Leadership According to the Evidence.* New York: Routledge.

Lemke, J. (2014). Uchange begins. Retrieved from http://www.jaylemke.com/.

Levin, B. (2009). 20 Minutes to change a life? *Phi Delta Kappan, 90*(5), 384–385. Retrieved from http://www.kappanmagazine.org/content/90/5/384.abstract?related-urls=yes&legid=pdk;90/5/384.

Levy, P. (1997). *Collective intelligence: Mankind's emerging world in cyberspace.* (R. Bononno Trans.). New York: Plenum Press.

Lipponen, L., & Kumpulainen, K. (2011). Acting as accountable authors: Creating interactional spaces for agency work in teacher education. *Teaching and Teacher Education, 27*(5), 812–819. doi: 10.1016/j.tate.2011.01.001.

Lodge, C. (2005). From hearing voices to engaging in dialogue: Problematising student participation in school improvement. *Journal of Educational Change, 6*(2), 125–146. doi: 10.1007/s10833-005-1299-3.

Løhre, A., Moksnes, U. K., & Lillefjell, M. (2014). Gender differences in predictors of school wellbeing? *Health Education Journal, 73*(1), 90–100. doi: 10.1177/0017896912470822.

REFERENCES

Loi, D., & Dillon, P. (2006). Adaptive educational environments as creative spaces. *Cambridge Journal of Education, 36*(3), 363–381. doi: 10.1080/03057640600865959.

Loughran, J. (2002). Effective reflective practice: In search of meaning in learning about teaching. *Journal of Teacher Education, 53*(1), 33–43. doi: 10.1177/0022487102053001004.

Louie, B. Y., Drevdahl, D. J., Purdy, J. M., & Stackman, R. W. (2003). Advancing the scholarship of teaching through collaborative self-study. *The Journal of Higher Education, 74*(2), 150–171. doi: 10.1353/jhe.2003.0016.

Lowenstein, M. (2005). If advising is teaching, what do advisors teach? *NACADA Journal, 25*(2), 65–73. Retrieved from http://www.nacada.ksu.edu/portals/0/Clearinghouse/AdvisingIssues/documents/25-2-Lowenstein-pp65-73.pdf.

Lyons, T., Cooksey, R., Panizzon, D., Parnell, A., & Pegg, J. (2006). *Science, ICT and mathematics education in rural and regional Australia: The SiMERR national survey.* Canberra: Department of Education, Science and Training.

Mahony, P., & Hextall, I. (2009, September). Building schools for the future and the implications for becoming a teacher. Paper presented at the European Conference on Educational Research, Vienna.

Mannay, D. (2010). Making the familiar strange: Can visual research methods render the familiar setting more perceptible? *Qualitative Research, 10*(1), 91–111. doi: 10.1177/1468794109348684.

Mårell-Olsson, E. (2012). Att göra lärandet synligt? Individuella utvecklingsplaner och digital dokumentation [Making Learning Visible? Personal Development Planning and Digital Documentation]. Unpublished doctoral dissertation. Umea University, Umea.

Markus, T. (1993). *Buildings and power: Freedom and control in the origins of modern building types.* London: Routledge.

Maslow, A. (1954). *Motivation and personality.* New York: Harper.

Matthew, C. T., & Sternberg, R. J. (2009). Developing experience-based (tacit) knowledge through reflection. *Learning and Individual Differences, 19*(4), 530–540. doi: 10.1016/j.lindif.2009.07.001.

McGregor, J. (2004a). Space, power and the classroom. *Forum. 46*(1), 13–18. doi: 10.2304/forum.2004.46.1.2.

McGregor, J. (2004b). Spatiality and the place of the materials in schools. *Pedagogy, Culture & Society, 12*(3), 347–372. doi: 10.1080/14681360400200207.

McLaughlin, C. (2008). Emotional wellbeing and its relationship to schools and classrooms: A critical reflection. *British Journal of Guidance & Counselling, 36*(4), 353–366. doi: 10.1080/03069880802364486.

McLoughlin, C., & Lee, M. (2010). Personalised and self-regulated learning in the Web 2.0 era: International exemplars of innovative pedagogy using social software. *Australasian Journal of Educational Technology, 26*(1), 28–43. Retrieved from http://www.ascilite.org.au/ajet/ajet26/mcloughlin.pdf.

McTighe, J., & Brown, J. (2005). Differentiated instruction and educational standards: Is détente possible? *Theory into Practice, 44*(3), 234–244. doi: 10.1207/s15430421tip4403_8.

McTighe, J., & Wiggins, G. (2004). *Understanding by design* (2nd ed.). Alexandria, VA: Association for Supervision and Curriculum Development.

Mercer, N. (2008). Talk and the development of reasoning and understanding. *Human Development, 51*(1), 90–100. doi: 10.1159/000113158.

Meyer, B., Haywood, N., Sachdev, D., & Faraday, S. (2008). *Independent learning: Literature review.* London: Department for Children, Schools, and Families.

Midgley, C., Maehr, M. L., Hruda, L. Z., Anderman, E., Anderman, L., Freeman, K. E., Gheen, M.... & Urdan, T. (2000). *Manual for the patterns of adaptive learning scales (PALS).* Ann Arbor, MI: University of Michigan.

Mitra, D. L. (2007). Student voice in school reform: From listening to leadership. In D. Thiessen & A. Cook-Sather (Eds.), *International handbook of student experience in elementary and secondary school* (pp. 727–744). Dordrecht, NL: Springer.

Mitra, D. L. (2009). Strengthening student voice initiatives in high schools: An examination of the supports needed for school-based youth-adult partnerships. *Youth and Society, 40*(3), 311–335. doi: 10.1177/0044118X08316211.

REFERENCES

Mitra, D., Serriere, S., & Stoicovy, D. (2012). The role of leaders in enabling student voice. *Management in Education, 26*(3), 104–112. doi: 10.1177/0892020612445678.
Moje, E. B. (2007). Developing socially just subject-matter instruction: A review of the literature on disciplinary literacy. In N L. Parker (Ed.), *Review of Research in Education.* (pp. 1–44). Washington, DC: American Educational Research Association.
Moos, R. H., & Trickett, E. J. (1987). *Classroom environment scale manual* (2nd ed.). Palo Alto, CA: Consulting Psychologists Press.
Murphy, E. & Rodriguez-Manzanares, M. (2008). Using activity theory and its principle of contradictions to guide research in educational technology. *Australasian Journal of Educational Technology, 24*(4), 442–457. Retrieved from http://www.ascilite.org.au/ajet/ajet24/murphy.html.
Muukkonen, H, & Lakkala, M. (2009). Exploring metaskills of knowledge-creating inquiry in higher education. *Computer-Supported Collaborative Learning, 4*(2), 187–211. doi: 10.1007/s11412-009-9063-y.
Nair, P. (2006). *Design strategies for tomorrow's schools in 21st century learning environments.* Paris: OECD.
Nair, P., & Fielding, R. (2005). *The language of school design: Design patterns for 21st century schools.* Mineapolis, MN: Designshare.
Needham, C. (2011). Personalization: From story-line to practice. *Social Policy and Administration, 45*(1), 54–68. doi: 10.1111/j.1467-9515.2010.00753.x.
Niska, J. (2013). A study of the impact of professional development on middle level advisors. *RMLE Online, 37*(5), 1–14. Retrieved from https://www.amle.org/portals/0/pdf/rmle/rmle_vol37_no5.pdf.
Norman, D. (1999). Affordance, conventions and design. *Interactions* 6(3), 38–43. doi: 10.1145/301153.301168.
Oates, T. (2011). Could do better: Using international comparisons to refine the national curriculum in England. *The Curriculum Journal, 22*(2), 121–150. doi: 10.1080/09585176.2011.578908.
O'Brien, M. (2008). *Wellbeing and post-primary schooling: A review of the literature and research.* Dublin, Ireland: National Council for Curriculum and Assessment. Retrieved from http://www.ncca.ie/en/Publications/Reports/Wellbeing_and_Post Primary Schooling_A_review_of_the_literature_and_research.pdf.
OECD. (2009). *Education at a glance.* Paris: OECD Publishing. doi: 10.1787/eag-2012-en.
OECD. (2010). *PISA 2009 Results: Overcoming social background – Equity in learning opportunities and outcomes (Volume II).* Paris: OECD Publishing. doi: 10.1787/9789264091504-en.
OECD. (2014). *PISA 2012 Results: What students know and can do: Student performance in mathematics, reading and science* (Vol. I, Revised ed., February 2014). Paris: OECD Publishing. doi: 10.1787/9789264201118-en.
Onyx, J., Wood, C., Bullen, P., & Osburn, L. (2005). Social capital: A rural youth perspective. *Youth Studies Australia, 24*(4), 21–27. Retrieved from http://www.acys.info/ysa/issues/v.24_n.4_2005/p21_-_J._Onyx_et._al.__December_2005.pdf.
O'Reilly, T. (2007). What is Web 2.0: Design patterns and business models for the next generation of software. *Communications & Strategies, 1*, 17–37. Retrieved from http://papers.ssrn.com/sol3/papers.cfm?abstract_id=1008839.
Ottesen, E. (2007). Teachers "in the making": Building accounts of teaching. *Teaching and Teacher Education, 23*(5), 612–623. doi: 10.1016/j.tate.2007.01.011.
Palombi, B. J. (1992). Psychometric properties of wellbeing instruments. *Journal of Counseling & Development, 71*(2), 221–225. doi: 10.1002/j.1556-6676.1992.tb02204.x.
Paludan, J. (2006). Personalised learning 2025. In *Schooling for tomorrow: Personalising education*, Paris: OECD Publishing, 83–100.
Parrish, A.-M., Okely, A., Stanley, R., & Ridgers, N. (2013). The effect of school recess interventions of physical activity. *Sports Medicine, 43*(4), 287–299. doi: 10.1007/s40279-013-0024-2
Pedersen, S., & Liu, M. (2003). Teachers' beliefs about issues in the implementation of a student-centered learning environment. *Educational Technology, Research and Development 51*(2), 57–76. doi: 10.1007/BF02504526.
Peirce, C. S. (1931–58). *Collected papers of Charles Sanders Peirce.* 8 Vols. (Hartshorne, C., Weiss, P. & Burks, A. W. Eds., Vols. 1–6), (Burks, A. W. Ed., Vols. 7–8). Cambridge, MA: Harvard University Press.

REFERENCES

Phillippo, K. (2009). A matter of alignment: An organizational analysis of the advisor role in three smalll urban high schools. Unpublished doctoral dissertation. Stanford University, Ann Arbor.

Phillippo, K. (2010). Teacher-advisors providing social and emotional support: A study of complex role enactment in small high schools. *Teachers College Record, 112*(8), 2258–2293. Retrieved from http://www.tcrecord.org/Content.asp?ContentId=15955.

Pintrich, P. (2004). A conceptual framework for assessing motivation and self-regulated learning in college students. *Educational Psychology Review, 16*(4), 385–407. doi: 10.1007/s10648-004-0006-x.

Pintrich, P. R., & De Groot, E. (1990). Motivated and self-regulated learning components of academic performance. *Journal of Educational Psychology, 82*(1), 33–40. doi: 10.1037/0022-0663.82.1.33.

Plowright, D. (2011). Using mixed methods: Frameworks for an integrated methodology. Thousand Oaks, CA: Sage.

Prain, V., Cox, P., Deed, C., Dorman, J., Edwards, D., Farrelly, C., Keeffe, M., . . .Yager, Z. (2013). Personalised learning: lessons to be learnt. *British Educational Research Journal, 39*(4), 654–676. doi: 10.1080/01411926.2012.669747.

Prain, V., Cox, P., Deed, C., Dorman, J., Edwards, D., Farrelly, C., Keeffe, M., . . .Yager, Z. (in press). Personalising Learning in Open-Plan Schools. Rotterdam: Sense Publishers.

Pridham, B., Deed, C., & Cox, P. (2013). Workplace-based practicum: Enabling expansive practices. *Australian Journal of Teacher Education, 38*(4). doi: 10.14221/ajte.2013v38n4.7.

Putnam, R. D. (1993). The properous community: Social capital and public life. *The American Prospect, 4*(13), 35–42. Retrieved from http://prospect.org/article/prosperous-community-social-capital-and-public-lifehttp://prospect.org/article/prosperous-.

Putnam, R. T., & Borko, H. (2000). What do new views of knowledge and thinking have to say about research on teacher learning? *Educational Researcher, 29*(1), 4–15. doi: 10.3102/0013189X029001004.

Pykett, J. (2009). Personalisation and de-schooling: Uncommon trajectories in contemporary education policy. *Critical Social Policy, 29*(3), 374–397. doi: 10.1177/0261018309105176.

Pykett, J. (2010). Personalised governing through behaviour change and re-education. Paper presented at the Political Studies Association Conference, Edinburgh.

Quenzel, G., & Hurrleman, K. (2013). The growing gender gap in education. *International Journal of Adolescence and Youth, 18*(2), 69–94. doi: 10.1080/02673843.2012.665168.

Ramstetter, C. L., Murray, R., & Garner, A. S. (2010). The crucial role of recess in schools. *Journal of School Health, 80*(11), 517–526. doi: 10.1111/j.1746-1561.2010.00537.x

Reay, D., & Arnot, M. (2002). Social inclusion, gender, class and community in secondary schooling. Paper presented at the BERA annual conference, University of Exeter.

Reh, S., Rabenstein, K., & Fritzsche, B. (2011). Learning spaces without boundaries? Territories, power and how schools regulate learning. *Social & Cultural Geography, 12*(1), 83–98. doi: 10.1080/14649365.2011.542482.

Robinson C., & Taylor C. (2007). Theorising student voice: Values and perspectives. *Improving Schools, 10*(1), 5–17. doi: 10.1177/1365480207073702.

Robinson, V., & Ward, L. (2005). Lay governance of New Zealand's schools: An educational, democratic or managerialist activity? *Journal of Educational Administration, 43*(2), 170–186. doi: 10.1108/09578230510586579.

Rogers. S. (2013). Personalisation and student voice. *Insights, 7*(Autumn), British Education Research Association. Retrieved from http://www.bera.ac.uk/wp-content/uploads/2013/12/Insights-7-Personalisation-Student-Voice-for-web-2.pdf.

Rowe, G., Hirsh, J. B., Anderson, A. K., & Smith, E. E. (2007). Positive affect increases the breadth of attentional selection. *PNAS Proceedings of the national Academy of Sciences of the United States of America, 104*, 383–388. doi: 10.1073/pnas.0605198104.

Rudduck, J., & Fielding, M. (2006). Student voice and the perils of popularity. *Educational Review, 58*(2), 213–231. doi: 10.1080/00131910600584207.

Rudduck, J., & McIntyre, D. (Eds.). (2007). *Improving learning through consulting pupils*. Teaching and Learning Research Programme (TLRP) Consulting Pupils Project Team. London: Routledge.

Rutter, M. (1990). Psychsocial resilience and protective mechanisms. In J. Rolf, A. Masten, D. Cicchetti, K. Nuechterlain, & S. Weintraub (Eds.), *Risk and protective factors in the development of psychopathology* (pp. 181–214). New York: Cambridge University Press.

REFERENCES

Sachs, J. (2003). *The Activist Teaching Profession*. Maidenhead: Open University Press.

Santoro, N., Reid, J., Mayer, D., & Singh, M. (2013). Teacher knowledge: continuing professional learning. *Asia-Pacific Journal of Teacher Education, 41*(2), 123–125. doi: 10.1080/1359866X.2013.777326.

Schlecty, P. (1997). *Inventing better schools: An action plan for educational reform*. San Francisco: Jossey-Bass.

Schon, D. (1983). *The Reflective practitioner: How professionals think in action*. New York: Basic Books.

Seaton, A. (2002). Reforming the hidden curriculum: The key abilities model and four curricular forms. *Curriculum Perspectives, 22*(1), 9–15. Retrieved from http://andrewseaton.com.au/reform.htm.

Sebba, J., Brown, N., Steward, S., Galton, M., James, M., Celentano, N., & Boddy, P. (2007). *An investigation of personalised leaning approaches used by schools*. Research Report RR843. Annesley, NG: DfES Publications.

Seligman, M., Ernst R., Gilham, J., Reivich K., & Linkins M. (2009). Positive education: Positive psychology and classroom interventions. *Oxford Review of Education, 35*(3), 293–311. doi: 10.1080/03054980902934563.

Sergiovanni, T. J. (2000). *The lifeworld of leadership: Creating culture, community and personal meaning in our schools*. San Francisco: Jossey-Bass.

Sfard, A. (1998). On two metaphors for learning and the dangers of choosing just one. *Educational Researcher, 27*(2), 4–12. doi: 10.3102/0013189X027002004.

Sharples, M. Taylor, J., & Vavoula, G. (2010). A theory of learning for the mobile age. In B. Bachmair (Ed.), *Medienbildung in neuen Kulturraumen* (pp. 87–99). Stuttgart: VS Verlag fur Sozialwissenschaften.

Shohel, M. (2012). Nostalgia, transition and the school: photographic images as a visual method in educational research. *International Journal of Research and Method in Education, 35*(3), 269–292. doi: 10.1080/1743727X.2012.713253.

Simon, H. A. (1976). *Administrative Behaviour*. (3rd ed.). New York: Free Press.

Skinner, E. A., & Belmont, N. J. (1993). Motivation in the classroom: Reciprocal effect of teacher behavior and student engagement across the school year. *Journal of Educational Psychology, 85*(4), 571–581. doi: 10.1037/0022-0663.85.4.571.

Skrtic, T. M., & Sailor, W. (1996). Voice, collaboration and inclusion. *Remedial and Special Education, 17*(3), 142–158. doi: 10.1177/074193259601700304.

Slavin, R. (1990). *Cooperative learning: Theory, research and practice*. Boston: Allyn & Bacon.

Slee, R. (2001). Driven to the margins: Disabled students, inclusive schooling and the politics of possibilities. *Cambridge Journal of Education, 31*(3), 385–397. doi: 10.1080/03057640120086620.

Smyth, J. (2006a). Educational leadership that fosters 'student voice'. *International Journal of Leadership in Education: Theory and Practice, 9*(4), 279–284. doi: 10.1080/13603120600894216.

Smyth, J. (2006b). "When students have power": Student engagement, student voice, and the possibilities for school reform around "dropping out" of school. *International Journal of Leadership in Education, 9*(4), 285–298. doi: 10.1080/13603120600894232.

Solvberg, A. & Rismark, M. (2012). Learning spaces in mobile learning environments. *Active Learning in Higher Education, 13*(1), 23–33. doi: 10.1177/1469787411429189.

Stafford, T. (2011). *Teaching visual literacy in the primary classroom*. New York: Routledge.

Sternberg, R. J., & Horvath, J. A. (1995). A prototype view of expert teaching. *Educational Researcher, 24*(6), 9–17. doi: 10.3102/0013189X024006009.

Stockhill, J. (2011). *Student focussed strategies: Supporting achievement. Research Associate Full Report*. National College for School Leadership. Retrieved from http://www.nationalcollege.org.uk/docinfo?id=151988&filename=student-focused-strategies-full-report.pdf.

Stradling, B., & Saunders, L. (1993). Differentiation in practice: responding to the needs of all pupils. *Educational Research, 35*(2), 127–137. doi: 10.1080/0013188930350202.

Strong, R., Silver, H., & Perini, M. (2001). *Teaching what matters most*. Alexandria, VA: Association for Supervision and Curriculum Development.

Subban, P. (2006). Differentiated instruction: A research basis. *International Education Journal, 7*(7), 935–947. Retrieved from http://ehlt.flinders.edu.au/education/iej/articles/v7n7/Subban/paper.pdf.

Sugarman, J., & Martin, J. (2011). Theorizing relational agency. *Journal of Constructivist Psychology, 24*(4), 283–289. doi: 10.1080/10720537.2011.593455.

REFERENCES

Sugarman, J., & Sokol, B. (2012). Human agency and development: An introduction and theoretical sketch. *New Ideas in Psychology, 30*(1), 1–14. doi: 10.1016/j.newideapsych.2010.03.001.

Sutherland, J. (2013). Going 'meta': Using a metadiscoursal approach to develop secondary students' dialogic talk in small groups. *Research Papers in Education.* doi: 10.1080/02671522.2013.850528.

Tashakkori, A., & Teddlie, C. (2010). *Mixed methods in social & behavioural research.* Los Angeles, CA: Sage.

Taylor, J., & Nelms, L. (2008). *Life chances at 16: Life stage study stage 8.* Melbourne: Brotherhood of St. Laurence.

Taylor, P., Fraser, B., & Fisher, D. (1997). Monitoring constructivist classroom learning environments. *International Journal of Educational Research, 27*(4), 293–302. doi: 10.1016/S0883-0355(97)90011-2.

Taylor, C., & Robinson, C. (2009). Student voice: Theorising power and participation. *Pedagogy, Culture and Society, 17*(2), 161–175. doi: 10.1080/14681360902934392.

Teddlie, C., & Tashakkori, A. (2009). Foundations of mixed methodology. Thousand Oaks, CA: Sage.

Thomson, S., & De Bortoli, L. (2008). *Exploring scientific literacy: How Australia measures up: The PISA 2006 survey of students' scientific, reading and mathematical literacy skills.* Retrieved from http://research.acer.edu.au/ozpisa/2.

Tienken, C. (2013). Conclusions from PISA and TIMSS testing. *Kappa Delta Pi Record, 49*(2), 56–58. doi: 10.1080/00228958.2013.786588.

Tomlinson, C. A. (1999). *The differentiated classroom: Responding to the needs of all learners.* Alexandria. VA: Association for Supervision and Curriculum Development.

Tomlinson, C. A. (2001). *How to differentiate instruction in mixed-ability classrooms.* Alexandria, VA: Association for Supervision and Curriculum Development.

Tomlinson, C. (2005). Grading and differentiation: Paradox or good practice. *Theory into Practice, 44*(3), 262–269. doi: 10.1207/s15430421tip4403_11.

Tomlinson, C. A., & Kalbfliesch, M. (1998). Teach me, teach my brain: A call for differentiated classrooms. *Educational Leadership* 56(3), 52–55. Retrieved from http://www.ascd.org/publications/educational-leadership/nov98/vol56/num03/Teach-Me,-Teach-My-Brain@-A-Call-for-Differentiated-Classrooms.aspx.

Tuttle, J. (2000). *Differentiated Classrooms.* Woodbury: Cedar Mountain Academy.

Tytler, R., Prain, V., Hubber, P., & Waldrip, B. (2013). *Constructing representations to learn in science.* Rotterdam: Sense Publishers.

Underwood, J., Baguley, T., Banyard, P., Coyne, E., Farrington-Flint, L., & Selwood, I. (2008). *Impact 2007: Personalising learning with technology: Final report.* Coventry: British Educational Communications and Technology Agency (BECTA).

UN General Assembly, *Convention on the Rights of the Child*, 20 November 1989, United Nations, Treaty Series, vol. 1577, p. 3. Retrieved from http://www.refworld.org/docid/3ae6b38f0.html.

Valeski, T. N., & Stipek, D. (2001). Young children's feelings about school. *Child Development, 72*(4), 1198–2013. doi: 10.1111/1467-8624.00342.

Van Petegem, K., Aelterman, A., Rosseel, Y., & Creemers, B. (2007). Student perception as moderator for student wellbeing. *Social Indicators Research, 83*(3), 447–463. doi: 1854/7689.

Van Petegem, K., Aelterman, A., Van Keer, H., & Rosseel, Y. (2008). The influence of student characteristics and interpersonal teacher behaviour in the classroom on students' wellbeing. *Social Indicators Research, 85*(2), 279–291. doi: 10.1007/s11205-007-9093-7.

Vaughan, W. (2002). Effects of cooperative learning on achievement and attitude among students of color. *The Journal of Educational Research, 95*(6), 359–364. doi: 10.1080/00220670209596610.

Velez, J. J., Sorenson, T., McKim, A., & Cano, J. (2013). Self-efficacy and task value motivation of students based on classroom, instructor and student variables. *NACTA Journal, 57*(4), 65–71. Retrieved from http://www.nactateachers.org/volume-57-num-4-dec-2013.

Verbert, K., Duval, E., Klerkx, J., Govaerts, S. & Santos, J. L. (2013). Learning analytics dashboard applications. American Behavioral Scientist, 57(10), 1500–1509. doi: 10.1177/0002764213479363.

Verloop, N., Van Driel, J., & Meijer, P. (2001). Teacher knowledge and the knowledge base of teaching. *International Journal of Educational Research, 35*(5), 441–461. doi: 10.1016/S0883-0355(02)00003-4.

Vygotsky, L. S. (1986). *Thought and language.* (A. Kozulin, Trans. & Ed.). Cambridge, MA: MIT Press.

REFERENCES

Vygotsky, L. S. (1997a). *Problems of the theory and history of psychology.* Vol. 3. *The collected works of L. S. Vygotsky.* New York: Plenum Press.
Vygotsky, L. S. (1997b). *Educational Psychology.* Boca Raton FL: St Lucie Press.
Vygotsky, L. S. (1998). *Child psychology.* Vol. 5. *The collected works of L. S. Vygotsky.* New York: Plenum Press.
Waldrip, B., Cox, P., Deed, C., Dorman, J., Edwards, D., Farrelly, C., Keefe, M. . . Yager, Z. (2014). Student perceptions of personalised learning: Validation and development of questionnaire with regional secondary students. *Learning Environments Research, 17*(2). doi: 10.1007/s10984-014-9163-0
Waldrip, B. G., Fisher, D. L., & Dorman, J. (2009). Identifying exemplary science teachers through their students' perceptions of the assessment process. *Journal of Science and Technology Education, 27*(1), 117–129. doi: 10.1080/02635140802658958.
Waxman, H. C., Sparks, K., Stillisano, J., & Lee, Y. H. (2009). The development and use of a learning environment instrument to evaluate teacher's professional development. Paper presented at the Annual Meeting of the American Educational Research Association, San Diego, CA.
Wellborn, J. G., & Connell, J. P. (1987). *Manual for the Rochester assessment package for schools.* Rochester, NY: University of Rochester.
Wharton, D., & Grant, J. (2005). *Teaching analysis of film language.* London: British Film Institute.
Wiggins, G., & McTighe, J. (1998). *Understanding by design.* Alexandria, VA: Association for Supervision and Curriculum Development.
Wittgenstein, L. (1972). *Lectures and conversations on aesthetics, psychology, and religious belief.* Berkeley: University of California Press.
Woods, P. A. (2004). Democratic leadership: Drawing distinctions with distributed leadership. *International Journal of Leadership in Education, 7*(1), 3–26. doi: 10.1080/1360312032000154522.
Woods, P., & Gronn, P. (2009). Nurturing democracy: The contribution of distributed leadership to a democratic organizational landscape. *Educational Management, Administration and Leadership, 37*(4), 430–451. doi: 10.1177/1741143209334597.
World Health Organisation (WHO). (1996). *Promoting health through schools.* Retrieved from http://www.who.int/iris/handle/10665/63367#sthash.Mj72gAhw.dpuf.
Wubbels, T., & Brekelmans, M. (2005). Two decades of research on teacher-student relationships in class. *International Journal of Educational Research, 43*(1–2), 6–24. doi: 10.1016/j.ijer.2006.03.003.
Yin, R. (2008). *Case study research: Design and methods.* Thousand Oaks: Sage.
Yost, D. S., Sentner, S. M., & Forlenza-Bailey, A. (2000). An examination of the construct of critical reflection: Implications for teacher education programming in the 21st century. *Journal of Teacher Education, 51*(1), 39–49. doi: 10.1177/002248710005100105.
Zeichner, K. (2006). Reflections of a university-based teacher educator on the future of college- and university-based teacher education. *Journal of Teacher Education, 57*(3), 326–340. doi: 10.1177/0022487105285893.
Zeichner, K. (2010). Rethinking the connections between campus courses and field experiences in college- and university-based teacher education. *Journal of Teacher Education, 61*(1–2), 89–99. doi: 10.1177/0022487109347671.
Zimmerman, B. (2008). Investigating self-regulation and motivation: Historical background, methodological developments, and future prospects. *American Educational Research Journal, 45*(1), 166–183. doi: 10.3102/0002831207312909.
Zou, X. (2011). What happens in different contexts and how to do learner autonomy better? *Teacher Development, 15*(4), 421–433. doi: 10.1080/13664530.2011.635268.

INDEX

A

Academic Efficacy, 16, 24, 26, 29, 39, 143, 144, 176, 195
Achievement
  academic, 31, 50
  in mathematics, 54
  importance of TA program, 72, 165
  in studio arts, 119
  student achievement, 52, 61
  and links with adolescent well-being, 169; *see also national* tests (NAPLAN)
Activity theory, 6, 200, 205–207, 209, 212, 215
Adaptation
  of teachers to up-scaled learning communities, 4, 5, 9, 17, 43, 109, 110, 123, 198, 211, 214
Affordance theory, 8, 79, 80, 82, 86, 87, 90–92, 107–109, 136, 202, 203, 218
Agency, 6, 7, 9, 52–54, 79–80, 83, 84, 90–93, 103–105, 137, 138, 141–143, 171, 172, 187, 190, 197–201, 206–209, 202, 225
Assessment, 14, 23–26, 29, 30, 33, 34, 39, 40, 45, 554–557, 82–84, 87, 88, 130–132, 212, 226; *see* Bendigo Education Plan, personalised learning, curriculum, PLEQ scales, differentiation, mathematics, literacy
Attendance, 10, 11, 19, 29, 36, 41, 85, 152, 153, 183, 186, 187, 195
Attitudes to School, 10, 35, 36, 55, 57, 176, 177, 185, 2012
Autism Spectrum Disorder, 183

B

Bendigo Education Plan
  context, strategies, 4, 5
  rationale including equity and social justice, 9–11, 13–17
  assessment, 28, 29, 31, 33, 34, 36
  school design, 61–64
  student voice, 143–147, 149–155, 157, 159–161
  outcomes, 195, 196, 205–209
  well-being issues, 173–179
Bullying, 10, 14,148, 164, 167, 175, 181, 182, 185

C

Capacity building: students, 45, 46,
  teacher professional learning 76, 171,178, 180, 219
  in distributed leadership, 104
Choice
  student choice, 12, 53–55, 83, 86, 110–112, 128, 129, 173, 179, 180, 184, 209, 220; *see* self-regulated learning; studio arts; self-directed learning.
Collaboration in open-plan settings; *see* team teaching
Co-regulated learning; *see* learning
Curriculum
  differentiated, 16, 17, 21, 23, 42, 57, 60, 61, 63–66, 77, 88, 128, 203, 205, 209, 229, 232, 233

D

Dashboard, 86–93, 153, 161, 183, 184, 225
Differentiated curriculum; *see* curriculum

INDEX

Distributed leadership, 9, 10, 15, 47, 52, 61, 95–98, 101–106, 163, 199, 201, 207, 209, 215, 218, 220, 226; *see* also capacity building

Division of labour, 6, 151, 154, 199, 200, 206; *see* activity theory, teacher roles, student roles

E

Ecosystems, 155; *see* threshold of change

Educational disadvantage, 34, 175; *see* Bendigo Education Plan

Embodied learning, 117, 143, 202; *see* also theoretical perspectives

Engagement
teacher, 129, 136
student, 10, 11, 26, 29, 30, 33, 38–40, 47, 48, 51, 92, 93, 101, 104, 110, 117, 143, 144, 160, 161, 180, 189–191, 202, 217, 219, 224; *see* also Bendigo Education Plan, students, teachers, pre-service teachers

Epistemic learning, 51, 110

Epistemological dimensions, 51, 111; *see* also domains, personalised learning, curriculum quality

Evaluation, *see* chapters 2 and 12; *see* also BEP strategies

F

Feedback, 7, 8, 10, 15, 21, 49, 56, 69, 81, 82, 99, 118, 122, 156, 171, 203, 213; *see* also curriculum, PLEQ scales, student, teacher

Frameworks, chapter 3; *see* theoretical perspectives

G

Games based learning, 86, 135, chapter 5; *see* also Grevillea College

Gender
differences in perceptions of well-being 144, 146; 170, 174, 179–181, 196, 211, 212, 220, 223

Goals
student learning, 14, 25, 26, 50–52, 86, 90, 97, 102, 153, 164, 165, 197–200, 202, 203; *see* Bendigo Education Plan

Grevillea College
academic attainment, 35
attitudes to school, 36
school structure, 64–66
school design, 74
vision statement, 73
game design project, 84–86
teacher advisor program, 98, 99, 102
student leadership; *see* chapter 9, engaging boys through technology, 135
student voice, 152, 162
student wellbeing, 178

H

Higher order thinking, 13, 39, 92; *see* also Bendigo Education Plan

I

Identity
student, 50, 75, 78, 143, 149, 212, 217
teacher and community, 73

Informal learning
student, 12, 13
encouraged by school design and structures, 62, 73, 79–81, 83, 84, 108, 128, 136, 138, 200, 202, 219

Information Communication Technology; *see* games based learning; dashboard; virtual learning

Ironbark College

228

INDEX

academic attainment, 35, 36
attitudes to school
distributed leadership, 101–105
school attendance, chapter 2, school structure, 64–66; chapters 4, 11,
school design, 71–73
vision statement, 70
teacher advisor program, 75, 156, 160, 162, 164, 166, 169–172
case study, 55
student leadership, chapter 9
student voice 153,
student wellbeing programs 178, 182, 185, 188–191
Inquiry; *see* pragmatism.

K

Knowledge; *see* pragmatism, theoretical perspectives, adaptation, teacher, pre-service teacher; epistemic; epistemological directions.

L

Leadership
distributed, 9, 10, 17, 47, 69, 198, 199, 201, 207–209, 202, 215, 216, 218, 219, 220, 224, 225, 226 chapter 6
teacher leadership, 74, 109, 205, chapter 11
student, 153, 221
traditional, chapter 6
transformational, chapter 6. *see* also distributed leadership, teachers, students, theoretical perspectives.
Learning
self-regulated, 49, 50, 52, 54, 153, 213, 215, 221, 223
co-regulated, 50 52, 56, 213
technologically mediated learning, *see* information communication technology; virtual learning: chapter 5;
see also informal, curriculum, differentiated curriculum;
see also Melaleuca College, Grevillea College, Whirrakee College, Ironbark College, mathematics case study, studio arts case study, personalised learning, Bendigo Education Plan, differentiated curriculum
Learning communities
structures of chapter 4; protocols in 13, 56, 73, 78, 100, 102, 108–110, 131–133, 137, 163, 188, 197, 198, 200; *see* affordances: constraints of, 54, 73, 79, 85, 107–9, 117; *see* upscaled learning communities, team teaching, distributed leadership in
Learning environment; *see* chapters 2, 11; *see* also open-plan settings; PLEQ research scales; well-being
Learning theory; *see* adaptation
Literacy, 3, 23
student achievement levels, 35
English case studies, *see* chapter 7; *see* also National Assessment Program-Literacy and Numeracy

M

Mathematics
student achievement levels, 35
mathematics case studies, chapters 3, 7; *see* also Bendigo Education Plan; Ironbark College; Waratah College
Measurement
data chapter, 2
effectiveness of BEP strategies, chapter 12; *see* PLEQ scales; *see* also NAPLAN, achievement; attendance, attitudes to school

229

INDEX

Melaleuca College
  academic attainment, 34, 35
  attitudes to school, 36
  distributed leadership, 100, 102
  school attendance, 37
  school structure, 65, 66, 75–77, 154, 184, 185
  vision statement, 75
  teacher advisor program, 162
  self-directed learning, 82
  studio arts case study, chapter 7; English case study, 110, 118
  student wellbeing programs, 178, 182
Mentoring
  students, 77, 105, 153
  pre-service teachers, 81
  teacher advisor as mentor, 99, 102, 126, 169–172
Multi-theoretic perspectives; *see* theoretical perspectives

N

National Assessment Program in Literacy and Numeracy (NAPLAN)
  explained, 23
  NAPLAN data 34, 55, 57–8, 121, 152, 212; *see also* mathematics, literacy
Nested agency 52, 54

O

Open-Plan Settings
  affordances of, 7, 8, 91–3, 109, 110, 120, 136, 197, 199, 201–203
  constraints of, 56, 78–80, 109, 110, effects on teachers practical reasoning, 48, 63, 73. 80–88, 123, 126, 129, 130, chapter 7, 138, 200
  effects on student learning, chapter 7; effects on student well-being, 33, 174, 178, 180
  varying gender effects of, 178–182
  increased visibility in, chapter 9, student perceptions of, 145–150, 152, 176–7, 185, 187, 188, 190; *see also* learning, distributed leadership,

P

Peer relationships; *see* teachers, students, relationships, relational agency.
Personalised learning experience questionnaire, 19, 23–25, 28, 29, 31, 33
  emergent model, chapter 2;
  survey results, 37, 143–6, 151–152, 176, 178–181, 196, 198
Personalised learning, 4, 8, 14–17
  definitions of, 20, 21–24, 33
  emergent model 38, 40,
  claims for, critiques of, enactment of, chapter 3, 197, 199, 203, 204, 208, 209, 212, 213, 214, 218, 219, 220; *see* literacy, mathematics, studio arts, games base d learning; assessment of, *see* assessment
Practical reasoning
  principals, teachers
Pragmatism; chapter 1. *See* theoretical perspectives
Pre-Service Teachers
  preparing for open-plan settings, chapter 8; case study, chapter 8; mentors for, chapter 8
Principals
  decision-making, chapter 4; distributing leadership, chapter 6; *see also* Grevillea College, Ironbark College, Melaleuca College, Whirrakee College

Professional learning; chapter.6; pre-service teachers, chapter 8; desirability of, chapter 12; challenges in continuity of, chapter 12
Physical environment
see open-plan settings, school design, well being, PLEQ scales

Q

Qualitative research,
see research methods theory, 5, 16, 57, 143, 159, 160, 173, 198, 217, 221
Quantitative research; chapter 2; *see* research methods PLEQ, NAPLAN, Attendance, Attitudes to School Survey.

R

Reflection; *see* pragmatism
Relational agency 7, 52–54, 56, 57, 79–80, 91–93, 107, 112, 117, 120, 143, 155, 165, 170–172, 187, 200, 205, 206, 208, 209, 202, 215, 219, 224
  importance of in promoting wellbeing, 190; *see also* theoretical perspectives.
Relationships in open-plan settings, 46, teacher/teacher, 47, 48, 70, 99
  student/teacher, 12, 14, 15, 20, 50, 62 68, 75, 78, 83, 90 98, 102, 103, 105, 108, 109, 117, 159–167, 173–179, 182–191, 201, 206
  student/student, 26, 29, 30, 61, 72, 73, 141–150, 206, 208, 213; *see also* teacher advisor, student voice
Research methods; *see* Qualitative, Quantitative research
Resilience
  building in students, chapter 10

S

Self-efficacy, 16, 26–9, 54, 176, 178, 183, 225
Self-regulated learning; *see* learning
Shared space; *see* open-plan, learning communities, learning environment
Sphere of influence, 6, 7, 13, 15, 51, 68–9, 73, 81, 83, 84, 91, 107–110, 112–3, 117, 118, 120, 141, 143, 190, 200
Statistical analyses; *see* PLEQ
Structures; *see* school design; team teaching, distributed leadership, teacher advisor
Students
  academic efficacy, 16, 20, 24, 26–29, 39, 40, 144, 195
  academic performance, 3, 10, 16, 19;28, 34, 41 73 78, 97, 101, 107, 152, 165, 180, 195, 196, 223
  perceptions, 6, 17, 19–24, 29–34, 39, 40, 49, 90, 117, 122–3, 141–145, 153, 160, 176–8, 181, 182, 188, 191, 196, 198, 199, 211, 215, 226
  socio-economic status, 3, 4, 10, 19, 20, 23, 49–51, 54, 58, 64, 65, 71, 72, 73, 84, 120, 122, 142, 173, 178, 195, 196, 198–200; *see also* agency; co-regulated learning; self-regulated learning; gender, academic attainment, attitudes to school, attendance
Student as researcher, 160, 167
Student voice
  rationale, chapter 9; challenges, chapter 9; perceptions of readiness for, chapters 2, 9; enablers, chapters 6, 9; constraints on, chapter 9; responses in BEP schools,

231

INDEX

chapter 9; future directions, chapter 9
Studio Arts, 118

T
Teacher advisor
   purpose, 14, 17, 43, 55, 70, 101–105, 150, 152, 153, 156
   TA curriculum, chapter 10; student effects of TA program, chapters 10, 11
Teacher perceptions, 15, 21, 90, 104, 107–109, 117
   action possibilities, chapters 5, 6, 7, 8; challenges
Teachers
   adaptive strategies, 9, 95, 108, 125–6, 136, 138, 197, 202
   practical reasoning; 3, 17, 61, 77–81, 138, 197
   capacity building 97–99, 159, 211; *see* professional learning
Team teaching; *see* adaptation, pre-service teachers; mathematics; literacy; studio arts
Technology; *see* ICT, games based learning, dashboard, Web 2.0 technologies
Theoretical perspectives; *see* relational agency, nested agency, pragmatism, activity theory, affordance theory, embodied learning, adaptation, threshold of change, sphere of influence

U
Upscaled learning communities, 5, 6, 9

V
Video methods: in student as researcher research, chapter 10; value of- theoretical perspectives, chapter 9
Virtual learning
Vistaed visibility
   affordances of, chapter 12; and effects on teacher practice, chapters 1, 7, 12; and effects on bullying, chapters 9, 11; and exposure of poverty of pedagogy, chapter 9; *see also* open-plan settings
Voice; *see* student voice

W
Waratah College
   case study, chapter 7; PLEQ results, chapter 2
Wattle College
   PLEQ results, chapter 2
Well-being
   theory, chapter 11; teacher understandingsof, chapter 11; programs for improved well-being, chapter 11; student experiences in BEP schools, chapters 9, 10, 11
Whirrakee College
   academic attainment, chapter 2, attitudes to school, chapter 2, dashboard case study, chapter 5; distributed leadership; chapter 4; school attendance, chapter 2; school structure; chapter 4, 11, school design, chapter 4; vision statement, chapter 4; teacher advisor program, chapter 10; English case study, chapter 7; student voice in, chapter 9; student wellbeing programs, chapter 11, year 10 independence, chapter 9

CPSIA information can be obtained
at www.ICGtesting.com
Printed in the USA
FFOW04n1405151015
17728FF